BANCO!
Here at last is the sensational sequel to PAPILLON—the
great story of escape and adventure that took the world by
storm.

Banco continues the adventures of Henri Charrière—nick-
named 'Papillon'—in Venezuela, where he has finally won his
freedom after thirteen years of escape and imprisonment.
Despite his resolve to become an honest man, Charrière is soon
involved in hair-raising exploits with goldminers, gamblers,
bank-robbers, revolutionaries—robbing and being robbed, his
lust for life as strong as ever. He also runs night clubs in
Caracas until an earthquake ruins him in 1967—when he
decides to write the book that brings him international fame.

BANCO is ferocious, funny, tender, crowded with incident
and excitement.

BANCO is as vibrantly alive as PAPILLON.

BANCO is the work of a born story-teller.

Also by Henri Charrière

Papillon

Henri Charrière

Banco

The Further Adventures of Papillon

Translated from the French by
Patrick O'Brian

A PANTHER BOOK

GRANADA
London Toronto Sydney New York

Published by Granada Publishing Limited in 1974
Reprinted 1974, 1975 (six times), 1976 (twice), 1977 (twice),
1979, 1980

ISBN 0 586 04010 2

First published in Great Britain by Hart-Davis,
MacGibbon Ltd 1973
Copyright © Editions Robert Laffont, S.A., 1972
This translation © Hart-Davis, MacGibbon 1973

Granada Publishing Limited
Frogmore, St Albans, Herts AL2 2NF
and
3 Upper James Street, London W1R 4BP
866 United Nations Plaza, New York, NY 10017, USA
117 York Street, Sydney, NSW 2000, Australia
100 Skyway Avenue, Rexdale, Ontario, M9W 3A6, Canada
PO Box 84165, Greenside, 2034 Johannesburg, South Africa
61 Beach Road, Auckland, New Zealand

Made and printed in Great Britain by
Richard Clay (The Chaucer Press) Ltd
Bungay, Suffolk
Set in Linotype Plantin

Granada ®
Granada Publishing ®

To the memory of Dr Alex Guibert-Germain,
to Madame Alex Guibert-Germain,
to my countrymen, the Venezuelans,
to my French, Spanish, Swiss, Belgian, Italian, Yugoslav,
German, English, Greek, American, Turkish, Finnish,
Japanese, Israeli, Swedish, Czechoslovak, Danish, Argentine,
Colombian, and Brazilian friends and all those friends who
are faceless but who have done me the honour of writing to me.

'What you think of yourself matters more than what others
think of you.'

(*author unknown to Papillon*)

Contents

	Translator's Introduction	9
1	First Steps into Freedom	13
2	The Mine	32
3	Jojo La Passe	51
4	Farewell to El Callao	82
5	Caracas	90
6	The Tunnel under the Bank	101
7	Carotte: the Pawn-Shop	115
8	The Bomb	132
9	Maracaibo: among the Indians	149
10	Rita—the Vera Cruz	166
11	My Father	187
12	I become a Venezuelan	200
13	My Childhood	212
14	The Revolution	236
15	*Camarones*	243
16	The Gorilla	247
17	Montmartre—My Trial	256

Translator's Introduction

MIDDLE-AGED, impoverished by an earthquake and worried about his future, Henri Charrière sat down to write a book to restore his fortunes: it was his first, and he called it *Papillon*, the name by which he had been known in the underworld of Paris and in the French penal settlements. He had no great opinion of himself as an author and he was quite willing to have it improved, cut about and put into 'good French'; but the first publisher he sent it to happened to employ a brilliant editor who at once realized the exceptional quality of the manuscript and who delivered it to an astonished public in its original state, merely tidying up the punctuation, the spelling and a very few points of style.

That was in 1970, the year of the *phénomène Papillon*, a phenomenon almost unparalleled in the annals of publishing: it was not only that an extraordinary number of people read the book (850,000 copies were sold in the first few months), but that the readers embraced the whole spectrum of literary opinion, from the Académie Française to those whose lips moved slowly as they made their fascinated way through the strange adventures of an indomitable man struggling against the society that had sent him to rot in the infamous tropical prisons of Guiana with a life-sentence for a murder that he had never committed.

They were all deeply moved by the burning sense of injustice that runs right through the book and that gives it its coherence and validity, but even more by Papillon's sheer narrative power, his innate genius for telling a story. 'This is a literary prodigy,' said François Mauriac. 'It is utterly fascinating reading . . . This new colleague of ours is a master!' And he pointed out that it was not enough to have been a transported convict and to have escaped again and again; extraordinary talent was required to give the book its ring of truth and to make its value 'exactly proportional to its immense success'.

The soundness of Mauriac's words can be seen not only from the immense quantities of hopeless manuscripts by other ex-prisoners (purple characters, but untouched by genius) that flow into publishers' offices every week, but also by the baldness of the following summary that is intended to put the reader of this second volume into the picture: the main facts are here, but I am the first to admit that the heart of the matter is lacking.

The facts, then: in 1931 Henri Charrière, alias Papillon, was sentenced to transportation for life and he was taken away with some hundreds of others in a prison-ship bound for South America, for French Guiana. Here he found himself in an appallingly tough and savage world where corruption, terrorism, sodomy and murder were commonplace; he was well equipped for survival in this world, being as tough as any man there, perfectly loyal to his friends and perfectly uncompromising in his hatred of the official establishment, and in time he could have carved out a respectable place for himself. But he had no intention of staying; he had sworn not to serve his unjust sentence, and forty-two days after his arrival he made a break. With two companions (one broke his leg in escaping) he made his way down the Maroni river in a crazy boat; at a remote lepers' island they changed boats and so rode out to sea, sailing under the broiling sun day after day until at last they reached Trinidad. On and on to Curaçao, where the boat was wrecked; on to Rio Hacha in Colombia, where the wind failed them and they were taken prisoner. Another break, this time with a Colombian friend, and eventually Papillon reached hostile Indian territory, alone and on foot. They took him in, gave him two wives, and then, when at last he would stay no longer, a bag of pearls. Back to Colombia, only to be arrested and imprisoned once more, and, after several abortive breaks, handed over to the French authorities. Then solitary confinement on the Île Saint-Joseph—a deeply moving account of the silence, the heat and the utter loneliness of that dim, timeless, underground cage—two years of it. When at last it was over and he was out in the light again, he began to make a raft for another break; but a fellow convict informed upon him, and having killed the informer he went back to solitary—an eight years' sentence cut to nineteen months for rescuing a little girl from the sharks. Another attempt to escape; transfer to Devil's Island and then the final break at last, riding two sacks of coconuts through the shark-infested sea to the mainland. A new boat and a new series of adventures brought him, by way of British Guiana (and a new wife), to Venezuela and to the Venezuelan penal settlement at El Dorado, where he was held on the charge of being a rogue and a vagabond. But a *coup d'état* in Caracas brought the promise of release, and the last pages of the book show Papillon, equipped with genuine papers at last, and dressed in good civilian clothes, ready to walk out into freedom after thirteen years of being in prison or on the run. That is where the present volume starts, and from now on his story is told in his own infinitely more living words.

But, before I leave Henri Charrière to tell his own story, perhaps I may be permitted to say a word about the translation. I had followed *Papillon*'s wild success; I had watched the splendid time the author was having (Papillon in a sledge with Brigitte Bardot, Papillon with an immense cigar and a diamond ring, Papillon in a dinner-jacket, painting Paris red) with delight and with admiration for his iron resistance; but I had been afraid that fame and wealth might alter his style and complicate my task. Not at all: as soon as I looked into *Banco* I recognized exactly the same voice: here and there a slightly more literary turn of phrase, here and there a literary allusion, but not the least change in the essential Papillon. So I made no alteration in the techniques I had adopted for translating his earlier book: of these the only one that seems to call for any explanation is my use of a somewhat archaic Americanized slang, particularly in the dialogue. This seemed to me the only way of rendering Papillon's equally archaic argot; and in the few cases where even American would not quite yield the liveliness of the French, I comforted myself with the proverb from Papillon's own country: 'If you cannot have thrushes to eat, then you must make do with blackbirds.'

PATRICK O'BRIAN

11

'GOOD luck, Frenchman! From this moment, you're free. *Adios!*'

The officer of the El Dorado penal settlement waved and turned his back.

And it was no harder than that to get rid of the chains I had been dragging behind me these thirteen years. I held Picolino by the arm and we took a few steps up the steep path from the river-bank, where the officer had left us, to the village of El Dorado. And now, sitting here in my old Spanish house on the night of 18 August 1971, to be exact, I can see myself with unbelievable clarity on that pebbly track; and not only does the officer's voice ring in my ears in just the same way, deep and clear, but I make the same movement that I made twenty-seven years ago—I turn my head.

It is midnight: outside, the night is dark. And yet it's not. For me, for me alone, the sun is shining: it's ten o'clock in the morning and I stare at the loveliest shoulders, the loveliest back I have ever seen in my life—my gaoler's back moving farther and farther away, symbolizing the end of the watching, the spying, the surveillance that had gone on every day, night, minute and second, never stopping for thirteen years.

A last look at the river, a last look beyond the warder at the island in the middle with the Venezuelan penal settlement on it, a last look at a hideous past that lasted thirteen years and in which I was trampled upon, degraded and ground down.

All at once pictures seemed to be forming against the mists raised from the water by the blazing tropical sun, to show me the road I had travelled these thirteen years, as though it were on a screen. I refused to watch the film; I caught Picolino by the arm, turned my back on the weird picture and led him quickly up the path, first giving myself a shake to get rid of the filth of the past for good and all.

Freedom? Yes, but where? At the far end of the world, way back in the plateaux of Venezuelan Guiana, in a little village deep in the most luxuriant virgin forest you can imagine. This was the south-east tip of Venezuela, close to the Brazilian frontier: an enormous sea of green broken only here and there by the waterfalls of the rivers and streams that ran through it—a green ocean with widely-scattered little communities with ways and customs worthy of biblical times, gathered round a chapel, where no priest even had to talk about love for all men and simplicity because that was the way they lived naturally, all the year round. Often these *pueblitos* are only linked to others, as remote as themselves, by a truck or two: and looking at the trucks, you wondered how they ever got so far. And in their way of life these simple, poetic people live just as people did hundreds and hundreds of years ago, free from all the taints of civilization.

When we had climbed up to the edge of the plateau where the village of El Dorado begins, we almost stopped; and then slowly, very slowly, we went on. I heard Picolino draw his breath, and like him I breathed in very deeply, drawing the air right down into the bottom of my lungs and letting it out gently, as though I were afraid of living these wonderful minutes too fast—these *first minutes of freedom*.

The broad plateau opened in front of us: to the right and the left, little houses, all bright and clean and surrounded by flowers. Some children had caught sight of us: they knew where we came from. They came up to us, not unfriendly at all; no, they were kind, and they walked beside us without a word. They seemed to understand how grave this moment was, and they respected it.

There was a little wooden table in front of the first house with a fat black woman selling coffee and *arepas*, maize cakes.

'Good morning, lady.'

'*Buenas días, hombres!*'

'Two coffees, please.'

'*Sí, señores.*' And the good fat creature poured us out two cups of delicious coffee: we drank them standing, there being no chairs.

'What do I owe you?'

'Nothing.'

'How come?'

'It's a pleasure for me to give you the first coffee of your freedom.'

'Thank you. When's there a bus?'

'Today's a holiday, so there's no bus; but there's a truck at eleven.'

'Is that right? Thanks.'

A black-eyed, light-skinned girl came out of a house. 'Come in and sit down,' she said with a lovely smile.

We walked in and sat down with a dozen people who were drinking rum.

'Why does your friend loll out his tongue?'

'He's sick.'

'Can we do anything for him?'

'No, nothing: he's paralysed. He's got to go to hospital.'

'Who's going to feed him?'

'Me.'

'Is he your brother?'

'No; my friend.'

'You got money, Frenchman?'

'Very little. How did you know I was French?'

'Everything gets known here in no time. We knew you were going to be let out yesterday: and that you escaped from Devil's Island and that the French police are trying to catch you to put you back there again. But they won't come and look for you here: they don't give orders in this country. We are the ones who are going to look after you.'

'Why?'

'Because ...'

'What do you mean?'

'Here, drink a shot of rum and give one to your friend.'

Now it was a woman of about thirty who took over. She was almost black. She asked me whether I was married. Yes, in France. If my parents were still alive. Only my father.

'He'll be glad to hear you are in Venezuela.'

'That's right.'

A tall dried-up white man then spoke—he had big, staring eyes, but they were kind—'My relation didn't know how to tell you why we are going to look after you. Well, I'll tell you. Because unless he's mad—and in that case there's nothing to be done about it—a man can be sorry for what he's done and he can turn into a good man if he's helped. That's why you'll be looked after in Venezuela. Because we love other men, and

15

with God's help, we believe in them.'

'What do you think I was a prisoner on Devil's Island for?'

'Something very serious, for sure. Maybe for having killed someone, or for a really big theft. What did you get?'

'Penal servitude for life.'

'The top sentence here is thirty years. How many did you do?'

'Thirteen. But now I am free.'

'Forget all that, *hombre*. As quick as you can forget everything you suffered in the French prisons and here in El Dorado. Forget it, because if you think about it too much you'll be forced to feel ill-will towards other men and maybe even hate them. Only forgetting will let you love them again and live among them. Marry as soon as ever you can. The women in this country are hot-blooded, and the love of the woman you choose will give you happiness and children, and help you forget whatever you have suffered in the past.'

The truck arrived. I thanked these kind, good people and went out, holding Picolino by the arm. There were about ten passengers sitting on benches in the back of the truck. In their kindness these humble people left us the best seats, next to the driver.

As we lurched wildly along the bumpy, pot-holed track, I thought about this strange Venezuelan nation. Neither the fishermen of the Gulf of Paria, nor the ordinary soldiers of El Dorado, nor the humble working-man who talked to me in that thatched mud hut had had any education. They could hardly read and write. So how did they come to have that sense of Christian charity and nobility of heart that forgives men who have done wrong? How did they manage to find just the right encouraging words, helping the ex-convict with their advice and what little they possessed? How did it come about that the heads of the penal settlement of El Dorado, both the officers and the governor—educated men, those—had the same ideas as the simple people, the idea of giving the man who is down his chance, whoever he is and however bad the thing he's done? Those were not qualities that could ever come from Europeans: so the Venezuelans must have got them from the Indians.

*

16

Here we are in El Callao. A big square: music. Of course: it is 5 July, the national holiday. People dressed in their best clothes, the motley crowd of tropical countries where all sorts of colours are mixed—black, yellow, white, and the copper of the Indians, whose race always comes out in the slightly slanting eyes and the lighter skin. Picolino and I got out, as well as some passengers from the back of the truck. One of them, a girl, came up to me and said, 'Don't pay: that has been looked after.' The driver wished us good luck and the truck set off again. With my little bundle in one hand and Picolino holding the other with the three fingers he had left, I stood there wondering what to do. I had some English pounds from the West Indies and a few hundred bolivars (one bolivar is worth about ten new pence) given me by my mathematical pupils at the penal settlement. And a few raw diamonds found among the tomatoes in the kitchen-garden I had made.

The girl who had told us not to pay asked me where we were going and I told her my idea was to find a little boarding-house.

'Come to my place first: then you can look around.'

We crossed the square with her and in a couple of hundred yards we reached an unpaved street lined with low houses; they were all made of baked clay, and their roofs were thatch or corrugated iron. At one of them we stopped.

'Walk in. This house is yours,' said the girl. She must have been about eighteen.

She made us go in first. A clean room with a floor of pounded earth; a round table; a few chairs; a man of about forty, medium height, smooth black hair, the same colour as his daughter's; Indian eyes. And three girls of about fourteen, fifteen and sixteen.

'My father and my sisters,' she said, 'here are some strangers I have brought home. They've come from the El Dorado prison and they don't know where to go. I ask you to take them in.'

'You're welcome,' said the father. And he repeated the ritual words, 'This house is yours. Sit down here, round the table. Are you hungry? Would you like coffee or rum?'

I didn't want to offend him by refusing so I said I'd like some coffee. The house was clean, but I could see from the

17

simple furniture that they were poor.

'My daughter Maria, who brought you here, is the eldest. She takes the place of her mother, who left us five years ago with a gold-prospector. I'd sooner tell you that myself, before you hear it from someone else.'

Maria poured coffee for us. Now I could look at her more closely, seeing she had come to sit down next to her father, right opposite me. The three sisters stood behind her. They looked closely at me, too. Maria was a girl of the tropics, with big black almond-shaped eyes. Her jet-black curling hair, parted in the middle, came down to her shoulders. She had fine features, and although you could make out the drop of Indian blood from the colour of her skin, there was nothing Mongolian about her face. She had a sensuous mouth: splendid teeth. Every now and then she showed the tip of a very pink tongue. She was wearing a white, flowered, wide-open blouse that showed her shoulders and the beginning of her breasts, hidden by a brassière that could be seen under the blouse. This blouse, a little black skirt and flat-heeled shoes were what she had put on for the holiday—her best. Her lips were bright red, and two pencilled lines at the corners of her huge eyes made them seem even larger.

'This is Esmeralda [Emerald],' she said, introducing her youngest sister. 'We call her that because of her green eyes. This is Conchita; and the other is Rosita, because she looks like a rose. She is much lighter coloured than the rest of us and she blushes at the least thing. Now you know the whole family. My father's name is José. The five of us are the same as one, because our hearts beat all together. And what's your name?'

'Enrique.' [Henri: in Spanish they say Enrique.]

'Were you in prison long?'

'Thirteen years.'

'Poor thing. How you must have suffered.'

'Yes: a great deal.'

'Papa, what do you think Enrique can do here?'

'I don't know. Do you have a trade?'

'No.'

'Well then, go to the gold-mine. They'll give you a job.'

'And what about you, José? What do you do?'

'Me? Nothing. I don't work—they pay you very little.'

Well, well, well. They were poor, sure enough; yet they were quite well dressed. Still, I couldn't very well ask him what he used for money—whether he stole instead of working. Wait and see, I said to myself.

'Enrique, you'll sleep here tonight,' said Maria. 'There's a room where my father's brother used to sleep. He's gone, so you can have his place. We'll look after the sick man while you go to work. Don't thank us; we're giving you nothing—the room's empty in any case.'

I didn't know what to say. I let them take my little bundle. Maria got up and the other girls followed her. She had been lying: the room was in use, because they brought out women's things and put them somewhere else. I pretended not to notice anything. No bed, but something better, something you see most of the time in the tropics—two fine wool hammocks. A big window with just shutters—no glass—opening on to a garden full of banana palms.

As I swung there in the hammock I could hardly believe what had happened to me. How easy this first day of freedom had been! Too easy. I had a free room and four sweet girls to look after Picolino. Why was I letting myself be led by the hand like a child? I was at the world's end, to be sure; but I think the real reason why I let myself be managed was because I had been a prisoner so long that obeying was the only thing I understood. Yet now I was free and I ought to make my own decisions; but still I was letting myself be led. Just like a bird when you open the door of its cage and it doesn't know how to fly any more. It has to learn all over again.

I went to sleep without thinking about the past, exactly as the humble man of El Dorado had advised me. Just one thought before I dropped off: these people's hospitality was something staggering and wonderful.

I had just breakfasted off two fried eggs, two fried bananas covered with margarine and black bread. Maria was in the bedroom, washing Picolino. A man appeared in the doorway: a machête in his belt.

'Gentes de paz,' said he. Men of peace, which is their way of saying I'm a friend.

'What do you want?' asked José, who had had breakfast

with me.

'The chief of police wants to see the men from Cayenne.'

'You don't want to call them that. Call them by their names.'

'OK, José. What are their names?'

'Enrique and Picolino.'

'Señor Enrique, come with me. I am a policeman, sent by the chief.'

'What do they want with him?' asked Maria, coming out of the bedroom. 'I'll come too. Wait while I dress.'

In a few minutes she was ready. As soon as we were in the street she took my arm. I looked at her, surprised, and she smiled at me. We soon reached the little administrative building. More police, all in plain clothes apart from two in uniform with machêtes hanging from their belts. In a room full of rifles, a black man with a gold-braided cap. He said to me, 'You're the Frenchman?'

'Yes.'

'Where's the other?'

'He's sick,' said Maria.

'I command the police. I'm here to be useful and to help you if you need it. My name's Alfonso.' And he held out his hand.

'Thanks. Mine's Enrique.'

'Enrique, the chief administrator wants to see you. You can't go in, Maria,' he added, seeing she was about to follow me. I went into the next room.

'Good morning, Frenchman. I am the chief administrator. Sit down. Since you're in compulsory residence here in El Callao I sent for you so that I could get to know you: because I'm responsible for you.' He asked me what I was going to do—where I wanted to work. We talked a while and then he said to me, 'If there's anything at all, come and see me. I'll help you work out as good a life as we can manage.'

'Thank you very much.'

'Oh, there's one thing. I must warn you that you're living with very good, honest girls; but their father, José—he's a pirate. Be seeing you.'

Maria was outside, at the station door, settled into that attitude of Indians when they are waiting, neither moving nor talking to anyone at all. She was not an Indian: yet in spite of everything, because of that little drop of Indian blood she had, the race came out. We took another way back to the house and walked through the whole village, her arm in mine.

'What did the chief want with you?' asked Maria, calling me *tu* for the first time.

'Nothing. He told me I could count on him to help me find a job or in case I was in a hole.'

'Enrique, you don't need anyone now. Nor does your friend.'

'Thanks, Maria.'

We passed by a pedlar's stall, full of women's trinkets—necklaces, bracelets, earrings, brooches, etc.

'Hey, look at this.'

'Oh, how pretty!'

I took her over to the stall and picked out the best necklace together with matching earrings, and three other smaller ones for her sisters. I gave thirty bolivars for these tinselly little things, paying with a hundred note. She put on the necklace and the earrings straight away. Her big black eyes sparkled with joy and she thanked me as though they were really valuable jewels.

We went back to the house, and the three girls shrieked with delight over their presents. I went to my room, leaving them. I had to be alone to think. This family had offered me their hospitality with a splendid generosity; but should I accept it? I had a little Venezuelan money and some English pounds, not to mention the diamonds. Reckoning it all together, I could live four months and more without worrying and I could have Picolino looked after.

All these girls were lovely, and like tropical flowers they were surely all warm, sexy, ready to give themselves only too easily, almost without thinking. I had seen Maria looking at me today almost as if she were in love. Could I resist so much temptation? It would be better for me to leave this too welcoming house, because I did not want my own weakness to bring trouble and suffering. On the other hand, I was thirty-seven and although I looked younger, that did not change my real age. Maria was not quite eighteen and her sisters were younger still. I ought to go, I thought. The best thing would be to leave Picolino in their care: paying for his board, of course.

'Señor José, I'd like to talk to you alone. Shall we go and have a rum at the café in the square?'

'All right. But don't call me señor. You call me José and I'll call you Enrique. Let's go. Maria, we're going out to the square for a minute.'

'Enrique, change your shirt,' said Maria. 'The one you've got on is dirty.'

I went and changed in the bedroom. Before we left, Maria said to me, 'Don't stay long, Enrique; and above all, don't you drink too much!' And before I had time to step back she kissed me on the cheek. Her father burst out laughing, and he said, 'That Maria—she's in love with you already.'

As we walked towards the bar I began, 'José, you and your family took me in the first day of my freedom, and I thank you more than I can say. I'm about your age; and I don't want to make you a bad return for your hospitality. You're a man, so you will understand that if I lived among your daughters it would be hard for me not to fall in love with one of them. But I'm twice as old as the eldest and I'm legally married in France. So let's go and have a drink or two together, and then you take me to some cheap little boarding-house. I can pay.'

'Frenchie, you're a real man,' said José, looking me straight in the eye. 'Let me shake your hand good and hearty, like a brother, for what you've just said to a poor guy like me. In this country, do you see, it's not like it is where you come from, maybe. Here almost nobody's married legally. You like one another, you make love, and if there's a child you set up house together. You join up as easily as you leave one another. It's very hot here, and on account of the heat the women are very full-blooded. They thirst for love and the pleasures of the flesh. They mature early. Maria's an exception; she's never had an affair although she's nearly eighteen. I think your country's morality is better than ours, because here there are any number of women who have children without a father, and that's a very serious problem. But what can you do about it? The good Lord says you must love one another and have children. In this country the women don't calculate when they give themselves to a man—they aren't after a social position.

They want to love and be loved, just like that, quite naturally: nothing more. They are faithful so long as they like you sexually. When that's over, it's another story. Yet they are wonderful mothers, willing to make any sacrifice at all for their children, even keeping them when they could work for themselves. So although I quite see you are surrounded by temptation all the time, I ask you again to stay with us. I'm glad to have a man like you in the house.'

We were in the bar before I answered. It was a bar and at the same time a grocer's shop. A dozen men were sitting about. We drank a few *Cuba Libres*, a mixture of rum and Coca-Cola. Several people came up to shake my hand and bid me welcome to their village. Each time José introduced me as a friend who was living at his house. We had a good many drinks. When I asked what they came to, José became almost annoyed. He wanted to pay for everything. Still, I did manage to persuade the barman to refuse his money and take mine.

Someone touched me on the shoulder: it was Maria. 'Come home. It's lunch-time. Don't drink any more: you promised me not to drink too much.' She was saying 'thee' to me now.

José was arguing with another man; she said nothing to him but took me by the arm and led me out.

'What about your father?'

'Let him be. I can never say anything to him when he's drinking and I never come to fetch him from the café. He wouldn't have it, anyway.'

'Why did you come and fetch me, then?'

'You're different. Be good, Enrique, and come along.' Her eyes were so brilliant and she said it so simply that I went back to the house with her.

'You deserve a kiss,' she said when we got there. And she put her lips to my cheek, too near my mouth.

José came back after we had had lunch together at the round table. The youngest sister helped Picolino eat, giving him his food little by little.

José sat down by himself. He was tolerably high, so he spoke without thinking. 'Enrique is frightened of you, my girls,' he said. 'So frightened he wants to go away. I told him that in my opinion he could stay, and that my girls were old enough to know what they were doing.'

Maria gazed at me. She looked astonished, perhaps disappointed. 'If he wants to go, Papa, let him. But I don't think he'd be better off anywhere else than he is here, where everyone likes him.' And turning to me she added, 'Enrique, don't be a coward. If you like one of us and she likes you, why should you run away?'

'On account of he's married in France,' said her father.

'How long since you saw your wife?'

'Thirteen years.'

'The way we see it, if you love a man you don't necessarily marry him. If you give yourself to a man, it's to love him, nothing more. But it was quite right of you to tell our father you were married, because like that you can't promise any of us anything at all, apart from love.' And she asked me to stay with them without committing myself. They would look after Picolino and I would be free to work. She even said I could pay a little, as if I were a lodger, to make me feel easier in my mind. Did I agree?

I had no time to think properly. It was all so new and so quick after thirteen years of life as a convict. I said, 'OK, Maria. That's fine.'

'Would you like me to go with you to the gold-mine this afternoon to ask for a job? We could go at five, when the sun is lower. It's a mile and a half from the village.'

'Fine.'

Picolino's movements and his expression showed how pleased he was that we were going to stay. The girls' kindness and their care had won his heart. My staying was chiefly on account of him. Because here I was pretty sure of having an affair before long: and maybe it would not suit me.

With all that had been going on inside my head these last thirteen years, with all that had stopped me sleeping these thirteen years on end, I was not going to come to a halt as quickly as all this and settle down in a village at the far end of the world just because of a girl's pretty face. I had a long road in front of me, and my stops must be short. Just long enough to get my wind and then full speed ahead. Because there was a reason why I had been fighting for my liberty these thirteen years and there was a reason why I had won the fight: and that reason was *revenge*. The prosecuting counsel, the false witness, the cop: I had a score to settle with them. And that was something I was never to forget. Never.

I wandered out to the village square. I noticed a shop with the name Prospéri over it. He must be a Corsican or an Italian, and indeed the little shop did belong to the descendant of a Corsican. Monsieur Prospéri spoke very good French. He kindly suggested writing a letter for me to the manager of La Mocupia, the French company that worked the Caratal gold-mine. This splendid man even offered to help me with money. I thanked him for everything and went out.

'What are you doing here, Papillon? Where the hell have you come from, man? From the moon? Dropped by parachute? Come and let me kiss you!' A big guy, deeply sunburnt, with a huge straw hat on his head, jumped to his feet. 'You don't recognize me?' And he took off his hat.

'Big Charlot! Stone the crows!' Big Charlot, the man who knocked off the safe at the Place Clichy Gaumont in Paris, and the one in the Batignolles station! We embraced like two brothers. Tears came into our eyes, we were so moved. We gazed at one another.

'A far cry from the Place Blanche and the penal, mate, eh? But where the hell have you come from? You're dressed like an English lord: and you've aged much less than me.'

'I'm just out of El Dorado.'

'How long were you there?'

'A year and more.'

'Why didn't you let me know? I'd have got you out straight away, signed a paper saying I was responsible for you. Christ above! I knew there were some hard cases in El Dorado, but I never for a moment imagined you were there, you, a buddy!'

'It's a bloody miracle we should have met.'

'Don't you believe it, Papi. The whole of Venezuelan Guiana from Ciudad Bolivar to El Callao is stuffed with right hard guys or detainees making a break. And as this is the first bit of Venezuelan territory you come across when you escape, there's no miracle in meeting anyone at all between the Gulf of Paria and here—every last son of a bitch comes this way. All those who don't come apart on the road, I mean. Where are you staying?'

'With a decent type called José. He has four daughters.'

'Yes, I know him. He's a good chap, a pirate. Let's go and get your things: you're staying with me, of course.'

'I'm not alone. I've got a paralysed friend and I have to look after him.'

'That doesn't matter. I'll fetch an ass for him. It's a big house and there's a negrita [a black girl], who'll look after him like a mother.'

When we had found the second donkey we went to the girls' house. Leaving these kind people was very painful. It was only when we promised we should come and see them and said they could come and see us at Caratal that they calmed down a little. I can never say too often how extraordinary it is, the Venezuelan Guianans' hospitality. I was almost ashamed of myself when I left them.

Two hours later we were at Charlot's 'château', as he called it. A big, light, roomy house on a headland looking out over the whole of the valley running down from the hamlet of Caratal almost to El Callao. On the right of this terrific virgin forest landscape was the Mocupia gold-mine. Charlot's house was entirely built of hardwood logs from the bush: three bedrooms, a fine dining-room and a kitchen; two showers inside and one outside, in a perfectly kept kitchen-garden. All the vegetables we had at home were growing there, and growing well. A chicken-run with more than five hundred hens; rabbits, guinea-pigs, two goats and a pig. All this was the fortune and the present happiness of Charlot, the former hard guy and specialist in safes and very delicate operations worked out to the second.

'Well, Papi, how do you like my shack? I've been here seven years. As I was saying in El Callao, it's a far cry from Montmartre and penal! Who'd ever have believed that one day I'd be happy with such a quiet, peaceful life? What do you say, buddy?'

'I don't know, Charlot. I'm too lately out of stir to have a clear idea. For there's no doubt about it, we've always been on the loose and our young days were uncommonly active! And then ... it sets me back a little, seeing you quiet and happy here at the back of beyond. Yet you've certainly done it all yourself and I can see it must have meant a solid dose of hard labour, sacrifices of every kind. And as far as I am concerned, you see, I don't feel myself up to it yet.'

When we were sitting round the table in the dining-room and drinking Martinique punch, Big Charlot went on, 'Yes, Papillon, I can see you're amazed. You caught on right away that I live by my own work. Eighteen bolivars a day means a small-time life, but it's not without its pleasures. A hen that hatches me a good brood of chicks, a rabbit that brings off a big litter, a kid being born, tomatoes doing well … All these little things we despised for so long add up to something that gives me a lot. Hey, here's my black girl. Conchita! Here are some friends of mine. He's sick; you'll have to look after him. This one's called Enrique, or Papillon. He's a friend from France, an old-time friend.'

'Welcome to this house,' said the black girl. 'Don't you worry, Charlot, your friends will be properly looked after. I'll go and see to their room.'

Charlot told me about his break—an easy one. When he reached penal in the first place he was kept at Saint-Laurent-du-Maroni, and after six months he escaped from there with another Corsican called Simon and a detainee. 'We were lucky enough to reach Venezuela a few months after the dictator Gomez died. These open-handed people helped us make a new life for ourselves. I had two years of compulsory residence at El Callao, and I stayed on. Little by little, I took to liking this simple life, you get it? I lost one wife when she was having a baby, and the daughter too. Then this black girl you've just seen, Conchita, she managed to comfort me with her real love and understanding, and she's made me happy. But what about you, Papi? You must have had a cruelly hard time of it: thirteen years is a hell of a stretch. Tell me about it.'

I talked to this old friend for more than two hours, spilling out everything these last years had left rankling in me. It was a wonderful evening—wonderful for us both to be able to talk about our memories. It was odd, but there was not a single word about Montmartre, not a word about the underworld, no reminders of jobs that were pulled off or that misfired, nothing about crooks still at large. It was as though for us life had begun when we stepped aboard *La Martinière*, me in 1933, Charlot in 1935.

Excellent salad, a grilled chicken, goat cheese and a delicious mango, washed down with good Chianti and all put on the table by the cheerful Conchita, meant that Charlot could welcome me properly in his house and that pleased him. He suggested going down to the village for a drink. I said it was so pleasant here I didn't want to go out.

'Thanks, my friend,' said my Corsican—he often put on a Paris accent. 'You're dead right: we are comfortable here. Conchita, you'll have to find a girl-friend for Enrique.'

'All right: Enrique, I'll introduce you to friends prettier than me.'

'You're the prettiest of them all,' said Charlot.

'Yes, but I'm black.'

'That's the very reason why you're so pretty, poppet. Because you're a thoroughbred.'

Conchita's big eyes sparkled with love and pleasure: it was easy to see she worshipped Charlot.

Lying quietly in a fine big bed I listened to the BBC news from London on Charlot's radio: but being plunged back into the life of the outside world worried me a little—I was not used to it any more. I turned the knob. Now it was Caribbean music that came through: Caracas in song. I did not want to hear the great cities urging me to live their life. Not this evening, anyway. I switched off quickly and began to think over the last few hours.

Was it on purpose we had not talked about the years when we both lived in Paris? No. Was it on purpose we had not mentioned the men of our world who had been lucky enough not to be picked up? No again. So did it mean that for tough guys like us what had happened before the trial no longer mattered?

I tossed and turned in the big bed. It was hot: I couldn't bear it any more and I walked out into the garden. I sat down on a big stone, from where I was I looked out over the valley and the gold-mine. Everything was lit up down there. I could see trucks, empty or loaded, coming and going.

Gold: the gold that came out of the depths of that mine. If you had a lot of it, in bars or turned into notes, it would give you anything on earth. This prime mover of the world, that cost so little to mine, since the workers had such miserable wages, was the one thing you had to have to live well. And there was Charlot who had lost his freedom because he had wanted a lot of it: yet now he hadn't even mentioned the stuff. He never told me whether the mine had plenty of gold in it or not. These days his happiness was his black girl, his house, his animals and his kitchen-garden. He had never even referred to money. He had become a philosopher. I was puzzled.

I remembered how they caught him—a guy by the name of Little Louis had tipped off the police; and during our short meetings in the Santé he never stopped swearing he would get him the first chance he had. Yet this evening he had not so much as breathed his name. And as for me—Christ, how strange!—I had not said a word about my cops, nor Goldstein, nor the prosecuting counsel, either. I ought to have talked about them! I hadn't escaped just to end up as a cross between a gardener and a working-man.

I had promised to go straight in this country and I'd keep my word. But that didn't mean I had given up my plans for revenge. Because you mustn't forget, Papi, that the reason why you're here today is not only that the idea of revenge kept you going for thirteen years in the cells but because it was your one religion too; and that religion is something you must never give up.

His little black girl was very pretty, all right; but still I wondered whether Big Charlot wouldn't be better off in a city than in this hole at the far end of creation. Or maybe it was me who was the square, not seeing that my friend's life had its charm. Or then again was it Charlot who was afraid of the responsibilities that modern big-town life would put upon him? That was something to chew over and reflect upon.

Charlot was forty-five, not an old man. Very tall, very strong, built like a Corsican peasant fed on plenty of good healthy food all his young days. He was deeply burnt by the sun of this country, and with his huge straw hat on his head, its brim turned up at the sides, he really looked terrific. He was a perfect example of the pioneer in these virgin lands, and he was so much one of the people and the country he did not stand out at all. Far from it: he really belonged.

Seven years he'd been here, this still-young Montmartre safe-breaker! He must certainly have worked more than two years to clear this stretch of plateau and build his house. He had to go out into the bush, choose the trees, cut them down, bring them back, fit them together. Every beam in his house was made of the hardest and heaviest timber in the world, the kind they call ironwood. I was sure all he earned at the mine had gone into it, because he must have had help and have paid for the labour, the cement (the house was concreted), the well and the windmill for pumping the water up to the tank.

That well-rounded young negrita with her big loving eyes: she must be a perfect companion for this old sea-dog on shore. I'd seen a sewing-machine in the big room. She must make those little dresses that suited her so well. Not many dress-maker's bills for Charlot, no sir.

Maybe the reason why he hadn't gone to the city was that he was not sure of himself, whereas here he enjoyed a life with no problems at all. You're a great guy, Charlot! You're the very picture of what a crook can be turned into. I congratulate you. But I also congratulate the people who helped you to change not only your life but even your way of seeing what a life can be or ought to be.

But still these Venezuelans are dangerous, with their gener-ous hospitality. Being surrounded with human kindness and good will all the time soon turns you into a prisoner if you let yourself be caught. I'm free, free, free, and I mean to stay that way for ever.

Watch it, Papi! Above all, no setting up house with a girl. You need love when you've been cut off from it for so long. But fortunately I'd already had a girl in Georgetown two years ago, my Hindu, Indara. So from that point of view I was not so vulnerable as if I'd come straight from penal, which was the case with Charlot. Yet Indara was lovely and I was happy; but it wasn't for that I had settled in Georgetown, living there in clover. Then again if the quiet life is too quiet, even though it's happy, it's not for me: that I know very well.

Adventure! Adventure so you feel alive, alive all through! Besides, that was why I left Georgetown and why I landed up at El Dorado. But that's the reason too why I'm here today, in this very spot.

OK. Here the girls are pretty, full-blooded and charming and I certainly cannot live without love. It's up to me to avoid complications. I must promise myself to stay here a year, since I'm forced to do so anyway. The less I own, the easier I'll be able to leave this country and its enchanting people. I'm an adventurer, but an adventurer with a shift of gear—I must get my money honestly, or at least without hurting anyone. Paris, that is my aim: Paris one day, to present my bill to the people who put me through so much suffering.

I was calmer now, and my eyes took in the setting moon as it dipped towards the virgin forest, a sea of black tree-tops with waves of different heights—but waves that never stirred. I went back to my room and stretched out on the bed.

Paris, Paris, you're still a great way off yet; but not so far that I shan't be there again one day, walking the asphalt of your streets.

2: The Mine

A WEEK later, thanks to the letter that Prospéri, the Corsican grocer, wrote for me, I was taken on at the Mocupia mine. Here I was, looking after the working of the pumps that sucked up the water from the shafts.

The mine looked like a coal-pit: the same underground galleries. There were no veins of gold and very few nuggets. The gold was found in very hard rock: they blasted this rock with dynamite and then broke the oversized lumps with a sledge-hammer. The pieces were put into trucks, and the trucks came to the surface in lifts; then crushers reduced the rock to a powder finer than sand. This was mixed with water, making a liquid mud that was pumped up into huge tanks as big as the reservoirs in an oil-refinery: these tanks had cyanide in them. The gold dissolved into a liquid heavier than the rest and sank to the bottom. Under heat, the cyanide evaporated, carrying off the particles of gold; they solidified and were caught by filters very like combs as they went past. Then the gold was collected, melted into bars, carefully checked for 24-carat purity and put into a strictly guarded store. But who did the guarding? I still can't get over it. Simon, no less, the hard guy who had made his break from penal with Big Charlot.

When my work was over, I went to gaze at the sight: I went to the store and stared at the huge pile of gold ingots neatly lined up by Simon, the ex-convict. Not even a strong-room: just a concrete store-house with walls no thicker than usual and a wooden door.

'OK, Simon?'

'OK. And what about you, Papi? Happy at Charlot's?'

'Yes, I'm fine.'

'I never knew you were in El Dorado. Otherwise I'd have come to get you out.'

'That's civil. Are you happy here?'

'Well, you know, I have a house: it's not as big as Charlot's, but it's made of bricks and mortar. I built it myself. And I've got a young wife, very sweet. And two little girls. Come and see me whenever you like—my house is yours. Charlot tells me your friend is sick: now my wife knows how to give injections, so if you need her don't hesitate.'

We talked. He too was thoroughly happy. He too never spoke of France or Montmartre, though he had lived there. Just like Charlot. The past no longer existed; the only thing that mattered was the present—wife, children, the house. He told me he earned twenty bolivars a day. Fortunately their hens gave them eggs for their omelettes and the chickens were on the house; otherwise they wouldn't have gone far on twenty bolivars, Simon and his brood.

I gazed at that mass of gold lying there, so carelessly stored behind a wooden door and these four walls only a foot thick. A door that two heaves on a jemmy would open without a sound. This heap of gold, at three bolivars fifty the gramme or thirty-five dollars the ounce, would easily tot up to three million five hundred thousand bolivars or a million dollars. And this unbelievable great fortune was within hand's reach! Knocking it off would be almost child's play.

'Elegant, my neat pile of ingots? Eh, Papillon?'

'It'd be more elegant still well salted away. Christ, what a fortune!'

'Maybe: but it's not ours. It's holy, on account of they've entrusted it to me.'

'Entrusted it to you, sure; but not to me. You must admit it's tempting to see something like that just lying about.'

'It's not just lying about, because I'm looking after it.'

'Maybe. But you aren't here twenty-four hours out of the twenty-four.'

'No. Only from six at night to six in the morning. But during the day there's another guard: maybe you know him—Alexandre, of the forged postal orders.'

'Oh yes, I know him. Well, be seeing you, Simon. Say hello to your family for me.'

'You'll come and see us?'

'Sure. I'd like to. *Ciao.*'

I left quickly, as quickly as I could to get away from this scene of temptation. It was unbelievable! Anyone would say they were yearning to be robbed, the guys in charge of this mine. A store that could hardly hold itself upright and two one-time high-ranking crooks taking care of all that treasure!

In all my life on the loose I'd never seen anything like it!

Slowly I walked up the winding path to the village. I had to go right through it to reach the headland with Charlot's château on it. I dawdled; the eight-hour day had been tough. In the second gallery down there was precious little air, and even that was hot and wet, in spite of the ventilators. My pumps had stopped sucking three or four times and I had had to set them right away. It was half past eight now and I had gone down the mine at noon. I'd earned eighteen bolivars. If I had had a working-man's mind, that wouldn't have been so bad. Meat was 2·50 bolivars the kilo; sugar 0·70; coffee 2. Vegetables were not dear either: 0·50 for a kilo of rice and the same for dried beans. You could live cheaply, that was true. But did I have the sense to put up with that kind of life?

In spite of myself, as I climbed up the stony path, walking easily in the heavy nailed boots they had given me at the mine—in spite of myself, and although I did my best not to think about it, I kept seeing that million dollars in gold bars just calling out for some enterprising hand to grab it. At night, there wouldn't be any difficulty in jumping on Simon and chloroforming him without being recognized. And then the whole thing was in the bag, because they carried their fecklessness to the point of leaving him the key of the store so he could take shelter if it rained. Criminal irresponsibility! All that would be left to do then was carry the two hundred ingots out of the mine and load them into something—a truck or a cart. I'd have to prepare several caches in the forest, all along the road, to salt the ingots away in little packets of a hundred kilos each. If it was a truck, then once it was unloaded I'd have to carry right on as far as possible, pick the deepest place in the river and toss it in. A cart? There were plenty in the village square. The horse? That would be harder to find, but not impossible. A night of very heavy rain between eight and six in the morning would give me all the time I needed for the job and it might even let me get back to the house and go to bed meek as a monk.

By the time I reached the lights of the village square, in my mind I had already brought it off, and was slipping into the sheets of Big Charlot's bed.

'*Buenos noches*, Francès,' called a group of men sitting at the village bar.

'Hello there, one and all. Good night, *hombres*.'

'Come and join us for a while. Have an iced beer: we'd like you to.'

It would have been rude to refuse so I accepted. And here I was sitting among these good souls, most of them miners. They wanted to know whether I was all right, whether I'd found a woman, whether Conchita was looking after Picolino properly, and whether I needed money for medicine or anything else. These generous, spontaneous offers brought me back to earth. A gold-prospector said that if I didn't care for the mine and if I only wanted to work when I felt like it I could go off with him. 'It's tough going, but you make more. And then there's always the possibility you'll be rich in a single day.' I thanked them all and offered to stand a round.

'No, Frenchman, you're our guest. Another time, when you're rich. God be with you.'

I went on towards the château. Yes, it would be easy enough to turn into a humble, honest man among all these people who lived on so little, who were happy with almost nothing, and who adopted a man without worrying where he came from or what he had been.

Conchita welcomed me back. She was alone. Charlot was at the mine—when I left for work so he came back. Conchita was full of fun and kindness: she gave me a pair of slippers to rest my feet after the heavy boots.

'Your friend's asleep. He ate well and I have sent off a letter asking for him to be taken into the hospital at Tumereno, a little town not far off, bigger than this.'

I thanked her and ate the hot meal that was waiting for me. This welcome, so homely, simple and happy, made me relax; it gave me the peace of mind I needed after the temptation of that ton of gold. The door opened.

'Good evening, everybody.' Two girls came into the room, just as if they were at home.

'Good evening,' said Conchita. 'Here are two friends of mine, Papillon.'

One was dark, tall and slim; she was called Graciela, and was very much the gypsy type, her father being a Spaniard. The other girl's name was Mercedes. Her grandfather was a

German, which explained her fair skin and very fine blonde hair. Graciela had black Andalusian eyes with a touch of tropical fire; Mercedes' were green and all at once I remembered Lali, the Goajira Indian. Lali ... Lali and her sister Zoraïma: what had become of them? Might I not try to find them again, now I was back in Venezuela? It was 1945 now, and twelve years had gone by. That was a long, long time, but in spite of all those years I felt a pain in my heart when I remembered those two lovely creatures. Since those days they must have made themselves a fresh life with a man of their own race. No, honestly I had no right to disturb their new existence.

'Your friends are terrific, Conchita! Thank you very much for introducing me to them.'

I gathered they were both free and neither had a fiancé. In such good company the evening went by in a flash. Conchita and I walked them back to the edge of the village, and it seemed to me they leant very heavily on my arms. On the way back Conchita told me both the girls liked me, the one as much as the other. 'Which do you like best?' she asked.

'They are both charming, Conchita; but I don't want any complications.'

'You call making love "complications"? Love, it's the same as eating and drinking. You think you can live without eating and drinking? When I don't make love I feel really ill, although I'm already twenty-two. They are only sixteen and seventeen, so just think what it must be for them. If they don't take pleasure in their bodies, they'll die.'

'And what about their parents?'

She told me, just as José had done, that here the girls of the ordinary people loved just to be loved. They gave themselves to the man they liked spontaneously, wholly, without asking anything in exchange apart from the thrill.

'I understand you, poppet. I'm as willing as the next man to make love for love's sake. Only you tell your friends that an affair with me doesn't bind me in any way at all. Once warned, it's another matter.'

Dear Lord above! It wasn't going to be easy to get away from an atmosphere like this. Charlot, Simon, Alexandre and no doubt a good many others had been positively bewitched. I saw why they were so thoroughly happy among these cheerful people, so different from ours. I went to bed.

'Get up, Papi! It's ten o'clock. And there's someone to see you.'

'Good morning, Monsieur.' A greying man of about fifty; no hat; candid eyes; bushy eyebrows. He held out his hand. 'I'm Dr Bougrat.* I came because they told me one of you is sick. I've had a look at your friend. Nothing to be done unless he goes into hospital at Caracas. And it'll be a tough job to cure him.'

'You'll take pot-luck with us, Doctor?' said Charlot.

'I'd like to. Thanks.'

Pastis was poured out, and as he drank Bougrat said to me, 'Well, Papillon, and how are you getting along?'

'Why, Doctor, I'm taking my first steps in life. I feel as if I'd just been born. Or rather as if I'd lost my way like a boy. I can't make out the road I ought to follow.'

'The road's clear enough. Look around and you'll see. Apart from one or two exceptions all our old companions have gone straight. I've been in Venezuela since 1928. Not one of the convicts I've known has committed a crime since being in this country. They are almost all married, with children, and they live honestly, accepted by the community. They've forgotten the past so completely that some of them couldn't tell you the details of the job that sent them down. It's all very vague, far away, buried in a misty past that doesn't matter.'

'Maybe it's different for me, Doctor. I have a pretty long bill to present to the people who sent me down against all justice—thirteen years of struggle and suffering. To see the bill is paid, I have to go back to France; and for that I need a lot of money. It's not by working as a labourer that I'm going to save up enough for the voyage out and back—if there is any return—quite apart from what my plan will cost. And then the thought of ending my days in one of these God-forsaken holes ... I like the idea of Caracas.'

* The hero of a well-known criminal affair in Marseilles during the twenties. A dead man was found in a cupboard in his consulting-room. Bougrat pleaded professional error in the amount of an injection. The court said it was murder. They gave him a life-sentence, but he soon escaped from Cayenne and made himself a new life in Venezuela.

'And do you think you're the only one of us with an account to settle? Just you listen to the story of a boy I know. Georges Dubois is his name. A kid from the slums of La Villette—alcoholic father, often inside with delirium tremens, the mother with six children: she was so poor she went around the North African bars looking for customers. Jojo, they called him; and he'd been going from one reformatory to the next since he was eight. He started with the crime of knocking off fruit outside shops—did it several times. First a few terms in the Abbé Rollet's homes, then, when he was twelve, a tough stretch in a really hard reformatory. I don't have to tell you that the fourteen-year-old Jojo, surrounded by young fellows of eighteen, had to look out for his arse. He was a weakly kid, so there was only one way of defending himself—a knife. One of these perverted little thugs got a stab in the belly, and the authorities sent Jojo to Esse—the toughest reformatory of the lot, the one for hopeless cases—until the age of twenty-one. Then they gave him his marching orders for the African disciplinary battalions, because with a past like his, he was not allowed into the ordinary army. They handed him the few francs he had earned and farewell, adieu! The trouble was that this boy had a heart. Maybe it hardened, but it still had some sensitive corners. At the station he saw a train destined for Paris. It was as if a spring had been triggered off inside him. He jumped in double quick, and there he was in Paris. It was raining when he walked out of the station. He stood under a shelter, working out how he would get to La Villette. Under this same shelter there was a girl; she too was keeping out of the rain. She gave him a pleasant sort of a look. All he knew about women was the chief warder's fat wife at Esse and what the bigger boys at the reformatory had told him—more or less true. No one had ever looked at him like this girl: they began to talk.

' "Where do you come from?"

' "The country."

' "I like you, boy. Why don't we go to a hotel? I'll be nice to you and we'll be in the warm."

'Jojo was all stirred up. To him this chick seemed something wonderful—and what's more her gentle hand touched his. Discovering love was a fantastic, shattering experience for him. The girl was young and very amorous. When they had made love until they could no more, they sat on the bed to smoke, and the chick said to him, "Is this the first time you've been to bed with a girl?"

' "Yes," he confessed.

' "Why did you wait so long?"

' "I was in a reformatory."

' "A long time?"

' "Very long."

' "I was in one too. I escaped."

' "How old are you?" asked Jojo.

' "Sixteen."

' "Where are you from?"

' "La Villette."

' "What street?"

' "Rue de Rouen."

'So was Jojo. He was afraid to understand. "What's your name?" he cried.

' "Ginette Dubois."

'It was his sister. They were completely overwhelmed and they both began to cry with shame and wretchedness. Then each told the road they had travelled. Ginette and her other sisters had had the same kind of life as Jojo—homes and reformatories. Their mother had just come out of a sanatorium. The eldest sister was working in a brothel for North Africans in La Villette—sweated labour. They decided to go and see her.

'They had scarcely left the hotel before a pig in uniform called out to the chick. "Now you little tart, didn't I tell you not to come soliciting on my beat?" And he came towards them. "This time I'll run you in, you dirty little whore."

'It was too much for Jojo. After everything that had just happened, he no longer really knew what he was doing. He brought out a many-bladed pocket-knife he had bought for the army and shoved it into the pig's chest. He was arrested and twelve "qualified" jurymen condemned him to death: he was reprieved by the President of the Republic and sent to the penal settlement.

'Well now, Papillon, he escaped and at present he's living at Cumana, a fair-sized port. He's a shoemaker, he's married, and he has nine children, all well cared for and all going to school. Indeed, one of the elder children has been at the university this last year. Every time I'm in Cumana I go and see them. That's a pretty good example, eh? Yet believe you me, he too had a long bill to present to society. You're no exception, Papillon, you see. Plenty of us have reasons for revenge. But as far as I know, not one of us has left this country to take it. I trust you, Papillon. Since you like the idea of Caracas, go there: but I hope you'll have the sense to live the city life without falling into any of its traps.'

Bougrat left very late that afternoon. My ideas were in a turmoil by having seen him. Why had he made such an impression on me? Easy to see why. During these first days of freedom I had met convicts who were happy and readjusted; but even so, there was nothing extraordinary about the lives they led. It was more a prudent, very small-time kind of living. Their position was way down—workmen or peasants. Bougrat was different. For the first time I had seen an ex-con who was now a monsieur, a gentleman. That was what had made my heart thump. Would I be a monsieur too? Could I become one? For him, as a doctor, it had been comparatively easy. It would be harder for me, maybe; but even if I didn't yet know how to set about it, I was sure that one day I was going to be a monsieur too.

Sitting on my bench at the bottom of the second gallery I watched my pumps: today they had run without a hitch. Keeping time with the engine I repeated Bougrat's words, 'I trust you, Papillon! Watch out for the pitfalls of the city.' There must be some, for sure; and it wouldn't be so easy to change my outlook either. I had had proof of that: only yesterday the sight of the gold store-house had knocked me absolutely flat. I had been out only a fortnight, and already, as I climbed up the path, dazzled by that fortune within hand's reach, I was working out the details of how to get hold of it. And I'd certainly not yet completely made up my mind to leave those ingots lying there in peace.

The thoughts ran pell-mell through my head. 'Papillon, I trust you.' But could I put up with living like my companions? I didn't think so. After all, there were plenty of other ways of getting enough money honestly. I was not forced to accept a life that was too small for me. I could carry on as an adventurer—I could prospect for gold or diamonds, vanish into the bush and come out some day with enough to set me up in the kind of position I was after.

It wouldn't be easy to give up running risks and taking chances. But I thought, in spite of the temptation of that heap of gold, you mustn't do it; you can't do it; you haven't the right to do it. A million dollars ... You get that, Papi? Especially, since the job's already in the bag. You don't even have to work it out—it can't miss. Tempting, by God, tempting. Lord above, they had no right to shove a mountain of gold right under a crook's nose and then say to him 'You mustn't touch.' The tenth part of that gold would be enough for me to carry out everything, revenge included—to carry out everything I'd dreamt of during those thousands of hours when I was buried alive.

At eight o'clock the hoist brought me up to the surface. I took the long way round so as not to go by the store-house. The less I saw of it, the better. I passed quickly through the village, greeting people and saying sorry to the ones who wanted me to stop—I was in a hurry; and I climbed fast to the house. Conchita was waiting for me, as black and cheerful as ever.

'Well, Papillon, and how are you doing? Charlot told me to pour you out a stiff pastis before dinner. He said you looked as though you had problems. What's wrong, Papi? You can tell me, your friend's wife. Would you like me to fetch Graciela for you, or maybe Mercedes if you like her better? Don't you think that would be a good idea?'

'Conchita, you're my little black pearl of El Callao, you're wonderful, and I see why Charlot worships you. Maybe you're right: maybe to set me up I need a girl beside me.'

'That's for sure. Unless it's Charlot who was right.'

'How do you mean?'

'Well, there was me saying that what you needed was to love and be loved. And he told me to hold on before I put a girl in your bed—perhaps it was something else.'

'How do you mean, something else?'

She hesitated for a moment and then all at once she said, 'I don't care if you do tell Charlot; but he'll box my ears.'

'I shan't tell him anything. I promise.'

41

'Well, Charlot says you aren't built for the same kind of life as he and the other Frenchmen here.'

'What else? Come on, Conchita; tell me the lot.'

'And he said you must be thinking that there's too much useless gold lying about at the mine and that you'd find something better to do with it. There! And he went on that you aren't a type that can live without spending a lot; and that you had a revenge you couldn't give up and for that you wanted a great deal of money.'

I looked her straight in the eye. 'Well, Conchita, your Charlot got it wrong, wrong, wrong. You're the one who was right. As for my future—no problem at all. You guessed it: what I want is a woman to love. I didn't like to say so, on account of I'm rather shy.'

'That I don't believe, Papillon.'

'OK. Go and fetch the blonde, and just you see if I'm not happy when I have a girl of my own.'

'I'm on my way,' she said, going into the bedroom to change her dress. 'Oh that Mercedes, how happy she will be!' she called. Before she had time to come back there was a knock at the door. 'Come in,' said Conchita. The door opened and there was Maria, looking a trifle confused.

'You, Maria, at this time of night? What a marvellous surprise! Conchita, this is Maria, the girl who took me in when Picolino and I first landed up in El Callao.'

'Let me kiss you,' said Conchita. 'You're as pretty as Papillon said you were.'

'Who's Papillon?'

'That's me. Enrique or Papillon, it's all one. Sit down by me on the divan and tell me everything.'

Conchita gave a knowing laugh. 'I don't think it's worth my while going out now,' she said.

Maria stayed all night. As a lover she was shy, but she reacted to the slightest caress. I was her first man. Now she was sleeping. The two candles I had lit instead of the raw electric light were guttering. Their faint glow showed the beauty of her young body even better, and her breasts still marked by our embrace. Gently I got up to make myself some coffee and to see what time it was. Four o'clock. I knocked over a saucepan and woke Conchita. She came out of

42

her room wearing a dressing-gown.

'You want some coffee?'

'Yes.'

'Only for you, I'm sure. Because she must be sleeping with those angels you've introduced her to.'

'You know all about it, Conchita.'

'My people have fire in their veins. You must have noticed it tonight. Maria has one touch of Negro, two touches of Indian and the rest Spanish. If you're not happy with a mixture like that, go and hang yourself,' she said, laughing.

The splendid sun was high in the sky when it saw Maria wake up. I brought her coffee in bed. There was a question already on my lips. 'Aren't they going to worry, not finding you at home?'

'My sisters knew I was coming here, so my father must have known an hour later. You aren't going to send me away to-day?'

'No, sweetie. I told you I didn't want to set up house, but between that and sending you away is a long chalk, if you can stay without any trouble. Stay as long as you like.'

It was close on twelve and I had to leave for the mine. Maria decided to go home, hitching a lift in a truck, and to come back in the evening.

'Hey there,' said Charlot. He was standing in the door of his room, wearing pyjamas; and he spoke to me in French. 'So you've found the chick you needed all by yourself. A luscious piece, too: I congratulate you, cock.' He added that as it was Sunday tomorrow we might drink to the marriage.

'Maria, tell your father and sisters to come and spend Sunday with us to celebrate this. And you come back whenever you like—the house is yours. Have a good day, Papi; watch out for the number three pump. And when you quit work, you don't have to drop in on Simon. If you don't see the stuff he is looking after so badly, you'll feel it less.'

'You dirty old crook. No, I shan't go and see Simon. Don't you worry, mate. *Ciao.*'

Maria and I walked through the village arm in arm, tight together, to show the girls she was my woman.

The pumps ran sweetly, even number three. But neither the hot, wet air nor the beat of the motor stopped me thinking about Charlot. He had grasped why I was so thoughtful, all right. It hadn't taken long for him, an old crook, to see that the heap of gold was at the bottom of it all. Nor for Simon either: and Simon must certainly have told him about our conversation. Those were the sort of friends a man should have—real friends, aglow with joy because I'd got myself a woman. They were hoping that this black-haired godsend would make me forget the blazing heap of loot.

I turned all this over and over in my head, and in time I began to see the position more clearly. These good guys were now as straight as so many rulers; they were leading blameless lives. But in spite of living like squares they had not lost the underworld outlook and they were utterly incapable of tipping off the police about anyone whatsoever, even if they guessed what he was up to and they knew for sure it would mean bad trouble for them. The two who would be taken in straight away if the thing came off were Simon and Alexandre, the men who guarded the treasure. Charlot would come in for his share of the wasps' nest too, because every single one of the ex-convicts would be trundled off to jail. And then farewell peace and quiet, farewell house, kitchen-garden, wife, kids, hens, goats and pigs. So I began to see how these former crooks must have quaked not for themselves but for their homes, when they thought how my caper was going to ruin everything. 'How I hope he doesn't go and bugger it all,' they must have said. I could see them holding a council of war.

I had made up my mind. I'd go and see Simon that evening and ask him and his family to the party tomorrow, and I'd tell him to invite Alexandre too if he could come. I must make them all think that for me having a girl like Maria was the finest thing in the world.

The hoist brought me up to the open air. I met Charlot on his way down and I said to him, 'The party's still on, mate?'

'Of course it is, Papillon. More than ever.'

'I'm going to ask Simon and his family. And Alexandre too, if he can come.'

Old Charlot was a deep one. He looked me straight in the eye and then in a rather flip tone he said, 'Why, that's a sweet idea, my friend.' Without another word he stepped into the hoist, and it took him down to where I had just come from. I went round by the store and found Simon.

'OK, Simon?'

'Fine.'

'I've dropped in to say hello, in the first place, and then to ask you to lunch with us on Sunday. Bring your family, of course.'

'That'll be great. What's the party for? Your being let out?'

'No, my marriage. I've found a girl. Maria from El Callao, José's daughter.'

'Congratulations, with all my heart. I truly hope you'll be happy, mate, upon my oath I do.' He shook my hand good and hard and I left him. Half way down the path I found Maria coming to meet me, and arms round each other's waists we went up to the château. Her father and sisters would be there around ten tomorrow morning to help get the food ready.

'So much the better, because there are going to be more of us than we had reckoned on. And what did your father say?'

'He said, "Be happy, daughter, but don't you kid yourself about the future. I only have to look at a man to know what he's like. The man you've chosen is a good one, but he won't stay here. He's not the sort to put up with a simple life like ours." '

'What did you say to that?'

'I said I'd do everything to keep you as long as ever I could.'

'Come and let me kiss you: you've got a lovely heart, Maria. Let's live in the present: the future can look after itself.'

Having eaten something we went to bed; we should have to be up early the next day to help Conchita kill the rabbits, make the big cake, fetch the wine, etc. This night was even more splendid and passionate and enchanting than the first. Maria really had fire in her veins. Straight away she learnt to call up and increase the pleasure she had been taught. We made love long and hard until we fell fast asleep wrapped tight together.

The next day was Sunday, and the party was a marvellous success. José congratulated us on loving one another and Maria's sisters whispered questions in her ear—full of curiosity. Simon and his fine family were there. And Alexandre too, since he had been able to find someone to fill in for him guarding the treasure. He had a charming wife, and a well-dressed little boy and girl came with them. The rabbits were delicious, and the huge cake, shaped like a heart, lasted no time at all. We even danced to the radio and the gramophone, and an old convict played the accordion.

After a good many liqueurs I set about my old crooks in French. 'Well, and what have you guys been thinking? Did you really believe I was going to pull something off?'

'Yes, mate,' said Charlot. 'We shouldn't have said a word if you hadn't brought it up yourself. But it's dead certain you had the notion of knocking off that ton of gold, right? Give the straight answer, Papillon.'

'You know I've been chewing over my revenge these thirteen years. Multiply thirteen years by three hundred and sixty-five days and then by twenty-four hours and each hour by sixty minutes and you still won't have the number of times I've sworn to make them pay for what I went through. So when I saw that heap of gold in such a place, why true enough, I did think of working out a job.'

'What then?' said Simon.

'Then I looked at the position from every side and I was ashamed. I was running the risk of destroying the happiness of you all. I came to see that this happiness of yours—a happiness I hope to have myself one day—was worth much more than being rich. So the temptation of knocking off the gold quite disappeared. You can take it for a certainty, and I give you my word: I shan't do anything here.'

'There you are, then,' said Charlot, grinning all over his face. 'So now we can sleep easy. It's not one of our crooks that would ever give way to temptation. Long live Papillon! Long live Maria! Long live love and freedom! And long live decency! Hard guys we were, hard guys we are still, but only towards the pigs. Now we're all of the same mind, including Papillon.'

Six months I'd been here. Charlot was right. On the day of the party I had won the first battle against my longing to pull something off. I had been drifting away from the 'road down the drain' ever since I had escaped. Now thanks to my friends' example I had gained an important victory over myself: I had given up the idea of grabbing that million dollars. One thing was sure: for the future it would not be easy for any job to tempt me. Once I'd given up a fortune like that, it would be very hard for anything else to make me change my ideas. Yet I wasn't entirely at peace with myself. I had to make my money some other way than stealing it, fair enough; but still I had to get enough together to be able to go to Paris and hand in my bill. And that was going to cost me a packet.

Boom-bom, boom-bom, boom-bom: all the time my pumps sucked up the water that flowed into the galleries. It was hotter than ever. Every day I spent eight hours down there in the bowels of the mine. At this time I was on duty from four in the morning until noon. When I knocked off I'd have to go to Maria's house in El Callao. Picolino had been there this last month, because in El Callao the doctor could see him every day. He was being given a course of treatment and Maria and her sisters looked after him wonderfully. So I was going to see him and to make love to Maria: it was a week since I'd seen her, and I wanted her, physically and mentally.

I found a lorry that gave me a lift. The rain was pouring down when I opened the door at about one o'clock. They were all sitting round the table, apart from Maria, who seemed to be waiting near the door. 'Why didn't you come before? A week's a long, long time. You're all wet. Come and change right away.'

She pulled me into the bedroom, took my clothes off and dried me with a big towel. 'Lie down on the bed,' she said. And there we made love, not minding about the others who were waiting for us the other side of the door, nor about their impatience. We dropped off to sleep, and it was Esmeralda, the green-eyed sister, who gently woke us up late that afternoon, when night was already coming on.

When we had all had dinner together, José the Pirate suggested going for a stroll.

'Enrique, you wrote to the chief administrator asking him to get Caracas to put an end to your *confinamiento* [compulsory residence]: is that right?'

'Yes, José.'

'He's had the reply from Caracas.'

47

'Good or bad?'

'Good. Your *confinamiento* is over.'

'Does Maria know?'

'Yes.'

'What did she say?'

'That you'd always said you wouldn't stay in El Callao.' After a short pause he asked me, 'When do you think you'll leave?'

Although I was bowled over by this news, I thought and then answered straight away, 'Tomorrow. The truck-driver who brought me said he was going on to Ciudad Bolivar tomorrow.' José bowed his head. '*Amigo mio*, are you sore at me?'

'No, Enrique. You've always said you'd never stay. But it's sad for Maria—and for me, too.'

'I'll go and talk to the driver if I can find him.'

I did find him: we were to leave tomorrow at nine. As he already had one passenger, Picolino would travel in the cab and myself on the empty iron barrels behind. I hurried to the chief administrator; he handed over my papers and, like the good man he was, he gave me some advice: and he wished me good luck. Then I went round seeing everybody who had given me their friendship and their help.

First to Caratal, where I picked up the few things I possessed. Charlot and I embraced one another, deeply moved. His black girl wept. I thanked them both for their wonderful hospitality.

'It's nothing, mate. You would have done the same for me. Good luck. And if you go to Paris, say hello to Montmartre from me.'

'I'll write.'

Then the ex-cons, Simon, Alexandre, Marcel, André. I hurried back to El Callao and there I said good-bye to all the miners and the gold- and diamond-prospectors and my workmates. All of them, men and women, said something from the heart to wish me good luck. It touched me a great deal and I saw even more clearly that if I had set up with Maria I should have been like Charlot and the others—I should never have been able to tear myself away from this paradise.

The hardest of all my farewells was to Maria. Our last

night, a mixture of love and tears, was more violent than anything we had ever known. Even our caresses broke our hearts. The horrible thing was that I had to make her understand there would be no hope of my coming back. Who could tell what my fate would be when I carried out my plans?

A shaft of sunlight woke me. My watch said eight o'clock already. I hadn't the heart to stay in the big room, not even the few moments for a cup of coffee. Picolino was sitting in a chair, tears running down his face. Esmeralda had washed and dressed him. I looked for Maria's sisters, but I couldn't find them. They'd hidden so as not to see me go. There was only José standing there in the doorway. He grasped me in the Venezuelan *abrazo* (one hand holds yours and the other is round your shoulders), as moved as I was myself. I couldn't speak, and he said only this one thing: 'Don't forget us; we'll never, never forget you. Good-bye: God go with you.'

With all his clean things carefully made up into a bundle, Picolino wept bitterly, and his movements and the hoarse sounds he uttered conveyed his wretchedness at not being able to bring out the millions of thanks he had in his heart. I led him away.

Carrying our baggage, we reached the driver's place. A splendid exit from the town, all right: his truck had broken down; no leaving today. We had to wait for a new carburettor. There was no way out of it—I returned to Maria's with Picolino. You can imagine the shrieks when they saw us coming back.

'God was kind to have broken the truck, Enrique! Leave Picolino here and walk around the village while I get the meal ready. It's an odd thing,' Maria added, 'but it could be you're not fated to go to Caracas.'

While I was strolling about I thought over this remark of Maria's. It worried me. I did not know Caracas, a big city, but people had talked about it and I could imagine what it was like. The idea certainly attracted me; but once I was there, what should I do, and how could I do it?

I walked slowly across the square of El Callao with my hands behind my back. The sun was blazing down. I went over to an almendron, a huge, very leafy tree, to shelter from the furious heat. Under the shade there stood two mules, and a little old man was loading them. I noticed the diamond-prospector's sieve and the gold-prospector's trough, a kind of Chinese hat they use to wash the gold-bearing mud in. As I gazed at these things—they were still new to me—I went on pondering. In front of me there was this biblical picture of a quiet, peaceful life with no sounds apart from those of nature and the patriarchal way of living; and I thought of what it must be like at that very moment in Caracas, the busy, teeming capital that drew me on. All the descriptions I had heard turned into exact images. After all, it was fourteen years since I had seen a big town! Since I could now do as I liked, there was no doubt about it—I was going to get there, and as quick as I could.

JESUS, the song was in French! And it was the little old prospector singing. I listened.

> The old sharks are there already
> They've smelt the body of a man.
> One of them chews an arm like an apple
> Another eats his trunk and tra-la-la
> The quickest gets it, the rest have none
> Convict farewell; long live the law!

I was thunderstruck. He sang it slowly, like a requiem. The 'tra-la-la' had an ironic merriment, and the 'long live the law' was full of the mockery of the Paris underworld: it sounded like an unanswerable truth. But to feel the full irony of it you had to have been there.

I looked closely at the man. The size of three apples one on top of the other: just five foot one, I learnt afterwards. One of the most picturesque ex-convicts I had ever come across. Snowy white hair with long, grey side-whiskers cut on the slant. Blue jeans; a big, broad leather belt; on the right, a long sheath with a curved handle coming out of it at the height of his groin. I walked over to him. He had no hat on—it was lying on the ground—so I could see his broad forehead, speckled with a red even darker than his old sun-baked pirate's tan. His eyebrows were so long and thick he surely had to comb them. Beneath them, steely grey-green eyes, gimlets that bored through me. I hadn't taken four steps before he said to me, 'You come from penal, as sure as my name's La Passe.'

'Right. My name's Papillon.'

'I'm Jojo La Passe.' He held out his hand and took mine frankly, just as it should be between men, not so hard it crushes your fingers the way the show-offs do, nor too flabby, like hypocrites and fairies. I said, 'Let's go to the bar and have a drink. It's on me.'

'No. Come to my place over the way, the white house. It's called Belleville, after where I lived when I was a kid. We can talk there in peace.'

Indoors it was swept and clean—his wife's field of action. She was young, very young; perhaps twenty-five. He—God knows: sixty at least. She was called Lola, a dusky Venezuelan.

'You're welcome,' she said to me, with a pleasant smile.

'Thanks.'

'Two pastis,' said Jojo. 'A Corsican brought me two hundred bottles from France. You'll see whether it's good or not.'

Lola poured it out and Jojo tossed back three-quarters of his glass in one gulp. 'Well?' said he, fixing me with his eye.

'Well what? You don't think I'm going to tell you the story of my life, do you?'

'OK, mate. But Jojo La Passe, doesn't that ring any bells?'

'No.'

'How quickly they forget you! Yet I was a big shot in penal. There was no one that came within miles of me for throwing the seven and eleven with dice just touched with a file—not loaded, of course. That wasn't yesterday, to be sure; but after all, men like us, we leave traces—we leave legends. And now according to what you tell me, in a few years it's all forgotten. Did not one single bastard ever tell you about me?' He seemed deeply outraged.

'Frankly, no.'

Once again the gimlets bored right into my guts. 'You stayed no great time in penal: you've scarcely got the face at all.'

'Thirteen years altogether, counting El Dorado. You think that's nothing?'

'It's not possible. You're scarcely marked, and only another con could tell that's where you come from. And even then, a con who was not a diabolically clever face-reader might get it wrong. You had it easy in penal, right?'

'It wasn't as easy as all that: the islands; solitary.'

'Balls, man, balls! The islands—they're a holiday camp! All they lack is a casino. For you, penal meant the sea-breeze, crayfish, no mosquitoes, fishing, and now and then a real treat—the pussy or the arse of some screw's wife kept too short of it by her bastard of a husband.'

'Still, you know . . .'

'Blah-blah-blah: don't you try to fool me. I know all about it. I wasn't on the islands, but I've been told about them.' This man, maybe he was picturesque, but things were likely to turn nasty for him: I felt my temper rising fast. He went on, 'Penal, the real penal, was Kilometre 24. That doesn't mean anything to you? No, it doesn't, and that's for sure. With your mug, you've certainly never pissed in those parts. Well, mate, I have. A hundred men, every one of them with diseased guts. Some standing, some lying down, some groaning like dogs. There's the bush in front of them, like a wall. But it's not them that are going to cut the bush down: it's the bush that's going to do the cutting. It's not a working camp. As the prison administration puts it, Kilometre 24 is a conveniently hidden little dell in the Guiana forest—you toss men into it and they never bother you again. Come, Papillon; don't try and stuff me up with your islands and your solitary. It won't wash with me. You've got nothing of the look of a dog with all the spirit beaten out of it, nor the hollow face of a skin-and-bones lag with a life-sentence, nor the dial you see on all those poor buggers who escaped from that hell by some miracle—unfortunate sods who look as if they'd been worked over with a chisel to give them an old man's face on a young man's head. There's nothing like that about you at all. So there's no possible mistake about my diagnosis: for you, penal meant a holiday in the sun.'

How he did nag on and on, this little old bastard. I wondered how our meeting was going to end.

'For me, as I've been telling you, it meant the hollow nobody ever comes out of alive—amoebic dysentery, a place where you gradually shit your guts out. Poor old Papillon: you didn't even know what penal was all about.'

I looked closely at this terribly energetic little man, working out just where to plant my fist on his face, and then all at once I shifted into reverse and decided to make friends. No point in getting worked up: I might need him. 'You're right, Jojo. My penal didn't amount to much, since I'm so fit it takes a really knowing type like you to tell where I come from.'

'OK, we're in agreement, then. What are you doing now?'

'I'm working at the Mocupia gold-mine. Eighteen bolivars a day. But I've got a permit to go wherever I like; my *confina-*

miento is over.'

'I bet you want to light off for Caracas and go on the loose again.'

'You're right: that's just what I want to do.'

'But Caracas, it's the big city; so trying to pull off anything there means a hell of a risk. You're scarcely out, and you want to go back inside again?'

'I've got a long bill for the sods who sent me down—the pigs, the witnesses, the prosecutor. A thirteen-year stretch for a crime I never committed: the islands, whatever you may think of them, and solitary at Saint-Joseph, where I went through the most horrible tortures the system could think up. And don't forget I was only twenty-four when they framed me.'

'Hell: so they stole the whole of your youth. Innocent, really innocent, cross your heart, or are you still pleading in the dock?'

'Innocent, Jojo. I swear by my dead mother.'

'Christ. Well, I see that must lay heavy on your chest. But you don't have to go to Caracas if you want dough to straighten out your accounts—come with me.'

'What for?'

'Diamonds, man, diamonds! Here the government is generous: this is the only country in the world where you can burrow wherever you like for gold or diamonds. There's only one thing: no machinery allowed. All they let you use is shovel, pickaxe and sieve.'

'And where's this genuine El Dorado? Not the one I've just come out of, I hope?'

'A good way off. A good way off in the bush. A good many days on a mule and then in a canoe and then on foot, carrying your gear.'

'It's not what you'd call in the bag; hardly child's play.'

'Well, Papillon, it's the only way of getting hold of a fat sack of dough. You find just one bomb and there you are, a wealthy man—a man who has women that smoke and fart in silk. Or, if you like it that way, a man who can afford to go and present his bill.'

Now he was in full flow; his eyes blazed; he was all worked up and full of fire. A bomb, he told me—and I'd already heard it at the mine—was a little mound no bigger than a peasant's handkerchief, a mound where by some mystery of nature a hundred, two hundred, five hundred, even a thousand carats of diamonds were clustered together. If a prospector found a bomb in some far-off hole, it didn't take long—presently men started coming in from north, south, east and west, as if they'd been told by some grapevine. A dozen, then a hundred, then a thousand. They smelt the gold or the diamonds like a starving dog smells a bone or an old bit of meat. They came flooding in from every point of the compass. Rough types with no trade who'd had enough of battering away with a pick at twelve bolivars a day for some employer. They got sick of it, and then they heard the call of the jungle. They didn't want their family to go on living in a rabbit-hutch, so they went off, knowing very well what they were in for—they were going to work from one sun to the next in a wicked climate and a wicked atmosphere, condemning themselves to several years of hell. But with what they sent home, their wife would have a light, roomy little house; the children would be properly fed and clothed and they'd go to school—even go on with their own schooling, perhaps.

'So that's what a bomb gives?'

'Don't talk balls, Papillon. The guy that finds a bomb never goes back to mining. He's rich for the rest of his life, unless he goes so crazy with joy that he feeds his mule with hundred-bolivar notes soaked in kummel or anis. No, the man I'm talking about, the ordinary guy, he finds a few little diamonds every day, even though they may be very, very small. But even that means ten or fifteen times what he gets in the town. Then again, he lives as hard as possible, right down to bed-rock; because out there you pay for everything in gold or diamonds. But if he lives hard, he can still keep his family better than before.'

'What about the others?'

'They come in every shape and size. Brazilians, types from British Guiana and Trinidad: they all of them escape from exploitation in the factories or cotton-plantations or whatever. And then there are the real adventurers, the ones who can only breathe when they're not hemmed in by the horizon, the ones who will always stake everything for the jackpot—Italians,

Englishmen, Spaniards, Frenchmen, Portuguese—men from all over. Christ, you can't imagine the types that come rushing into this promised land! The Lord above may have filled it with piranhas and anacondas and mosquitoes and malaria and yellow fever, but He's also scattered gold, diamonds, topazes and emeralds and such all over its surface. There's a swarm of adventurers from everywhere in the world, and they stand there in holes up to their bellies in the water, working so hard they never feel the sun nor the mosquitoes nor hunger nor thirst, digging, tossing out the slimy earth and washing it over and over again, straining it through the sieve to find the diamonds. Then again, Venezuela has enormous frontiers and there you won't meet anyone who asks you for your papers. So there's not only the charm of the diamonds, but you can be sure of the pigs leaving you in peace. A perfect place to lie up and get your breath if you're on the run.'

Jojo stopped. There was nothing he had forgotten: I now knew the lot. A quick moment of thought and then I said, 'You go off alone, Jojo. I can't see myself working like a Trojan. You'd have to be possessed—you'd have to believe in your bomb like you believe in God Almighty to stand it in that kind of a hell. Yes, you go off by yourself. I'll look for my bomb in Caracas.'

Once again his hard eyes pierced me through and through. 'I get it: you haven't changed. Do you want to know what I really think?'

'Go ahead.'

'You're quitting El Callao because it makes you sick, knowing there's an unprotected heap of gold at La Mocupia. Right or wrong?'

'Right.'

'You're leaving it alone because you don't want to muck things up for the old lags who are living here in retirement. Right or wrong?'

'Right.'

'And you think that when it comes to finding the bomb there where I said, it's a matter of many are called and few are chosen? Right or wrong?'

'Right.'

'And you'd rather find the bomb in Caracas, wrapped up

and prepared, the diamonds already cut—find it in a jeweller's shop or a gem wholesaler's?'

'Maybe: but that's not certain. Remains to be seen.'

'On my oath, you're a right adventurer; nothing will cure you.'

'That's as it may be. But don't you forget this thing that keeps eating me all the time—this revenge. For that I really think I'd do anything at all.'

'Adventure or revenge, you still need dough. So come along into the bush with me. It's terrific, you'll see.'

'With a pickaxe and a shovel? Not for me.'

'You got a fever, Papillon? Or has it turned you into a lemon, knowing that you can go where you like since yesterday?'

'I don't feel that way.'

'You've forgotten the main thing—my name. Jojo *La Passe*: Jojo the Craps.'

'OK, so you're a professional gambler: but I don't see what that's got to do with this notion of labouring away like brutes.'

'Nor do I,' said he, doubling up with laughter.

'How come? We aren't going to the mines to dig up diamonds? Where do we get them from, then?'

'Out of the miners' pockets.'

'How?'

'By shooting craps every night, and by sometimes losing.'

'I get you, mate. When do we leave?'

'Wait a minute.' He was very pleased with the effect of his words: slowly he stood up, pulled a table out into the middle of the room, spread a blanket over it and brought out six pairs of dice. 'Have a good look.' Very carefully I examined them. They were not loaded.

'No one could say those dice were cogged, could they?'

'Nobody.'

He brought a gauge out of a felt case, gave it to me and said, 'Measure.' One of the sides had been carefully filed and polished, reducing it less than a tenth of a millimetre. All you could see was shine. 'Try and throw seven or eleven.' I rolled the dice. Neither seven nor eleven. 'My turn now.' Jojo deliberately made a little ruck in the blanket. He held the dice with the tips of his fingers. 'That's what we call the nippers,' he observed. 'Here we go! And there's seven! And there's eleven! And eleven! And seven! You want six! Boom, there's six! Six with four and two or five and one? There you are. Is the gentleman satisfied?'

I was fascinated, utterly fascinated. I'd never seen such a thing: it was extraordinary. You couldn't make out the slightest false move.

'Listen, mate, I've been shooting craps for ever. I started on the Butte when I was eight. I've risked shooting them, mate, I've risked shooting them with dice like that, and do you know where? On the crap-table at the Gare de l'Est, in the days of Roger Sole and Co.'

'I remember. There were some very quaint specimens there.'

'You don't have to tell me. And among the regulars, as well as the wide boys and the pimps and the odds and sods, there were cops as famous as Jojo-le-Beau, the pimp-cop from La Madeleine, and specialists from the gambling squad. And they were done as brown as the rest. So you see there's no coming unstuck if you shoot these craps in a miners' camp.'

'True enough.'

'But get this: the one place is as dangerous as the other. At the Gare de l'Est the crooks were as quick on the draw as the miners. Just one difference: in Paris you shoot and you light out as quick as you can. At the mine, you shoot and stay put. There are no pigs: the miners make their own laws.' He paused, slowly emptied his glass, and went on, 'Well now, Papillon, are you coming with me?'

I reflected for a moment; but not for long. The adventure tempted me. It was risky, without doubt; those miners would not be choir-boys—far from it; but there might be big money to be picked up. Come on, Papillon, banco on Jojo! And again I said to him, 'When do we leave?'

'Tomorrow afternoon, if you like: at five, after the heat of the day. That'll give us time to get things together. We'll travel by night at first. You got a gun?'

'No.'

'A good knife?'

'No knife.'

'Never mind. I'll look after that. *Ciao.*'

I went back to the house, thinking about Maria. She'd certainly rather I went into the bush than to Caracas. I'd leave Picolino with her. And then tomorrow, on my way for the diamonds! And seven! And eleven! *Once, siete! Et sept, et onze!* I was there already: all I had left to do was to learn all the numbers in Spanish, English, Brazilian and Italian.

I found José at home. I told him I'd changed my mind. Caracas would be for another time; at present I was going off with an old white-haired Frenchman called Jojo to the diamond-mines.

'What are you going with him as?'

'As his partner, of course.'

'He always gives his partners half his winnings.'

'That's the rule. Do you know men who've worked with him?'

'Three.'

'Did they make plenty of money?'

'I don't know. I dare say they did. Each one of them made three or four trips.'

'And what about after those three or four trips?'

'After? They never came back.'

'Why not? Did they settle down there at the mines?'

'No. They were dead.'

'Is that right? Fever?'

'No. Killed by the miners.'

'Oh. Jojo must be a lucky guy, if he always got out of it.'

'Yes. But Jojo, he's very knowing. He never wins much himself: *he works it so that his partner wins.*'

'I see. So it's the other man who's in danger; not him. It's as well to know. Thanks, José.'

'You're not going, now that I've told you that?'

'One last question, and give me the straight answer: is there a chance of coming back with a lot of dough after two or three trips?'

'Sure.'

'So Jojo is rich. Why does he go back there, then? I saw him loading the mules.'

'To begin with Jojo doesn't risk anything, as I said. Secondly, he was certainly not going off. Those mules belong to his father-in-law. He made up his mind to go because he met you.'

'But what about the stuff he was loading, or getting ready to load?'

'How do you know it was for him?'

'Oh-ho. What other advice have you got?'

'Don't go.'

'Not that. I've made up my mind to go. What else?'

José bent his head as if to think. A long pause. When he looked up again his face was bright. His eyes shone with intelligence, and slowly, drawing out his words, he said, 'Listen to the advice of a man who knows that world through and through. Every time there's a big game, a real big game— when there's a heap of diamonds in front of you and everything is at the boiling-point, get up unexpectedly and don't sit there with your winnings. Say you've got a belly-ache and go straight to the john. You don't come back, of course; and that night you sleep somewhere else, not in your own place.'

'Pretty good, José. And what else?'

'Although the buyers at the mine pay a good deal less than the ones in El Callao or Ciudad Bolivar, you want to sell them all the diamonds you win—sell them every day. And *don't ever take the cash*. Make them give you receipts in your name so as to cash them at El Callao or Ciudad Bolivar. Do the same with foreign banknotes. You say you're afraid of losing everything you've won in a single day and so you avoid the risk by never having much on you. And you tell everybody just what you're doing, so it becomes well known.'

'So that way I'll have a chance of coming back?'

'Yes. You'll have a chance of coming back alive, if God wills.'

'Thanks, José. *Buenas noches*.'

Lying in Maria's arms, exhausted with love, my head in the hollow of her shoulder, I felt her breath on my cheek. In the darkness, before I closed my eyes, I saw a heap of diamonds in front of me. Gently I picked them up, as though I were playing with them, and put them into the little canvas bag that all miners carry; then I got up right away and having looked round I said to Jojo, 'Keep my place. I'm going to the john. I'll be back in a minute.' And as I dropped off, there were José's knowing eyes, shining full of light—only people who live very close to nature have eyes like that.

The morning passed quickly. Everything was settled. Picolino was to stay there: he would be well cared for. I kissed everybody. Maria shone with delight. She knew that if I went to the mines I should have to come back this way, whereas Caracas never gave back the men who went to live there. She went with me as far as the meeting-place. Five o'clock; Jojo was there, and in great form. 'Hello there, mate! OK? You're prompt—fine, fine! The sun will be down in an hour. It's better that way. There's no one who can follow you at night.'

A dozen kisses for my true love and I climbed into the saddle. Jojo fixed the stirrups for me and just as we were setting off Maria said to me, 'And above all, *mi amor*, don't forget to go to the lavatory at the right moment.'

I burst out laughing as I dug my heels into the mule. 'You were listening behind the door, you Judas!'

'When you love, it's natural.'

Now we were away, Jojo on a horse and me on a mule. The virgin forest has its roads, and they are called *piques*. A *pique* is a passage about two yards wide that has gradually been cut out through the trees; and the men who pass along keep it clear with their machêtes. On either side, a wall of green: above, a roof of millions of plants, but too high to be reached with a machête even if you stand in your stirrups. This is the *selva*, the tropical forest. It is made up of an impenetrable tangle of two kinds of vegetation: first comes a mixture of creepers, trees and plants that does not rise much above twenty feet, then over that, mounting to seventy-five or a hundred feet, there are the splendid great tops of the huge trees that climb higher and higher to reach the sun. But although their tops are in the sunlight, the foliage of their wide, leafy branches makes a thick screen, keeping off all but a dim, filtered day. In a tropical forest you are in a wonderful landscape that bursts into growth all over, so as you ride along a *pique* you have to hold the reins in one hand and keep slashing at everything that gets in your way. A *pique* where a certain number of people keep coming and going always looks like a well-kept corridor.

There's nothing that gives a man such a sense of freedom as

being in the bush and well armed. He has the feeling of being as much part of the landscape as the wild animals. He moves cautiously, but with unbounded self-confidence. He seems to be in the most natural of all possible elements, and all his senses are on the alert—hearing, sight and smell. His eyes dart perpetually from point to point, sizing up everything that moves. In the bush there is only one enemy that matters, the beast of beasts, the most intelligent, the cruellest, the wickedest, the greediest, the vilest and also the most wonderful—man.

We travelled all that night, going fairly well. But in the morning, after we had drunk a little coffee from the Thermos flask, my whore of a mule started dragging its feet, dawdling along sometimes as much as a hundred yards behind Jojo. I stabbed its arse with all kinds of thorns, but nothing did any good. And to aggravate matters, Jojo started bawling out, 'Why, you know nothing about riding, man. It's easy enough. Watch me.' And he would just touch his creature with his heel and set off at a gallop. And he'd stand in his stirrups and bellow, 'I'm Captain Cook' or 'Hey there, Sancho! Are you coming? Can't you keep up with your master, Don Quixote?'

This riled me and I tried everything I could think of to make the mule get along. At last I hit on a terrific idea and straight away it broke into a gallop. I dropped a lighted cigar-end into its ear. It tore along like a thoroughbred; I rejoiced, full of glee; I even passed the Captain, waving as I went flashing by. But a mule being a vicious brute this only lasted the length of the gallop. It rammed me up against a tree, nearly crushing my leg, and there I was on the ground, my arse filled with the prickles of some plant. And there was old Jojo, screeching with laughter like a child.

I won't tell the whole story of chasing the mule (two hours!) nor its kicking and farting and all the rest. But at last, out of breath, full of thorns, perishing with heat and weariness, I did manage to hoist myself on to the back of that cross-grained, obstinate bastard. This time it could go just as it chose: I was not going to be the one to cross it. The first mile I rode not sitting but lying on its back, with my arse in the air, trying to get the fiery thorns out of it.

The next day we left the pig-headed brute at a *posada*, an

inn: then two days in a canoe, and then a long day's walk with packs on our back brought us to the diamond-mine.

I dumped my load on the log table of an open-air eating-house. I was at the end of my tether, and I could have strangled old Jojo—he stood there with no more than a few drops of sweat on his forehead, looking at me with a knowing grin. 'Well, mate, and how are you feeling? OK?'

'Fine, fine! Is there any reason why I shouldn't be feeling fine? But just you tell me this: why have you made me carry a shovel, a pickaxe and a sieve all day long when we aren't going to do any digging at all?'

Jojo put on a sorrowful air. 'Papillon, you disappoint me. Think a little: use your loaf. If a guy turned up here, not carrying these tools, what would he have come for? That's the question everybody would ask—all these eyes that watched you coming into the village through the holes in the walls and the tin roofs. With you loaded as you were, no questions. You get it?'

'I get it, man.'

'It's the same for me, since I'm carrying nothing. Suppose I turn up with my hands in my pockets and I set up my table without doing anything else: what are the miners and their girls going to say, eh, Papi? This old French type is a professional gambler, that's what they are going to say. Well now, you'll see what I'm going to do. If I can, I'll try and find a secondhand motor-pump here in the village: otherwise I'll send for one. And twenty yards of big piping and two or three sluices. A sluice is a long wooden box with divisions, and these divisions have holes in them. You pump the mud into it, and that means a team of seven men can wash fifty times more earth than a dozen working the old-fashioned way. And it's still not looked upon as machinery. Then as the owner of the pump I get twenty-five per cent of the diamonds; and what's more, I have a reason for being here. No one can say I live off gambling, because I live off my pump. But since I'm a gambler *as well*, I don't stop gambling at night. That's natural, because I don't take part in the actual work. You get it?'

'It's as clear as gin.'

'There's a bright boy. Two *frescos*, Señora.'

A fat, friendly old light-skinned woman brought us glasses full of a chocolate-coloured liquid with an ice-cube and a bit of lemon swimming in it.

'That'll be eight bolivars, *hombres*.'

'More than two dollars! Hell, life is not cheap here.'

Jojo paid. 'How are things going?' he asked.

'So-so.'

'Are there any or are there not?'

'Men in plenty. But very, very few diamonds. They found this place three months ago, and since then four thousand men have come rushing in. Too many men for so few diamonds. And what about him?' she said, jerking her chin towards me. 'German or French?'

'French. He's with me.'

'Poor soul.'

'How come, poor soul?' I asked.

'Because you're too young and too good-looking to die. The men who come with Jojo never have any luck.'

'You shut your trap, you old fool. Come on, Papi, let's go.'

As we stood up, the fat woman said to me by way of good-bye, 'Look out for yourself.'

Of course, I'd said nothing about what José had told me, and Jojo was amazed that I did not try to find out what there was behind her words. I could feel him waiting for the questions that didn't come. He seemed upset and he kept glancing at me sideways.

Pretty soon, after he had talked to various people, Jojo found a shack. Three small rooms; rings to hang our hammocks; and some cartons. On one of them, empty beer and rum bottles; on another, a battered enamel bowl and a full watering-can. Strings stretched across to hang up our clothes. The floor was pounded earth, very clean. The walls of this hutch were made of planks from packing-cases—you could still read Savon Camay, Aceite Branca, Nestlé's Milk. Each room was about ten foot by ten. No windows. I felt stifled and took off my shirt.

Jojo turned, deeply shocked. 'Are you crazy? Suppose somebody came in? You've got a wicked mug already, and now if you go and show your tattooed hide, man it's as if you were advertising the fact that you're a crook. Behave yourself.'

'But I'm stifling, Jojo.'

'You'll get used to it—it's all a matter of habit. But behave yourself, almighty God: above all, behave yourself.'

I managed to keep myself from laughing: he was a priceless old party, that Jojo.

We knocked two rooms into one. 'This will be the casino,' said Jojo, with a grin. It made a room twenty foot by ten. We swept the floor, went out to buy three big wooden crates, some rum and paper cups to drink out of. I was eager to see what the game would be like.

I didn't have to wait long. Once we had been round a number of wretched little drinking-joints, to 'make contact' as Jojo put it, everyone knew that there would be a game of craps in our place at eight that evening. The last joint we went to was a shed with a couple of tables outside, four benches and a carbide lamp hanging from a covering of branches. The boss, a huge, ageless redhead, served the punch without a word. As we were leaving he came over to me and, speaking French, he said, 'I don't know who you are and I don't want to know. But I'll just give you this tip. The day you feel like sleeping here, come along. I'll look after you.'

He spoke an odd sort of French, but from his accent I realized he was a Corsican. 'You a Corsican?'

'Yes. And you know a Corsican never betrays. Not like some guys from the north,' he added, with a knowing smile.

'Thanks. It's good to know.'

Towards seven o'clock, Jojo lit the carbide lamp. The two blankets were laid out on the ground. No chairs. The gamblers would either stand or squat. We decided I shouldn't play that night. Just watch, that's all.

They started to arrive. Extraordinary mugs. Few short men: most were huge, bearded, moustachio'd types. Hands and faces were clean; they didn't smell; yet their clothes were all stained and very nearly worn out. But every single one of the shirts—mostly short-sleeved—was spotlessly clean.

In the middle of the cloth, eight pairs of dice were neatly arranged, each in a little box. Jojo asked me to give each player a paper cup. There were about twenty of them. I poured out the rum. Not a single guy there jerked up the neck of the bottle to say enough. After just one round, three bottles vanished.

Each man deliberately took a sip, then put his cup down in front of him and laid an aspirin tube beside it. I knew that there were diamonds in those tubes. A shaky old Chinese set up a little jeweller's scales in front of him. Nobody said much. These men were shagged out: they'd been labouring under the blazing sun, some of them standing in water up to their middles from six in the morning till the sun went down.

Ha, things were beginning to move! First one, then two, then three players took up a pair of dice and examined them carefully, pressing them tight together and passing them on to their neighbour. Everything must have seemed to be in order, because the dice were tossed back on to the blanket without anything being said. Each time, Jojo picked up the pair and put them back in their box, all except for the last, which stayed there on the blanket.

Some men who had taken off their shirts complained of the mosquitoes. Jojo asked me to burn a few handfuls of damp grass, so that the smoke would help to drive them out.

'Who kicks off?' asked a huge copper-coloured guy with a thick black curly beard and a lopsided flower tattooed on his right arm.

'You, if you like,' said Jojo.

Out of his silver-mounted belt, the gorilla—for he looked very like a gorilla—brought an enormous wad of bolivar-notes held in an elastic band.

'What are you kicking off with, Chino?' asked another man.

'Five hundred bolos.' Bolos is short for bolivars.

'OK for five hundred.'

And the craps rolled. The eight came up. Jojo tried to shoot the eight.

'A thousand bolos you don't shoot the eight with double fours,' said another player.

'I take that,' said Jojo.

Chino managed to roll the eight, by five and three. Jojo had lost. For five hours on end the game continued without an exclamation, without the least dispute. These men were uncommon gamblers. That night Jojo lost seven thousand bolos and a guy with a game leg more than ten thousand.

It had been decided to stop the game at midnight, but

everyone agreed to carry on for another hour. At one o'clock Jojo said this was the last crack.

'It was me that kicked off,' said Chino, taking the dice. 'I'll close it. I lay all my winnings, nine thousand bolivars.'

He had a mass of notes and diamonds in front of him. He covered a whole lot of other stakes and rolled the seven first go.

At this terrific stroke of luck, for the first time a murmur went round. The men stood up. 'Let's get some sleep.'

'Well, you saw that, mate?' said Jojo when we were alone.

'Yes: and what I noticed most were those right hard mugs. They all carry a gun and a knife. There were even some who sat on their machêtes, so sharp they could take your head off in one swipe.'

'That's a fact: but you've seen others like them.'

'Even so ... I ran the table on the islands, but I tell you I never had such a feeling of danger as tonight.'

'It's all a matter of habit, mate. Tomorrow you'll play and we'll win: it's in the bag. As you see it,' he added, 'which are the guys to watch closest?'

'The Brazilians.'

'Well done! That's how you can tell a man—the way he spots the ones who may turn lethal from one second to another.'

When we had locked the door (three huge bolts) we threw ourselves into our hammocks, and I dropped off right away, before Jojo could start his snoring.

The next day, a splendid sun arose fit to roast you—not a cloud nor the least hint of a breeze. I wandered about this curious village. Everyone was welcoming. Disturbing faces on the men, sure enough, but they had a way of saying things (in whatever language they spoke) so there was a warm human contact right away. I found the enormous Corsican redhead again. His name was Miguel. He spoke fluent Venezuelan with English or Brazilian words dropping into it every now and then, as if they'd come down by parachute. It was only when he spoke French, which he did with difficulty, that his Corsican accent came out. We drank coffee that a young brown girl had strained through a sock. As we were talking he said to me, 'Where do you come from, brother?'

'After what you said yesterday, I can't lie to you. I come from penal.'

'Ah? You escaped? I'm glad you told me.'

'And what about you?'

He drew himself up, six foot and more, and his redhead's face took on an extremely noble expression. 'I escaped too, but not from Guiana. I left Corsica before they could arrest me. I'm a bandit of honour—an *honourable* bandit.'

His face, all lit up with the pride of being an honest man, impressed me. He was really magnificent to see, this honourable bandit. He went on, 'Corsica is the paradise of the world, the only country where men will give their lives for honour. You don't believe it?'

'I don't know whether it's the only country, but I do believe you'll find more men in the maquis who are there on account of their honour than just plain bandits.'

'I don't care for town-bandits,' he said thoughtfully.

In a couple of words I told him how things were with me; and I said I meant to go back to Paris to present my bill.

'You're right; but revenge is a dish you want to eat cold. Go about it as carefully as ever you can; it would be terrible if they picked you up before you had had your satisfaction. You're with old Jojo?'

'Yes.'

'He's straight. Some people say he's too clever with the dice, but I don't believe he's a wrong 'un. You've known him long?'

'Not very; but that doesn't matter.'

'Why, Papi, the more you gamble the more you know about other men—that's nature; but there's one thing that worries me for you.'

'What's that?'

'Two or three times his partner's been murdered. That's why I said what I did yesterday evening. Take care: and when you don't feel safe, you come here. You can trust me.'

'Thanks, Miguel.'

Yes, a curious village all right, a curious mixture of men lost in the bush, living a rough life in the middle of an explosive landscape. Each one had his story. It was wonderful to see them, wonderful to listen to them. Their shacks were sometimes no more than a roof of palm-fronds or bits of corrugated iron, and God knows how they got there. The walls were strips of cardboard or wood or sometimes even cloth. No beds; only hammocks. They slept, ate, washed and made love almost in the street. And yet nobody would lift a corner of the canvas or peer between the planks to see what was going on inside. Everybody had the utmost respect for others' privacy. If you wanted to go and see anyone, you never went nearer than a couple of yards before calling out, by way of ringing the bell, 'Is there anyone at home?' If there was and he didn't know you, you said, '*Gentes de paz*,' the same as saying I'm a friend. Then someone would appear and say politely, '*Adelante. Esta casa es suya.*' Come in; this house is yours.

A table in front of a solid hut made of well-fitting logs. On the table, necklaces of real pearls from Margarita Island, some nuggets of virgin gold, a few watches, leather or expanding metal watch-straps, and a good many alarm-clocks. Mustafa's jewellery shop.

Behind the table, there was an old Arab with a pleasant face. We talked a while: he was a Moroccan and he'd seen I was French. It was five in the afternoon, and he said to me, 'Have you eaten?'

'Not yet.'

'Nor have I. I was just going to. If you'd like to share my meal . . .?'

'That would be fine.'

Mustafa was a kind, cheerful guy. I spent a very pleasant hour with him. He was not inquisitive and he didn't ask me where I came from.

'It's odd,' he said, 'in my own country I hated the French, and here I like them. Have you known any Arabs?'

'Plenty. Some were very good and others were very bad.'

'It's the same with all nations. I class myself among the good ones. I'm sixty, and I might be your father. I had a son of thirty: he was killed two years ago—shot. He was good-looking; he was kind.' His eyes brimmed with tears.

I put my hand on his shoulder: this unhappy father so moved by the memory of his son reminded me of my own—he too, retired in his little house in the Ardèche must have his eyes filled with tears when he thought of me. Poor old Papa.

Who could tell where he was, or what he was doing? I was sure he was still alive—I could feel it. Let's hope the war had not knocked him about too much.

Mustafa told me to come to his place whenever I felt like it—for a meal or if ever I needed anything: I'd be doing a kindness if I asked him a favour.

Evening was coming on: I said thank you for everything and set off for our shack. The game would soon be beginning.

I was not at all on edge about my first game. 'Nothing ventured, nothing gained,' Jojo had said, and he was quite right. If I wanted to deliver my trunk filled with dynamite at 36, quai des Orfèvres and to deal with the others I needed dough, plenty of dough. I'd be getting my hands on it precious soon: and that was a certainty.

As it was a Saturday, and as the miners religiously took their Sundays off, the game was not to begin before nine, because it would last until sunrise. The men came crowding to the shack, too many of them to get inside. It was impossible to find room for them all, so Jojo sorted out the ones who could play high. There were twenty-four of them: the rest would play outside. I went to Mustafa's, and he very kindly lent me a big carpet and a carbide lamp. As the big-time gamblers dropped out, so they could be replaced from outside.

Banco, and banco again! On and on: every time Jojo rolled the dice so I kept covering the stakes. 'Two to one he won't shoot six with double threes ... ten with double fives ...' The men's eyes were ablaze. Every time one of them lifted his cup an eleven-year-old boy filled it with rum. I'd asked Jojo to let Miguel supply the rum and the cigars.

Very soon the game heated up to boiling-point. Without asking his permission, I changed Jojo's tactics. I laid not only on him but also on the others, and that made him look sour. Lighting a cigar, he muttered angrily, 'Stuff it, man. Don't scatter the gumbo.' By about four in the morning I had a pile of bolivars, cruzeiros, American and West Indian dollars, diamonds and even some little gold nuggets in front of me.

Jojo took the dice. He staked five hundred bolivars. I went in with a thousand.

And he threw the seven!

I left the lot, making two thousand bolivars. Jojo took out

the five hundred he had won. And threw the seven again! Once more he pulled out his stake. And seven again!

'What are you going to do, Enrique?' asked Chino.

'I leave the four thousand.'

'Banco alone!' I looked at the guy who had just spoken. A little thickset man, as black as boot-polish, his eyes bloodshot with drink. A Brazilian for sure.

'Put down your four thousand bolos.'

'This stone's worth more.' And he dropped a diamond on the blanket, just in front of him. He squatted there in his pink shorts, bare to the waist. The Chinese picked up the diamond, put it on his scales and said, 'It's only worth three and a half.'

'OK for three and a half,' said the Brazilian.

'Shoot, Jojo.'

Jojo shot the dice, but the Brazilian grabbed them as they rolled. I wondered what was going to happen: he scarcely looked at the dice but spat on them and tossed them back to Jojo. 'Shoot them like that, all wet,' he said.

'OK, Enrique?' asked Jojo, looking at me.

'If that's the way you want it, *hombre*.'

Jojo hitched the fold in the blanket deeper with his left hand, and without wiping the dice he shot them—a long, long roll. And up came the seven again.

As if he was jerked by a spring, the Brazilian leapt to his feet, his hand on his gun. Then quietly he said, 'It's not my night yet.' And he went out.

The moment he shot up like a jack-in-the-box my hand darted to my gun—it had a round in the breech. Jojo never stirred nor made a move to defend himself. And yet it was him the black man was aiming at. I saw I still had a lot to learn before I knew the exact moment when to draw and fire.

At sunrise we stopped. What with the smoke of the damp grass and the cigars and cigarettes, my eyes stung so much they ran. My legs were completely numb from having squatted like a tailor more than nine hours on end. But there was one thing that pleased me: I hadn't had to get up and piss, not once, and that meant I was entirely in control of my nerves and of my life.

We slept until two in the afternoon. When I woke up, Jojo

wasn't there. I put on my trousers—nothing in the pockets! Shit! Jojo must have swiped the lot. But we hadn't settled our accounts yet: he shouldn't have done that. He was taking too much upon himself—coming it the boss, and coming it a trifle high. I wasn't and never had been a boss; but I couldn't bear people who thought themselves superior—who thought they could get away with anything. I went out and I found Jojo at Miguel's, eating a dish of macaroni and mince. 'OK, buddy?' he said to me.

'Yes and no.'

'How come, no?'

'Because you never ought to have emptied my pockets when I wasn't there.'

'Don't talk balls, boy. I know how to behave and the reason why I did that is on account of everything depends on mutual trust. Don't you see, during a game you might very well stuff the diamonds or the liquid some place else besides your pockets, for example? Then again, you don't know what I won either. So whether we empty our pockets together or not, it's all one. A matter of confidence.'

He was right: let's say no more. Jojo paid Miguel for the rum and the tobacco of last night. I asked whether the guys wouldn't think it odd that he paid for them to drink and smoke.

'But I'm not the one who pays! Each man who wins a packet leaves something on the table. Everyone knows that.'

And night after night this life went on. We'd been here two weeks, two weeks in which every night we played high and wild, gambling with the dice and gambling with our lives too.

Last night an appalling rain came hurtling down. Black as ink. A gambler got up after winning a fair pile. He went out at the same time as a huge guy who'd been just sitting there for some time, not playing any more for want of the wherewithal. Twenty minutes later the big guy who had been so unlucky came back and started gambling like crazy. I thought the winner must have lent him the dough, but still it seemed queer he should have lent him so much. When daylight came they found the winner dead, stabbed less than fifty yards from our place. I talked to Jojo about it, telling him what I thought.

'It's nothing to do with us,' he said. 'Next time, he'll watch out.'

'You're gaga, Jojo. There'll be no next time for him, on account of he's dead.'

'True enough: but what can we do about it?'

I was following José's advice, of course. Every day I sold my foreign notes, the diamonds and the gold to a Lebanese buyer, the owner of a jeweller's shop in Ciudad Bolivar. Over the front of his hut there was a notice 'Gold and diamonds bought here: highest prices given'. And underneath it 'Honesty is my greatest treasure'.

Carefully I packed the credit-notes payable on sight to my order in a balata'd envelope—an envelope dipped in raw latex. They could not be cashed by anyone else nor endorsed in any other name. Every gallowsbird in the village knew what I was doing, and if there was any type who made me feel too uneasy or who didn't speak French or Spanish, I showed him. So the only time I was in danger was during the game or when it ended. Sometimes that good guy Miguel came and fetched me when we stopped for the night.

For the last two days I'd had the feeling the atmosphere was getting tenser, more mistrustful. I'd learnt the smell in penal: when trouble was brewing in our barrack on the islands, you realized it without being able to tell how. When you're always on the alert, do you pick up waves put out by the guys getting ready for the rough stuff? I don't know. But I've never been wrong about things like that.

For example, yesterday four Brazilians spent the whole night propped up in the corners of the room, in the darkness. Very occasionally one of them would come out of the shadows into the hard light that shone on the blanket and lay a few ridiculous little bets. They never took the dice nor asked for them. Something else: *not one of them had a weapon that could be seen*. No machête, no knife, no gun. And that just didn't go with their killers' faces. It was on purpose, no doubt of it.

They came back this evening. They wore their shirts outside their pants, so they must have their guns up against their bellies. They settled into the shadows, of course, but still I could make them out. Their eyes never left the players' move-

73

ments. I had to watch them without their noticing it; and that meant I must not stare straight at them. I managed by coughing and leaning back, covering my mouth with my hand. Unfortunately there were only two in front of me. The others were behind, and I could only get quick glances of them by turning round to blow my nose.

Jojo's coolness was something extraordinary. He remained perfectly unmoved. Still, from time to time he did bet on other men's throws, which meant the risk of winning or losing by mere unaided chance. I knew that this kind of gambling set him on edge, because it forced him to win the same money two or three times before keeping it for good. The disadvantage was when the game grew red-hot he became too eager to win and passed me over great wads of dough too fast.

As I knew these guys were watching me, I left my pile there in front of me for everyone to see. I didn't want to behave like a living safe-deposit today.

Two or three times I told Jojo, in quick crook's slang, that he was making me win too often. He looked as if he didn't understand. I had worked the lavatory trick on them yesterday and I had not come back; so it was no good doing it now—if these four types meant to move in tonight, they were not going to wait for me to return: they'd get me between the shack and the shit-house.

I felt the tension mount: the four images in each corner were more on edge than ever. Particularly one who kept smoking cigarette after cigarette, lighting one from the butt of the other.

So now I started making bancos right and left, in spite of Jojo's ugly looks. To crown it all I won instead of losing and, far from shrinking, my pile kept on piling up. It was all there in front of me, mostly in five-hundred-bolivar notes. I was so keyed up that as I took the dice I put my cigarette down on them and it burnt two holes in a folded five hundred. I played and lost this note together with three others in a two-thousand-bolo banco. The winner got up, said, 'See you tomorrow,' and went out.

In the heat of the game I took no notice of how the time passed, and then all at once to my amazement I saw the note there on the blanket again. I knew perfectly well who'd won it, a very thin bearded white man of about forty with a pale mark on the lobe of his left ear, standing out against the sunburn. But he was not here any more. In a couple of seconds I had put the scene together again: he'd gone out alone, I was certain of that. Yet not one of those four types had stirred. So that meant they had one or two accomplices outside. They must have a system of signalling from where they were that a guy was coming out loaded with cash and diamonds.

There were a good many men gambling standing up, so I could not make out who had come in since the thin guy left. As for the ones sitting down, they had been the same for hours and the place of the thin guy with the burnt note had been filled the moment he left.

But who had played the note? I felt like picking it up and asking. But that would be very risky.

I was in danger: no doubt about that. There before my eyes was the proof that the thin guy had got himself killed. My nerves were tense but they were under control; I had to think very fast. It was four in the morning: no daylight before six-fifteen, because in the tropics the sun comes up straight away, some time after six. So if something was going to happen, it would be between four and five. Outside it was as dark as hell: I knew, because I had just got up, saying I wanted a breath of fresh air in the doorway. I'd left my pile there where I sat, neatly stacked. I saw nothing unusual outside.

I came back and sat down calmly, but all my senses were on the alert. The back of my neck told me there were two pairs of eyes drilling into it.

Jojo rolled the dice, and I let other people cover his stakes. And now he began to have a fair-sized pile in front of him—something he hated.

The temperature was rising, rising; I felt that for sure, and in a very natural voice, not as if I were taking precautions, I said to Jojo in French, 'I'm dead certain there's trouble in the air, man: I can smell it. Get up at the same time as me and let's cover the lot with our guns.'

Jojo smiled as though I were saying something pleasant: he no more bothered about me than about someone else understanding French, and he said, 'My good friend, what's the sense of this damn-fool attitude? And just who's to be covered

75

in particular?'

True enough. Cover who? And what reason could you give? Yet the balloon was just going to go up, that was certain. The guy with the everlasting cigarette had two full cups of rum and he tossed them straight off, one after the other.

It would be no good going out alone in the inky darkness, even holding a gun. The men outside would see me and I wouldn't see them. Go into the room next door? Worse still. Nine chances out of ten there was already a guy there: he could easily have got in by lifting one of the planks in the wall.

There was only one thing to do and that was to openly put all my winnings into my canvas bag, leave the bag there where I was sitting and go out and have a piss. They would not signal because I wouldn't have the dough on me. There was more than five thousand bolos in my pile. Better lose them than my life.

Anyhow, there was no choice. It was the only way to get out of this trap, which might snap to any minute.

I'd worked all this out very quickly, of course: it was now seven minutes to five. I gathered everything together, notes, diamonds, the aspirin tubes and all: everyone saw me. I deliberately stuffed this little fortune into the canvas bag. As naturally as could be I pulled the strings tight, put the bag down about a foot from me, and so that everybody should understand I said in Spanish, 'Keep an eye on the bag, Jojo. I don't feel so good: I'm going to take a breath of air.'

Jojo had been watching all my movements; he held out his hand and said, 'Give it me. It'll be better here than anywhere else.'

Unwillingly, I held it out, because I knew he was putting himself in danger, immediate danger. But what could I do? Refuse? Impossible: it would sound very strange.

I walked out, my hand on my gun. I could see no one in the darkness, but I didn't have to see them to know they were there. Quickly, almost running, I made for Miguel's place. There was just a chance that by coming back with him and a big carbide lamp we might avoid the crunch. Unfortunately Miguel's was more than two hundred yards from our shack. I began to run.

'Miguel! Miguel!'

'What's the matter?'

'Get up quick! Bring your gun and your lamp. There's trouble.'

Bang! Bang! Two shots in the pitch-black night.

I ran. First I got the wrong shack—insults from inside and at the same time they asked me what the shooting was about. I ran on. Here was our shack—all lights out. I flicked my lighter. People came running with lamps. Nobody left in the room. Jojo was lying on the ground, blood pouring from the back of his neck. He was not dead, but in a coma. An electric torch they'd left behind showed just what had happened. First they'd shot out the carbide lamp, at the same time knocking Jojo out. Using the torch, they'd swept up the pile lying in front of Jojo—my bag and his winnings. His shirt had been torn off and the canvas belt he wore next to his skin ripped open with a knife or a machête.

All the gamblers had escaped, of course. The second shot had been fired to make them move faster. Anyhow, there had not been many of us left when I'd got up. Eight men sitting down, two standing, the four types in the corners and the kid who poured out the rum.

Everybody offered to help. Jojo was carried to Miguel's hut, where there was a bed made of branches. He lay there in a coma all the morning. The blood had clotted; it no longer ran out, and according to an English miner that was a good sign but also a bad one, because if the skull was fractured, the bleeding would go on inside. I decided not to move him. A miner from El Callao, an old friend of Jojo's, set off for another mine to fetch a so-called doctor.

I was all in. I explained everything to Mustafa and Miguel, and they comforted me by saying that since the whole business had been as you might say signalled hours ahead, and since I had given Jojo a clear warning, he ought to have followed my lead.

About three in the afternoon, Jojo opened his eyes. We made him drink a few drops of rum, and then, the words coming hard, he whispered, 'It's all up with me, mate: I know it. Don't let me be moved. It wasn't your fault, Papi; it was mine.' He paused for a while and then went on, 'Miguel, there's a can buried behind your pig-sty. Let the one-eyed guy take it to Lola, my wife.' His mind was clear for a few minutes after that, and then he relapsed into coma. He died at sunset.

Doña Carmencita, the fat woman from the first joint, came to see him. She brought a few diamonds and three or four notes she had found on the floor at our place during the morning. God knows hundreds of people had been there, yet not one of them had touched either the money or the diamonds.

Almost the whole of the little community came to the funeral. The four Brazilians were there, still wearing their shirts outside their trousers. One of them came up to me and held out his hand; I pretended not to see it and gave him a friendly shove in the belly. Yes: I had been right. The gun was just there, where I had thought it would be.

I wondered whether I ought to deal with them. Do it now? Later? Do what? Nothing: it was too late.

I wanted to be alone, but after a burial it was the custom to go and have a drink at every joint whose owner had turned up at the graveyard. They always came, all of them.

When I was at Doña Carmencita's she came and sat by me, with her glass of anis in her hand. When I put mine to my lips, she raised hers too, but only to hide the fact that she was talking to me. 'It was better him than you,' she said. 'Now you can go wherever you want in peace.'

'What do you mean, in peace?'

'Because everybody knows you always sold your winnings to the Lebanese.'

'Yes, but suppose the Lebanese is killed?'

'That's true. One more problem.'

I told Doña Carmencita the drinks were on me and walked off by myself, leaving my friends sitting there. Without really knowing why, I took the path that led to what they called the graveyard, a piece of cleared ground of about fifty square yards.

Eight graves there in the cemetery: Jojo's was the latest. And there in front of it stood Mustafa. I went over to him. 'What are you doing, Mustafa?'

'I've come to pray for an old friend—I was fond of him—and to bring him a cross. You forgot to make one.'

Hell, so I had! I'd never thought of it. I shook the good old Arab's hand and thanked him.

'You're not a Christian?' he asked. 'I didn't see you pray when they threw the earth on to him.'

'Well, I mean ... there's certainly a God, Mustafa,' I said, to please him. 'And what's more, I thank Him for having looked after me instead of sending me down the line with Jojo. And I do more than say prayers for this old man; I forgive him: he was a poor little kid from the Belleville slums, and he was only able to learn just one profession—shooting craps.'

'What are you talking about, brother? I don't understand.'

'It doesn't matter. But just remember this: I'm really sorry he's dead. I did try to save him. But no one should ever think he's brighter than the rest, because one day he'll find a man who moves faster than him. Jojo is fine here. He'll sleep for ever with what he loved, adventure and the wild landscape; and he'll sleep with God's forgiveness.'

'Yes, God will forgive him for sure, because he was a good man.'

'That's a fact.'

I walked slowly back to the village. It was true that I did not feel resentful towards Jojo, although he had very nearly been the death of me. His enthusiasm, his prodigious energy, and, in spite of his sixty years, his youth, and his underworld good breeding—'Behave properly, God almighty, behave properly!' And then I'd been warned. I'd willingly send up a little prayer to thank José for his advice. Without him I shouldn't be here.

Swinging gently in my hammock and smoking fat cigar after fat cigar, as much to soak myself in nicotine as to chase the mosquitoes away, I cast up my accounts.

Right. I had ten thousand dollars after only a few months of freedom. And both here and at El Callao I had met men and women of all races and backgrounds, every one of them full of human warmth. Because of them and this life in the wild, in this atmosphere so unlike that of the city, I'd come to know how wonderful freedom was, the freedom I'd fought for so hard.

Then again the war had come to an end, thanks to Charlie de Gaulle and the Yankees; in all this churning about of millions of people, a convict didn't amount to much. So much the better for me: with all these problems to settle, they would have other things to do apart from worrying about what I had been.

I was thirty-seven: thirteen years of penal settlement, fifty-three months of solitary confinement, counting the Santé, the Conciergerie and Beaulieu as well as the prison on the islands, the Réclusion. It was hard to put a label on me. I was neither a poor bastard only capable of working with a pick or a shovel or an axe, nor was I a type with a real trade that would let me earn a decent living anywhere in the world, as a mechanic or an electrician, say. On the other hand, I couldn't take on important responsibilities; I hadn't enough education for that. At the same time as your schooling, you ought always to learn a good manual trade: if school goes wrong, you can then always look after yourself in life. It was not that you felt better than a street-sweeper if you had a certain amount of education—I had never despised any man, apart from screws and pigs—but you couldn't sustain your role. You were between two stools—you felt that you had it in you to be happy, but that you couldn't get there. I had both too much education and not enough. Hell, that was hardly the brightest outlook in the world.

Then again, if you were an ordinary, normal man, how could you control your deep-down urges? I ought to look for peace and quiet, and live like the retired lags of El Callao; but what I felt right down inside me was a kind of explosion, a terrific thirst for life. Adventure drew me on with such force that I wondered whether I should ever be able to live a quiet life.

And it was true that I had to take my revenge, too: it was true I could not possibly forgive the people who had done me and my family so much harm. Calm down, Papi, calm down. You've got plenty of time. You must gradually learn to trust in the future. For although you've sworn to go straight in this country, here you are right out on the loose, forgetting your promise.

How hard it was to live like other people, obey like other people, walk in step with everybody else, rigidly conforming to the rules.

Take your choice, Papi: either you make up your mind to obey the law in this, God's own country, and you give up your revenge, or you decide you can't put your obsession behind you. And in that case, since you'll need much more money than you'll ever make by working, you must go on the loose again.

And after all I could very well go and look for this essential cash *outside Venezuela*. That's not such a bad idea, man. But it needs thinking over first. Let's get some sleep.

But before that I couldn't help going to the doorway and gazing for a long while at the stars and the moon and listening to the countless noises coming from the mysterious bush that surrounded the village with a wall as dark as the moon was brilliant.

And then I slept, rocking gently in my hammock, happy to the core in the knowledge that I was free, free, free, and *master of my fate*.

AT about ten the next morning I went to see the Lebanese. 'So I go to El Callao or Ciudad Bolivar, to the addresses you've given me, and they pay me your bills of exchange?'

'That's right: you can go off with an easy mind.'

'But what if they kill you too?'

'It doesn't matter, as far as you're concerned. You will be paid whatever happens. You're going to El Callao?'

'Yes.'

'What part of France are you from?'

'Round Avignon: not far from Marseilles.'

'Why, I've got a friend from Marseilles: but he lives a great way off. Alexandre Guigue is his name.'

'Well, what do you know! He's a close friend of mine.'

'Of mine, too. I'm glad you know him.'

'Where does he live, and how can I get there?'

'He's at Boa Vista. A very long and complicated journey.'

'What does he do there?'

'He's a barber. Easy to find him—you just ask for the French barber-dentist.'

'So he's a dentist too?'

I couldn't help laughing. Because I knew Alexandre Guigue very well: an extraordinary guy. He was sent down the same time as me, in 1933; we made the crossing together, and he had all the time in the world to tell me every last detail of his job.

One Saturday night in 1929 or 1930, Alexandre and a friend climbed quietly down from the ceiling of Lisbon's biggest jewel-shop. They had broken into a dentist's flat on the next floor up. To fix the geography of the building, to make sure the dentist went away every week-end with his family, and to take the prints of the lock of the front door and the surgery, they had had to go there several times and have stoppings put in their teeth.

'Very good work he did, too,' Alexandre told me, 'seeing the stoppings are still there. In two nights we had all the time we needed to shift the jewels and open two safes and a little steel cabinet, doing it neatly and without any noise. There was no identikit in those days, but the dentist must have been fantastic at describing people, because as we were on the platform leaving Lisbon the pigs jumped on us without any hesitation at all. The Portuguese court sent us down for ten and twelve years. So there we were, a little while later, at their penal in Angola, down under the Belgian and French Congo. No problem about escaping: our friends came to fetch us in a taxi. Like an idiot I went to Brazzaville: my mate, he chose Leopoldville. A few months later I was picked up by the French police. The French wouldn't give me back to the Portuguese: they sent me back to France and there I copped a twenty-year stretch instead of the ten they'd given me in Portugal.'

He made a break from Guiana. I'd heard that he had passed through Georgetown, and that he'd gone to Brazil through the bush, riding on an ox.

What if I went to see him? Yes: I'd go to Boa Vista. That was a brilliant idea!

I set off with two men. They said they knew how to get to Brazil, and they were to help me carry the food and bedding. For ten days and more we wandered about the bush without even managing to reach Santa Helena, the last mining village before the Brazilian frontier: and after a fortnight we found ourselves at Aminos, a gold-mine almost on the edge of British Guiana. With the help of some Indians we reached the Cuyuni river, and that led us to a little Venezuelan village called Castillejo. There I bought machêtes and files as a present for the Indians, and I left my so-called guides. I had to control myself so as not to smash their faces in, because in fact they no more knew those parts than I did.

In the end I found a man in the village who really did know the country and who agreed to guide me. Four or five days later I reached El Callao.

At last, exhausted, worn out, thin as a lath, I knocked on Maria's door at nightfall.

'He's here! He's here!' shrieked Esmeralda at the top of her voice.

'Who?' asked Maria from another room. 'And why do you

shout so?'

All stirred up by finding this sweetness again after the weeks I had just been through, I caught hold of Esmeralda and put my hand over her mouth to stop her answering.

'Why all this noise about a visitor?' asked Maria, coming in. A cry, a cry from the bottom of her heart, a cry of joy, of love, of hope fulfilled, and Maria threw herself into my arms.

When I had embraced Picolino and kissed Maria's other sisters—José was away—I lay there a long, long while beside Maria. She kept asking me the same questions: she couldn't believe I had come straight to her house without stopping at Big Charlot's or at any of the village cafés.

'You're going to stay a little while in El Callao, aren't you?'

'Yes. I'll fix things so I stay for some time.'

'You must take care of yourself and put on weight: I'll cook such dishes for you, sweetheart. When you go, even if it wounds my heart for ever—not that I blame you in any way, since you warned me—when you go, I want you to be strong, so that you can avoid the snares of Caracas as well as you can.'

El Callao, Uasipata, Upata, Tumeremo: little villages with names strange for a European, tiny points on the map of a country three times the size of France, lost at the back of beyond, where the word progress has no meaning and where men and women, young and old, live as people lived in Europe at the beginning of the century, overflowing with genuine passions, generosity, joy in life and kindness ... Almost all the men who were then more than forty had had to bear the most terrible of all dictatorships, the rule of Gomez. They were hunted down and beaten to death for nothing: any man in authority could flog them with a bull's pizzle. When they were between fifteen and twenty in the years 1925 to 1935, all of them were hunted like animals by the army's recruiting agents dragged off to the barracks. Those were the days when a pretty girl might be picked out and kidnapped by an important official and thrown into the street when he was tired of her; and if her family raised a finger to help her they were wiped out.

Now and then, to be sure, there were risings, suicidal revolts by men who were determined to have their revenge even if they died for it. But the army was always there at once, and those who escaped with their lives were so tortured they were crippled for the rest of their days.

And yet in spite of all that, the almost illiterate people of these little backward villages here still retained the same love for other men and the same trust in them. For me it was a continual lesson, and one that touched me to the bottom of my heart.

I thought of all this as I lay there beside Maria. I had suffered, that was true; I had been condemned unjustly, and that was true again; the French warders had been as savage as the tyrant's police and soldiers, and maybe even more devilish; but here I was, all in one piece, having just gone through a terrific adventure—a dangerous adventure, certainly, but how utterly fascinating! I'd walked, paddled my canoe, ridden through the bush; but as I lived it each day was a year, so full it was; that life of a man with no laws, free from all restraints, from all moral limits, all obedience to orders from outside.

So I wondered whether I was doing the right thing, going to Caracas and leaving this corner of paradise behind me. Again and again I asked myself that question.

The next day, bad news. The correspondent of the Lebanese, a little jeweller who specialized in gold orchids with Margarita pearls and in all kinds of other truly original little ornaments, told me he couldn't pay anything on my notes of credit because the Lebanese owed him a huge sum of money. OK, so I'd go and get my money at the other address in Ciudad Bolivar.

'Do you know this man?' I asked.

'Only too well. He's a crook. He's run off, taking everything, even some choice pieces I'd left with him on trust.'

If what this goddamn fool said was true, then I was even more broke than before I went off with Jojo. Fine, fine! Fate —what a mysterious business. These sort of things only happened to me. And done by a Lebanese, into the bargain!

Bowed down and dragging my feet, I came back to the house. To win those wretched ten thousand dollars I'd risked my life ten and twenty times over; and now not the smell of a sou was left to me. Well, well: that Lebanese did not have to load the dice to win at craps. Better still, he did not even bother to move—he sat there at home, waiting for the cash to be brought to him.

But my zest for life was so strong that I bawled myself out. You're free, free, free, man, and here you are whining about fate! You must be doing it for the laugh: you can't be serious. So maybe you did lose your banco; but what a marvellous caper it was! Lay your bets! The bank is broke! In a few weeks' time I'll be a rich man or a corpse! The furious suspense, as if I was sitting on the edge of a volcano keeping watch on the crater, but knowing that other craters might open up too—wasn't it worth losing ten thousand dollars for all that?

I was in control again now and I could see the position clearly enough. I'd have to hurry back to the mine, before the Lebanese buggered off. And since time is money, don't let's lose any. I'd go and find a mule, some stores and be on my way! I still had my gun and my knife. The only question was, would I find the way? I hired a horse—Maria thought it far better than a mule. The one thing that worried me was the idea of taking the wrong *pique*, because there were places where others came in from all directions.

'I know the paths: would you like me to go with you?' asked Maria. 'Oh how I should love that! I'd only come as far as the *posada*, where you leave the horses before taking to the canoe.'

'It's too dangerous for you, Maria. Above all, too dangerous coming back alone.'

'I'll wait for somebody who's returning to El Callao. That way I'll be safe. Please say yes, *mi amor*!'

I talked it over with José, and he agreed she should go. 'I'll lend her my revolver. Maria knows how to use it,' he said.

And that's how we came to be sitting there alone on the edge of the *pique*, Maria and I, after a five hours' ride—I had hired another horse for her. She was wearing breeches, a present from a friend, a *llanera*. The Venezuelan *llana* is a huge plain, and the women who live there are brave and untameable; they fire a rifle or a revolver like a man, wield the machête like a fencer and ride like an Amazon—yet in spite of that they are capable of dying for love.

Maria was exactly the opposite. She was gentle and sensual

86

and so close to nature you felt she was part of it. Not that that prevented her from knowing how to look after herself, with a weapon or without: she was courageous.

Never, never shall I forget those days of travelling before we reached the *posada*. Unforgettable days and nights when it was our hearts that sang after we were too tired to speak our happiness.

Never shall I be able to describe the delight of those dream-like halts when we played in the coolness of the crystal-clear water and then, still wet and mother-naked, made love on the grassy bank with butterflies and humming-birds and dragon-flies all round us.

We would go on, tottering with love and sometimes so filled with ecstasy that I felt myself to make sure I was still all in one piece.

The nearer we came to the *posada* the more closely I list-ened to Maria's pure natural voice singing love songs. And as the distance shortened, the more often I pulled in my horse and found excuses for another rest.

'Maria, I think we ought to let the horses cool a while.'

'At this pace, he's not going to be the one who's tired when we get there, Papi: we're the ones who'll be worn out,' she said, breaking into a laugh that showed her pearly teeth.

We managed to spend six days on the road before we came in sight of the *posada*. When I saw it, in a flash I was over-come with a longing to spend the night there and then go back to El Callao. The idea of having the purity of those six days of passion all over again suddenly seemed to me a thousand times more important than my ten thousand dollars. The desire was so strong it made me tremble. But even stronger, there was a voice that said, 'Don't be a lemon, Papi. Ten thousand dollars is a fortune, the first big wad of the amount you need to carry out your plan. You must not give it up.'

'There's the *posada*,' said Maria.

And against myself, against everything I thought and felt, I said the opposite of what I wanted to say. 'Yes, there's the *posada*. Our journey's over: tomorrow I leave you.'

Four good men at the paddles, and in spite of the current the canoe raced over the water. Every stroke took me farther from

Maria: and standing on the bank she watched me disappear.

Where was peace, where was love, where perhaps was the woman with whom I was fated to build a home and a family? I forced myself not to look back, for fear I should call out to the paddlers 'Let's turn around!' I had to go on to the mine and get my money and then head for other adventures as soon as possible so as to make enough for the great journey to Paris and back: if there was to be any return.

Just one promise: I'd not hurt the Lebanese. I'd just take what belonged to me, neither more nor less. He'd never know he owed this forgiveness to six days of travelling through paradise with the most wonderful girl in the world, Maria, the nymph of El Callao.

'The Lebanese? But I'm pretty sure he's gone,' said Miguel, having crushed me in his embrace.

I had found the shack closed, true enough, but the wonderful sign was still there: 'Honesty is my greatest treasure'.

'You think he's gone? Oh, the bleeding shit!'

'Calm down, Papi. We'll soon find out.'

My doubt did not last long, nor my hope. Mustafa confirmed that the Lebanese had gone: but where had he gone? It was only after two days of inquiry that a miner told me he had lighted out for Brazil with three bodyguards. 'All the miners say he's an honest man, for sure.' Then I told the story of El Callao and all I'd learnt about the disappearing Lebanese in Ciudad Bolivar. Four or five guys, including an Italian, said that if I was right, then they were broke. There was only one old character from Guiana who would not see it our way. According to him, the real thief was the Ciudad Bolivar Greek. We turned it this way and that for quite a time, but in my heart of hearts I felt I'd lost the whole packet for good and all. What was I going to do?

Go to see Alexandre Guigue at Boa Vista? It was a long way off, Brazil. You had to reckon about three hundred miles through the bush to reach Boa Vista. My last experience had been too risky—just a little farther, and it would have been my last journey. No: I'd fix things so I was in contact with the mine, and as soon as I learnt the Lebanese had come to the surface again I'd pay him a visit. Once that was settled, I'd be on my way for Caracas, picking up Picolino as I went by. That was the most sensible answer. Tomorrow I'd set off for El Callao.

A week later, there I was with José and Maria. I told them everything. Gently, kindly, Maria found the right words to restore my spirits. Her father urged me to stay with them. 'We'll raid the Caratal mine, if you like.' I smiled, and patted him on the shoulder.

No, really that did not appeal to me: I mustn't stay here. It was only my love for Maria and hers for me that could keep me in El Callao. I was more hooked than I had believed and more than I wanted. It was a strong, genuine love; but still it wasn't powerful enough to overcome my desire for revenge.

Everything was settled: I had fixed with a truck-driver and we were to leave at five the next morning.

While I was shaving, Maria slipped out and hid in her sisters' room. That mysterious sense that women possess had told her that this time it was the real parting. Picolino was sitting there at the table in the big room, washed and tidy, with Esmeralda standing next to him, her hand on his shoulder. I took a step towards the room where Maria was. Esmeralda stopped me. 'No, Enrique.' Then all at once she too darted to the door and disappeared.

José went with us as far as the truck. We did not say a word.

Caracas, and as quick as you can make it.

Farewell, Maria, little flower of El Callao: in love and tenderness you gave me much more than all the gold that ever came from the mines.

IT was a tough journey, particularly for Picolino. Six hundred miles and more; twenty hours of driving, not counting the stops. We spent a few hours in Ciudad Bolivar, and then having crossed the splendid Orinoco on a ferry, we tore along, the truck racing like crazy, driven by a man with nerves of steel; which was just as well.

The next afternoon at four o'clock we reached Caracas. And straight away there I was in the big city. The movement, the crowds, the coming and going of thousands and thousands of people, sucked me right in.

1929, Paris. 1946, Caracas. Seventeen years had gone by without my having seen a genuine big city. A lovely city, Caracas, beautiful with its one-storey colonial houses; and it stretched right down the valley with the Avila mountains rising all round it. A city three thousand feet up, with an everlasting spring, neither too hot nor too cold.

'I trust you, Papillon,' said Dr Bougrat's voice in my ear, just as though he were there, watching us drive into this huge, swarming city.

Crowds of people everywhere, of all colours from the darkest to the lightest, without any complexes about race. All these people, black, brick-red or purest white, were alive with a happiness that went to my head in the first moments.

With Picolino leaning on my arm, we walked towards the middle of the city. Big Charlot had given me the address of an ex-lag who kept a boarding-house, the Pension Maracaibo.

Yes, seventeen years had gone by and a war had shattered the lives of hundreds of thousands of men of my age in a great many lands, including my own country, France. Between 1939 and 1945 Frenchmen had been prisoners, or they had been killed or maimed. And you are here, Papillon, here in a big city! You are thirty-seven, you are young and strong: look around you at all these people, some of them poorly dressed— they are laughing aloud. The singing was not just the sound of the hit-songs played on records, it was in the hearts of all the people. Of almost all, for of course you saw right away there were some who were dragging not a ball and chain but something worse—the misfortune of being poor and of not knowing how to look after themselves in the jungle of a big town.

How beautiful it is, a great city! And it was only four o'clock now. What must it be like at night, with its millions of electric stars? Yet we were still only in a working-class district, and a pretty tough one, at that. I'd spend a little money for once. 'Hey there, taxi!'

Sitting there beside me, Picolino laughed and dribbled like a kid. I wiped his poor mouth; he thanked me with shining eyes, trembling, he was so moved. For him, being in a town, a great capital like Caracas, meant above all the hope of finding hospitals and doctors who could turn the wreck he had become into a normal man once more. The miracle of hope. He held my hand, while outside the streets went by and then still more streets with people and still more people, so many of them they entirely hid the pavement. And the cars, and the hooters, and the siren of an ambulance, the clang of a fire-engine, the bawling of the hawkers and the newsboys selling the evening papers, the shriek of a lorry's brakes, the ting-a-ling of the trams, the bicycle bells—all these shouts and the deafening noise around made us feel almost drunk. The din, made up of hundreds of different sounds, destroys some people's nerves, but it had the opposite effect on us; it woke us up and made us thoroughly understand that we were right back in the crazy rhythm of modern mechanical life and instead of being tensed up we felt wonderfully happy.

There was nothing surprising about the fact that it was the noise that struck us most. We had lived in silence so long. For it was silence that I'd known these last seventeen years, the silence of the prisons, the silence of the penal settlement, the more than silence of solitary confinement, the silence of the bush and of the sea, the silence of the little remote villages where happy people live.

I said to Picolino, 'We are coming into a foretaste of Paris —Caracas, a real city. Here they'll make you well, and as for me, I'll find my right path and work out my fate: you can be sure of that.'

His hand squeezed mine; a tear ran from his eye. His hand was so brotherly and affectionate that I held on to it so as not to lose that marvellous contact; and since his other arm was dead, it was I that wiped away my friend's tear.

At last we reached the place run by Emile S., the lag, and settled in. He was not there, but as soon as his wife, a Venezuelan, heard we were from El Callao she grasped what we were and gave us a room with two beds right away, and some coffee.

Having helped Picolino to have a shower I put him to bed. He was tired and over-excited. When I left he made violent signs: I knew he meant to say 'You'll come back, won't you? You won't leave me in the lurch, all by myself?'

'No, Pico! I'll just spend a few hours in the town: I'll be back soon.'

And here I was in Caracas. It was seven o'clock when I walked down the street towards the Plaza Simon Bolivar, the biggest in the city. An explosion of light everywhere, a magnificent pouring out of electricity, neon signs of every colour. What enchanted me most was the advertisements in coloured lights, flaming dragons that came and went like will-o'-the-wisps, flashing on and off like a ballet run by a magician.

It was a splendid square, with a huge bronze statue of Simon Bolivar on an enormous horse in the middle of it. He looked terrific, and the statue showed how noble he must have been. I walked right round him, the man who set Latin America free, and I could not help greeting him in my bad Spanish, speaking low so no one would hear. '*Hombre!* What a miracle it is for me to be here at your feet—at the feet of the Man of Freedom. A poor bastard like me, who has been fighting all the time for that freedom you personify.'

The *pension* was a quarter of a mile from the square, and I went back twice before I found Emile S. He said Charlot had written to tell him we were coming: we went out to have a drink so we could talk quietly.

'It's ten years now I've been here,' said Emile. 'I'm married, with a daughter, and my wife owns the *pension*. That's why I can't put you up for nothing; but you'll only pay half-price.' The wonderful solidarity of ex-cons when one of them is in a jam! He went on, 'Is he an old friend, that poor guy with you?'

'You've seen him?'

'No, but my wife's been telling me about him. She says he's an absolute wreck. Is he gaga?'

'Far from it, and that's what's so terrible. His mind is as clear as a bell, but his tongue and his mouth and his right side down to the waist are paralysed. That's the way he was when I first knew him in El Dorado. Nobody knows who he is or whether he's a con or a detainee.'

'I can't see why you want to drag this unknown type around with you. You don't even know if he's a right guy or not. And then on top of that, he's a burden to you.'

'I've realized that, these eight months I've been looking after him. In El Callao I found some women who took charge. Even so, it's not easy.'

'What are you going to do with him?'

'Get him into hospital if I can. Or find a room—rough, if need be, but with a shower and a lavatory—to look after him until I can find a place for him somewhere.'

'You got dough?'

'A little, but I've got to take care; because although I understand all they say, I speak Spanish badly and it's not going to be so simple to make things work out.'

'You're dead right: it's not easy here—more people wanting work than there are jobs. But anyhow, Papi, don't you worry: you can stay in my place the few days you'll need to find something.'

I got the message. Emile was generous, but he was unhappy about the whole thing. His wife must have drawn a pretty picture of Picolino with his tongue lolling out and his animal grunts. She must have thought of the impression he would make on the boarders.

Tomorrow I'd carry his meals up to our room. Poor Picolino, sleeping there next to me in your little iron bed. Although I pay for your board and lodging, they don't want you. People who are well don't like to see the sick, you understand. With your twisted face in front of them, they don't feel like laughing. That's life, all right. The group only accepts you if your personality brings it something, or else if you're so null and void you don't worry anybody at all. They'll put up with a living piece of furniture. But don't you worry, mate. Even if I'm not as gentle as the El Callao girls, you'll always have me by you; something better than a friend—a crook who's adopted you and who'll do everything he can to prevent you dying like a dog.

Emile gave me several addresses, but there was no job for me anywhere. And twice I went to the hospital to try to get Picolino in. Nothing doing. According to them there were no empty beds; and his papers, saying he'd been let out of El Dorado, were no help at all. Yesterday they asked me how he came to be under my care and why, and what was his nationality and so on. When I told the little shit of a clerk that the chief of El Dorado had put him in my charge and that I had undertaken to look after him, this is what the bastard produced: 'Well then, since he's been let out because you agreed to take care of him, all you have to do is to keep him where you live and have him treated there. If you can't do that, you ought to have left him at El Dorado.'

When he asked for my address I gave him a false one. I did not trust the silly bugger, an international example of the small-time official who wants to throw his weight about.

I moved Picolino: I moved him quick. I was desperate, both for him and for me. I felt I couldn't stay at Emile's any longer; his wife was moaning about having to change Picolino's sheets every day. Yet I did wash the dirty places every morning as well as I could in the washbasin; but they took a long time to dry and it was soon noticed. So I bought an iron and dried the places I had washed with it.

What was to be done? I couldn't be sure. One thing was certain—I had to find an answer quick. Now for the third time I'd tried to get him into a hospital with no result. It was eleven o'clock when we came out. Since that was the way things were, we'd have to set about it properly: I decided to devote the whole of that fine afternoon to my friend. I led him to the Calvario, a wonderful garden filled with tropical plants and flowers on a little hill plumb in the middle of Caracas.

Sitting there on a bench and admiring the splendid view, we ate *arepas* with meat in them and drank a bottle of beer. Then I lit two cigarettes, one for Pico, one for me. It was hard for Picolino to smoke: he drooled on his cigarette. He felt this was an important moment and that I meant to tell him something that might hurt him badly. His eyes were full of anxiety and they seemed to say 'Speak, speak right away. I can feel you've taken a big decision. Tell me; I beg you to tell me.' Yes: I could read all that in his eyes as plain as if it was written. It made me wretched, and I hesitated. At last I brought it out. 'Pico, it's three days now I've been trying to get you into a hospital. There's nothing to be done: they don't want you. You understand?'

'Yes,' said his eyes.

'On the other hand, we can't go to the French consulate without the risk of them asking the Venezuelans for an extradition order.' He shrugged his good shoulder. 'Listen: you've got to get well, and to get well you've got to be treated. That's the main thing. But you know I haven't got enough money to have you looked after. So this is what we'll do: we'll spend the evening together, and I'll take you to the cinema. Then tomorrow morning I'll take you to the Plaza Bolivar without any papers on you. There you lie at the foot of the statue and you don't stir. If they want you to stand or to sit up, you refuse. It's dead certain that after a minute they'll call a cop and he'll call an ambulance. I'll follow in a cab to see what hospital they take you to. Then I'll wait two days before coming to see you, and I'll come in visiting hours so as to mix with the crowd. The first time maybe I shan't talk to you, but as I go past your bed I'll leave you some cigarettes and a little money. OK? You agree?'

He put his good arm on my shoulder and looked straight into my face. His expression was an extraordinary mixture of sadness and gratitude. His throat contracted: he made a superhuman effort to force his twisted mouth to bring out a hoarse sound very like 'Yes, thank you.'

Next day, everything happened just as I had foretold. Less than a quarter of an hour after Picolino lay down at the foot of the Bolivar statue, three or four old men sitting under the shade of the trees told a cop. Twenty minutes later an ambulance came for him. I followed in a cab.

Two days later—no difficulty about mingling with the visitors and finding him—he was in the third ward I went through. A piece of luck: he was between two very sick patients and I could talk to him a while without any risk. He was flushed with joy at seeing me, and maybe he jerked about a little too much.

'They look after you all right?'

He nodded yes.

I looked at the chart at the foot of his bed. 'Paraplegia or malaria with secondary complications. To be checked every two hours.' I left him six packets of cigarettes, matches and twenty bolivars in change.

'Be seeing you, Pico!' Seeing his desperate and imploring eyes I added, 'Don't worry, mate; I'll come back and see you.' I mustn't forget that I'd grown absolutely necessary to him. I was his one link with the world.

I'd been here a fortnight, and the hundred-bolivar notes were disappearing fast. Fortunately I had decent clothes when I got to Caracas. I found a little room, cheap, but still too dear for me. No women anywhere on the horizon. Yet the girls of Caracas were lovely to look at, intelligent and full of life. The difficulty was getting to know them. This was 1946, and it wasn't the custom for women to sit in a café alone.

A big city has its secrets. To be able to take care of yourself, you have to know them; and to know them, you have to know the bright guys. And just who are these bright guys of the streets? A whole mysterious tribe with its own language, laws, customs and vices; its own ways of managing to make enough to live on for twenty-four hours every day. Earning a living, as honestly as possible: that was the problem, and it wasn't easy.

Like all the others, I had my own little ways, often good for a hearty laugh and far from wicked. For example, one day I met a Colombian I'd known in El Dorado.

'What are you doing?'

He told me just then he was earning his living by running a lottery for a magnificent Cadillac.

'Hell, so you've made your fortune already? You must have, to own a Cadillac.'

He choked with laughter: then he explained the job. 'The Cadillac belongs to the director of a big bank. He drives himself, gets there at nine prompt and parks like a good citizen a hundred or a hundred and fifty yards from the bank. There are

96

two of us. One—not always the same, so we don't get spotted —follows him to the door of the bank where he sits on his arse all morning. If there's a hitch, a whistle you can't mistake for anything else: it's only happened once. So between the time he gets there and the time he goes, which is round about one, we put an elegant white streamer on the Cadillac, with red letters saying "On sale here: tickets that may win you this Cadillac. Winning numbers the same as the Caracas lottery. Draw next month." '

'Man, that's way out of the common run. So you sell tickets for a Cadillac that isn't yours? Christ, what a nerve! What about the pigs?'

'They're never the same; and seeing there's no vice in them, it never comes into their heads that maybe it's a swindle. And if they get a little too interested we give them a ticket or two and off they go, dreaming perhaps they'll win a Cadillac. If you want to make a little money with us, come along and I'll introduce you to my partner.'

'You don't think it stinks a trifle, clipping the poor?'

'Never on your sweet life. The tickets cost ten bolivars, so it's only well-off folk that can afford them. So there's no harm done.'

Once the partner had had a look at me, there was I, busy with this ploy. It's not very elegant, but you have to eat, sleep and be if not well dressed then at least clean. And I had to hold on to my reserve as long as possible—the few diamonds I'd brought from El Dorado and two five-hundred-bolivar notes that I hoarded like a miser in my charger, just as if I were still in penal. Because my charger was something I'd never left off carrying inside me, and for two reasons: my hotel was in a pretty rough part of the town and I might be robbed; and if I carried it in my pocket, I might lose it. In any case, it was fourteen years now I had had this charger in my colon, so a year more or less did not matter and that way I was easy in my mind.

The selling of the lottery tickets lasted more than a fort-night, and it would be going on still but for the fact that one day a very eager customer bought two tickets and examined every detail of this marvellous car he dreamt of winning. All at once he straightened up and cried, 'But doesn't this car belong to

Dr Fulano, the bank-director?'

Without batting an eyelid, the Colombian replied coolly, 'Just so. He put it into our hands to dispose of like this. He reckons a lottery will bring him in a better price than a straight sale.'

'Odd . . .' said the customer.

'But above all, don't mention it to him,' went on the Colombian, still very calm. 'He made us promise to say nothing, because he'd find it awkward if it was known.'

'I can't understand it: it's really most unusual for a man of his kind.'

As soon as he'd got far enough away, moving in the direction of the bank, we whipped off the streamer and folded it up. The Colombian vanished, carrying it, and I went to the door of the bank to tell our partner we were striking camp. Inside myself I was laughing like a hyena and I couldn't help hanging about not far from the door so as not to miss what I expected would be the sequel. It came off, all right. Three minutes later, there was the director together with the suspicious customer. He was waving his arms wildly and walking so fast I knew he was in a right fury.

They saw there was nobody left around the Cadillac, and surprised, no doubt, they came back slower, stopping at a café to have a drink at the bar. As the customer had not spotted me, I went in too to hear what they would say, for the laugh.

'By God, that was a nerve! Don't you think that was an infernal nerve, Dr Fulano?'

But the owner of the Cadillac, who, like all good Caraqueños, had a sense of humour, burst out laughing and said, 'When I think that if I had walked by they might have offered me a ticket for my own car! And that sometimes I'm so absent-minded that I might actually have bought it. You must admit it makes you laugh.'

Naturally enough, that was the end of our lottery. The Colombians vanished. For my part. I'd made close on fifteen hundred bolivars, enough to live on for over a month; which was important.

The days went by, and it was not at all easy to find anything worth while to do. This was the period when Pétain's supporters and the men who had collaborated with the Germans

98

started reaching Venezuela from France, on the run from the justice of their own country. Seeing I didn't know enough about the possible distinction between collaborators and Pétainists, I lumped them all together under the label of ex-Nazis. So I did not associate with them.

A month went by and nothing much happened. At El Callao I had never thought it would be so hard to get myself going. I was reduced to selling coffee-pots from door to door; they were supposed to be specially designed for offices.

My patter was so glib and so bloody silly it nauseated me. 'You see, Señor Director, whenever your employees go out for a coffee [a usual custom in all Venezuelan offices] they waste an enormous amount of time, particularly when it's raining; and during this time you are losing money. With a coffee-pot in the office, you gain all round.' Maybe he might gain all round, but I didn't, because several of the bosses answered, 'Oh, in Venezuela, you know, we take life quietly, even in business. Indeed, that's why our people are allowed to go out for a *cafecito* in working hours.'

Then again, you look rather foolish walking about the streets with a coffee-pot in your hand: and I was doing just that when I bumped into Paulo the Boxer, an old Montmartre acquaintance.

'Why, what do you know? You must be Paulo the . . .'

'And you're Papillon?'

He grabbed my arm and towed me into a café.

'Well, talk of coincidence—this is a coincidence, all right.'

'What are you up to, walking around the street with that coffee-pot?'

'I'm selling them: it's a bleeding disaster. What with getting it out and shoving it back again, the box tore just now.' I told him how things were with me and then I said, 'How about you?'

'Let's drink our coffee. I'll tell you somewhere else.'

We paid and stood up; I reached for my coffee-pot.

'Leave that where it is. You won't want it any more, I give you my oath.'

'You don't think so?'

'I know it, man.'

I left the vile pot on the table and we went out.

An hour later, in my room, after we had tossed memories of Montmartre to and fro, Paulo came to the point. He had a big job in a country not far from Venezuela. He knew he could rely on me. If I agreed, he'd take me on as one of his team.

'It's as easy as falling off a log—it's in the bag, man! I tell you very seriously, there are going to be so many dollars you'll need an iron to iron them out flat, so they don't take up too much room.'

'And where is it, this prodigious job?'

'You'll know when you get there. I can't say anything before.'

'How many will there be of us?'

'Four. One's already on the spot. I came here to fetch the other. You know him, by the way. He's a friend of yours: Gaston.'

'Right. But I've lost touch with him.'

'Not me,' said Paulo, laughing.

'You really can't tell me any more about the job?'

'Impossible, Papi. I've got my reasons.'

I thought quickly. Placed as I was, there wasn't much choice. Either I went on dragging about with a coffee-pot or some other goddamn nonsense in my hand or I went on the loose, with the possibility of getting hold of a packet and getting hold of it quick. I'd always known that Paulo was a sober, reflecting type, and if in his opinion there had to be four of us, then that meant this job was serious too. Technically, it would be a pretty piece of work. And that, I must admit, tempted me too. So what about it, Papi—banco?

'Banco!'

The next day we set off.

6: The Tunnel under the Bank

MORE than seventy-two hours of driving. We relieved one another at the wheel. Paulo took endless precautions: every time we filled up, the man who was driving put the others down three hundred yards from the pump and picked them up afterwards.

Gaston and I had been waiting half an hour in the driving rain, waiting for Paulo to come back. I was furious. 'You really think all this act is necessary, Paulo? Just look at us. We'll catch our bleeding deaths.'

'What a bleeding bore you are, Papi, I had air put in the tyres, changed a back wheel and filled up with oil and water. You can't do that in five minutes.'

'I never said you could. But I tell you straight, I don't see the point of all these precautions.'

'Well I do, and I'm the boss. You may have had a thirteen-year-stretch in penal, but I copped ten of solitary in our loving homeland; so I don't think you can ever do enough in the way of precautions. Suppose there's a tip about a car, a Chevrolet with one man in it, say—well, it's not the same as a car with three men in it.'

He was right. Let's say no more about it. Ten hours later we reached the town we were aiming for. Paulo dropped us at the end of a road with villas on either side of it.

'Take the pavement on the right. The villa's called Mi Amor; it's along there. Walk in like you owned it, and inside you'll find Auguste.'

There was a garden with flowers, and a neat path leading to the door of a pretty little house. The door was shut: we knocked.

'Hi there, brothers, come right in,' said Auguste, opening the door. He was in shirt-sleeves; he was covered with sweat, and his hairy arms had earth on them. We told him Paulo had gone to park the car at the other end of the town. It made sense not to have a Venezuelan number-plate seen too often in the road.

'Did you have a good run?'

'Yes.'

No more than that. We sat down in the dining-room. I felt the decisive moment was coming and I was rather tense. Gaston had no more idea than I what the job was all about. 'It's a matter of trust,' Paulo had said in Caracas. 'Either you come along or you don't. Take it or leave it. Just one thing: it means more liquid cash than you've ever dreamt of.' OK: but now it was all going to have to be clear, open and exact.

Auguste gave us coffee. Apart from a few questions about our journey and how we were, not a word that shed any light at all. They were prudent, tight-mouthed, in this family.

I heard a car door slam in front of the house. It must be Paulo who'd hired a car with a local number-plate. Just so.

'Here we are,' cried Paulo, coming in and taking off his leather jacket. 'Everything's going just fine, boys.' Calmly he drank his coffee. I said nothing: I was waiting. He asked Auguste to put the cognac bottle on the table. Without any hurry, and still looking thoroughly pleased with life, he poured some for us; and then at last he came to the point. 'Well, boys, here you are on the spot: this is where we work. Listen, now: just in front of this little house, on the other side of the street you came by, there's the back of a bank. Its main entrance is on the big avenue that runs parallel with our little road. And the reason why you see Auguste's arms all covered with clay is because he knew you were idle, no-account bums, and he set to work so there would be less for you to do.'

'Do what?' asked Gaston, who was no fool but who was not very quick on the uptake.

'Not much,' said Paulo, smiling. 'Just dig a tunnel. It starts in the room next to this; it'll go under the garden, then under the street and come out just beneath the bank's strong-room. If my calculations are right. If they're not, then maybe we'll find ourselves nearer the street side. If that happens, we go deeper and try again for under the very middle of the strong-room.' A short silence; and then he said, 'What do you say about it?'

'Just a second, man. Give me time to think. It's not quite the kind of job I was expecting.'

'Is it a big bank?' asked Gaston: this was not one of his brighter days. If Paulo had set all this going, and on such a scale, it was certainly not just for three tins of liquorice.

'You walk by the bank tomorrow, and you'll have something to say,' said Paulo, roaring with laughter. 'Get this: there are eight cashiers. That gives you some idea of what they must handle by way of notes in the course of a day.'

'Christ!' said Gaston, slapping his thigh. 'So it's a real bank! Well, I am pleased. For once I'll be in on a big-time job, in keeping with my title of top-line crook.'

Still with his broad grin of happiness, Paulo turned to me. 'You got nothing to say, Papillon?'

'I don't need any titles. I'd rather stay just plain mister with enough dough to carry out a job I have in mind. I don't need millions. I'll tell you what I think, Paulo: it's a prodigious job, and if it comes off—*when* it comes off, I should say, because you must always believe in a job—we're set up for the rest of our lives with enough for the rent and the telephone. But ... There are a good many buts to get round. I can ask questions, boss?'

'As many as you like, Papi. I meant to talk over every part of the job with you anyhow. For although I'm the top man, since it was me who worked it out, each one of us is risking his freedom and maybe his life. So ask all the questions you want.'

'Right. The first is this: from the room next door, where the shaft is, how far is it to the pavement on this side of the road?'

'Exactly eighteen yards.'

'Second, how far from the edge of the pavement to the bank?'

'Ten yards.'

'Third, inside the bank, have you worked out exactly where the door to the strong-room is?'

'Yes. I've hired a safe in the customers' room. It's just next to the bank's own strong-room and separated from it by an armoured door with two wheel-locks. There's only one way in, and that's from the customers' room. You go from there into the main strong-room. One day, after I'd been down there a good many times, I was waiting for them to give me the second key of my safe and I saw the armoured door open. As it swung round, I caught a glimpse of the strong-room and the big safes lined up all round it.'

'Could you get an idea of how thick the wall was between

the two rooms?'

'It was hard to tell on account of the steel casing.'

'How many steps down to the strong-room door?'

'Twelve.'

'So the strong-room floor is about ten foot below street-level. What's your plan?'

'We must try and hit just under the wall between the two rooms. We can guide ourselves by the bolts under the floor of the strong-room—the ones that hold the safes. That way we get into both rooms at once with just one hole.'

'Yes, but since the safes stand right against the wall, you're likely to come out under one of them.'

'I hadn't thought of that. If that happens, all you have to do is to make the hole larger towards the middle of the room.'

'I think two holes would be better: one in each room, and each in the middle, if possible.'

'I think so too, now,' said Auguste.

'OK, Papi. We aren't there yet, you know: but it's just as well to think of these things well ahead. What next?'

'How deep's the tunnel going to be?'

'Three yards.'

'How wide?'

'Two foot six. You have to be able to turn round inside.'

'Have you reckoned the height?'

'A yard.'

'The height and the width are fine; but I don't agree with the depth. Six feet of earth overhead isn't solid enough. If a heavy truck goes by, or a steam-roller, it might collapse.'

'I dare say, Papi; but there's no reason why trucks or heavy stuff should come along this street.'

'Sure. But it doesn't cost us anything to make a shaft four yards deep. You do that, and you've got three yards of earth between the top of the tunnel and the street. Any objection? The only extra work is digging the shaft a yard deeper. It doesn't change anything about the tunnel itself. Then four yards down, you're almost certain of reaching the bank at the level of its foundations or even lower. How many storeys in the building?'

'Ground-floor and one over it.'

'The foundations can't be very deep, then.'

'You're right, Papi. We'll go down to four yards.'

'How are you going to cope with the strong-room? What about the alarm system?'

'As I see it, Papi, that's the main snag. Still, looking at it logically, systems are set up *outside* strong-rooms. So long as you don't touch a door, either of the bank or of the strong-room, it oughtn't to go off. And there can hardly be one right inside the rooms. Still, I think we'd better not touch the safes either side of the door to the customers' room nor the ones by the armoured door.'

'I agree with you. There is one risk, of course, and that is when you get to work on the safes the vibration might set things off. But taking precautions like you said, we've a pretty good chance.'

'Is that the lot, Papi?'

'You've thought of lining the tunnel?'

'Yes. There's a work-bench and everything we need in the garage.'

'Fine. What about the earth?'

'First we'll spread it out right over the whole garden, and then we'll make raised beds, and lastly a platform all along the walls a yard wide and as high as it'll go without looking queer.'

'Are there any inquisitive bastards round here?'

'On the right everything's fine. A tiny little old couple who apologize every time they see me, because their dog shits just outside our garden gate. On the left, not so hot. There are two kids of eight and ten who never quit their swing for an instant, and the silly little buggers fly so high they can easily look over the wall and see what's happening in our place.'

'But however high they swing they can't see more than part of the garden—they can't possibly see the stretch against their own wall.'

'True enough, Papi. OK. Now suppose we've made the tunnel and we're under the strong-room. There we'll have to make a big hollow, a kind of room, so as to hold the tools and be able to work properly, perhaps two or three of us together. And then once we've hit the centre of the rooms we'll make a space under each, two yards square.'

'Right. And what are you going to cut the steel of the safes with?'

'That's something we'll have to talk over.'

'You start.'

'Well, the job could be done with oxyacetylene: that's something I understand—it's my trade. Or there's the electric welder, and I understand that too. But there's a snag—you need 220 volts and this villa only has 120. So I decided to let another guy in on the job. But I don't want him to work on the tunnel: he'll come a couple of days before we move in.'

'What'll he come with?'

'Here comes my big surprise. Thermite is what he'll come with. He's a positive artist in the thermite line. What do you say to that, everybody?'

'It'll make five shares instead of four,' said Gaston.

'There'll be more than you can carry, Gaston! five or four, it's all one.'

'As for me, I'm in favour of the thermite guy; because if there are a dozen safes to open, it goes quicker with thermite than with anything else at all.'

'Well then, there's the all-over plan. Are you all in agreement?'

Everyone said yes. Paulo said one other thing: neither Gaston nor I should show our noses out of doors during the daytime on any pretext whatsoever. We could go out at night from time to time, but as little as possible and then very carefully dressed, with a tie and all. Never all four of us together.

We went into the room next door: it had once been an office. They had already dug a hole a yard across and three deep, and I was admiring the sides, as straight as a wall, when the thought of ventilation came to me. 'And what have you laid on for air down there?'

'We'll pump it down with a little compressor and plastic tubing. If the one working begins to suffocate, someone'll hold the tube to his face while he gets on with the job. I bought a compressor in Caracas—it's almost silent.'

'What about an air-conditioner?'

'I thought of that, and I've got one in the garage; but it blows the fuses every time you switch it on.'

'Listen, Paulo. Nobody can tell what may happen to the thermite guy. If he doesn't turn up, the oxyacetylene is slow and the electric welder is the only thing for the job. We have to install 220 volts. To make it look natural, you say you want a deep-freeze and air-conditioning, etc., and a little circular saw in the garage as well, because you like arsing around with wood. There shouldn't be any difficulty.'

'You're right. There's everything to be said for putting in 220 volts. Well now, that's enough about the job for the moment. Auguste's the spaghetti king; as soon as it's ready, let's eat.'

Dinner was very cheerful. After we'd exchanged a few unpleasant memories, we all agreed that when talking about the past we'd never bring up stories about inside—only about happy things like women, the sun, the sea, games in bed, etc. We laughed like a pack of kids. Nobody had a second's remorse at the idea of attacking society in the shape of the greatest symbol of its selfish power, *a bank*.

There was no difficulty about installing the 220-volt current, because the transformer was close to the house. No problem at all. To finish the shaft, we gave up the short-handled pick, which was too awkward in such a confined space. Instead we cut out blocks of earth with the circular saw, prising out each block with a handy trowel and putting it into a bucket.

It was a titanic job, but little by little it advanced. In the house you could scarcely make out the zim-zim of the circular saw at the bottom of the shaft, now four yards deep. From the garden you heard absolutely nothing; there was nothing to be feared.

The shaft was finished. Today we started the tunnel, and it was Paulo, compass in hand, who dug the first yard through the very wet clayey earth that stuck to everything. We no longer worked half naked but in dungarees that come down under your feet. So when you came out and took the dungarees off, there you were as clean as a butterfly coming out of its cocoon. Apart from your hands, of course.

According to our calculations, we still had thirty cubic yards of earth to bring out.

'This is genuine convict's work,' said Paulo, when he was feeling rough.

But gradually we pushed on. 'Like moles or badgers,' said Auguste.

'We'll get there, mates! And we'll roll in cash for the rest of our lives. Isn't that right, Papillon?'

'Sure, sure! And I'll have the prosecutor's tongue and I'll get my false witness and I'll spring such a firework-display at 36, quai des Orfèvres! On with the job, boys—this is no time to talk bullshit or play belote. Here, lower me down the hole. I'm going to work another couple of hours.'

'Calm down, Papi. We're all of us on edge. Sure, it's not going fast, but we're getting on, and the jackpot's only fifteen yards ahead of us. Besides, we all have our problems. Look at this letter my friend Santos sent me from Buenos Aires.'

Paulo brought a letter out of his pocket and read it aloud. '"Dear Paulo: Do you believe in miracles, mate? It's more than six months now and not only haven't you come to see your two chicks but you haven't even sent them a line either, not so much as a postcard. You just don't understand the world. They don't know whether you're dead or alive or what part of the globe you're in. It's no fun for me to go and collect in these conditions. Every Monday the battle gets worse—Hey there! Where's our man?—What's he doing? He's on a job, I swear it!—Oh, he's a bleeding wonder with his big-time jobs! He'd do better to stay here with us: we're sick of going to bed with the pillow—This is the last time we ever hand over our takings, you get that? Either he comes or we divorce!

'"So come on now, Paulo: make an effort and send a line. Don't you believe in miracles? One of these days you're going to lose your two chicks, and then no more dough. Your buddy, Santos." Well, I do believe in miracles, and the miracle's right there, ahead of us. And you and I, mates, with our intelligence and our guts, we're the ones who'll work this miracle. Still, let's hope my lovebirds will hold out long enough; we need their dough to finish off the job.'

'We'll all give them a present,' said Auguste, beaming at the idea.

'That's my pigeon,' said Paulo. 'I'm the artist who's carrying out one of the most elegant jobs ever conceived by a crook; and without knowing it, they provide the financial backing. After all, that's a very great honour for them.'

A big laugh, drinks all round, and I agreed to take a hand at belote-bridge to please the others and to relax a trifle.

No difficulty about carrying the earth out into the garden; it was eighteen yards long and ten wide, and we spread the stuff out over the whole width except for the garage path. But seeing the earth we dug was not the same as the topsoil, we had a truck-load of good garden loam brought in from time to time. Everything was going fine.

How we dug, and how we heaved up the buckets full of earth! We laid a wooden floor in the tunnel, because the water seeping in turned it to mud; and the buckets slid easily on these planks when you heaved on the rope.

This is how we worked. There was one man at the far end of the tunnel: with the circular saw and a little pick he filled a bucket with the earth and stones; another stood at the bottom of the shaft and pulled the bucket back along the tunnel; and at the top there was a third who hauled it up and emptied it into a rubber-wheeled barrow. We broke through the wall that divided the house from the garage, so the fourth man only had to take the barrow, wheel it out through the garage and appear quite naturally in the garden.

We worked for hours on end, spurred on by a furious urge to win—an enormous pouring out of energy. The far end of the tunnel was very hard to bear in spite of the air-conditioner and the blast of pure air coming down the pipe we carried rolled round our neck so as to take a suck every now and then. I was covered with little red heat-pimples; there were great blotches of them all over my body. It looked like nettle-rash, and it itched horribly. The only one who did not have it was Paulo, because he just looked after the barrow and spread the earth in the garden. When we came out of that hell-hole it took over an hour to recover even after a shower; then, breathing normally and covered with Vaseline and cocoa-butter, at last we felt more or less all right. 'Anyhow, we were the ones who started this labour of Hercules. Nobody makes us do it. So help yourself, bear it, shut your trap and Heaven will help you.' That's what I said to myself and what I said two or three times a day to Auguste whenever he began to beef about having got himself mixed up with this kind of a job.

For slimming, there's nothing to touch digging a tunnel under a bank. It's amazing how supple you get, bending, craw-

109

ling and turning yourself inside out. In that tunnel, we sweated as much as if we had been in a sauna. If you do exercises in every conceivable position there's no danger of being over-weight; and you work up splendid muscles too. So there was everything to be said for it; and what's more, there at the end of the tunnel a magnificent prize was waiting—other people's money.

Everything was fine, except for the garden. With the level rising and rising, the flowers did not seem to grow but rather to sink; and that did not look altogether natural. If we went on, soon nothing would be seen but their petals. We hit on a remedy: we stuffed the flowers into pots and kept them flush with the earth as we dug it out. With the pots well covered nothing could be seen, and the plants looked as if they were coming right out of the surface.

This party was beginning to last rather too long. If only we could take turns at having a rest ... But there was no question of that. We all four had to be there to keep things running smoothly. With only three of us it would never end: and we'd have to store the earth in the house for the time being, which would be dangerous.

The trap-door over the shaft fitted to within a sixteenth of an inch. When we were resting, we could leave the room door open—not a thing could be seen. As for the hole in the garage wall, we covered it on the garage side with a huge wooden panel with handyman's tools hung on it, and on the house side with an immense Spanish colonial chest. So when Paulo had to have someone come to the house, he could do so without worrying at all. Gaston and I just hid in our first-floor bed-room.

For two days there had been non-stop torrential rain and the tunnel was flooded. There was close on a foot of water, so I suggested that Paulo should go and buy a hand-pump and the necessary piping. An hour later it was set up. Pumping as hard as we could (another form of exercise) we sucked up the water and poured it down the drain. A long, tough day's work for nothing.

December was coming nearer. If we could be ready by the end of November with our little room dug out and shored up, under the bank, that would be perfect. And if the thermite specialist appeared, there was no doubt Father Christmas would cram our stockings to the brim. If he did not turn up, then we'd decided to work with the electric welder. We knew where to find a set complete with all its fittings. General Electric turned out some terrific models. We'd buy it in another town much safer.

The tunnel crept on. Yesterday, 24 November, we reached the foundations of the bank. Only three yards to go and the room to make, that is to say about twelve cubic yards of earth to bring out. We celebrated with champagne, genuine *brut* from France.

'It tastes a bit green,' said Auguste.

'All the better. That's a good sign—it's the colour of dollars!'

Paulo summed up what there was left to do. Six days for bringing out the earth if there's not too much of it. Three days for the casing. Total, nine. 'It's 24 November today, so that brings us to 4 December. That's the big day, and we'll be sitting pretty. The bank shuts at seven in the evening on Friday, so we go into action at eight. We'll have the whole of Friday night, all day Saturday, Saturday night and the whole of Sunday. If all goes well, we ought to be able to quit the hideout at two in the morning on Monday. That makes fifty-two hours of work altogether. Everyone agreed?'

'No, Paulo, I don't agree at all.'

'Why not, Papi?'

'The bank opens at seven for the cleaners. At that moment the whole thing may turn sour for some reason or another: at seven in the morning, that is to say not long after we've left. This is what I suggest: we fix things so as to have finished the job by six on Sunday evening. By the time we've shared it out, it'll be round about eight. If we leave at eight, that will give us at least eleven hours' start if the thing blows up at seven, and thirteen hours if it hangs fire till nine.'

In the end everybody fell in with my suggestion. We drank our champagne, and as we drank it we put on records Paulo had brought—Maurice Chevalier, Piaf, the Paris of the little dance-halls ... Sitting there with his glass, each of us dreamt of the great day. It was there, so close you could almost touch it with your finger.

Your bill, Papi, the bill you've got there engraved on your heart, you'll be able to have it paid in Paris pretty soon. If all goes well and if luck's with me, I'll come back from France to El Callao and fetch Maria. My father: that would be for later on. Poor, wonderful Dad! Before I go and embrace him I'll first have to have buried the man I was, the man on the loose ... It won't take long once I've had my revenge and I'm fixed up properly.

It was two days after our champagne celebration that the thing happened, but we didn't know it until the day after that. We'd been to look at a General Electric welding and cutting set in a neighbouring town. My mate and I, dressed very smoothly, set out on foot and joined up with Paulo and Auguste in the car about a mile away.

'We've deserved this trip, boys. Breathe it in, breathe it in deep: this is the wonderful air of freedom!'

'You're dead right, Paulo; we've certainly deserved it. Don't drive too fast; let's have time to admire the countryside.'

We split up and stayed in two different hotels, spending three days in this charming port stuffed with ships and swarming with cheerful, motley crowds. Every evening we all met. 'No night-clubs, no brothels, no girls off the street; this is a business trip, mates,' said Paulo. He was right.

Paulo and I went to look at the set, taking our time about it. It was terrific but it had to be paid for in cash and we hadn't the necessary. Paulo wired Buenos Aires and fortunately he gave the address of the hotel in the port where he was staying. He decided to take us back to the villa and then return by himself a day or two later to get the dough and the welder. We drove back, thoroughly set up by these three days of holiday.

Paulo dropped Gaston and me at the corner of our little road as usual. The villa was a hundred yards away. We were walking calmly along, pleased with the idea of seeing our masterpiece of a tunnel again, when all at once I grabbed Gaston's arm and stopped him dead. What was going on outside the villa? There were cops, a dozen people milling around, and then I saw two firemen heaving earth out of the middle of the road. I didn't have to be told what had happened. The tunnel had been discovered!

Gaston began to tremble as though he had a fever, and then with his teeth chattering he stammered out, 'They've staved in our lovely tunnel! Oh, the bloody shits! Such a lovely tunnel!'

At this very moment a type with a pig's face you could tell a mile off was watching us. But the entire situation seemed to me so comic I burst out in such cheerful, genuine, open laughter that if the pig had had some slight doubt about us, it passed off straight away. Taking Gaston's arm I said out loud in Spanish, 'What a bleeding great tunnel those robbers have dug!'

And slowly we turned our backs on our masterpiece and walked away from the road—no hurry and no hitch. But now we'd got to get moving quick. I said to Gaston, 'How much have you got on you? I've nearly six hundred dollars and fifteen hundred bolivars. What about you?'

'Two thousand dollars in my charger,' said Gaston.

'Gaston, the best thing to do is for us to part right here in the street.'

'What are you going to do, Papi?'

'I'll go back to the port we came from and try to get a boat for no matter where—straight for Venezuela, if possible.'

We could not embrace one another there in the open street, but Gaston's eyes were as wet with emotion as mine as we shook hands. There's nothing that makes such a bond between men as the experience of danger and adventure.

'Good luck, Gaston.'

'Same to you, Papi.'

Paulo and Auguste went home by different roads, the one to Paraguay, the other to Buenos Aires. Paulo's girls no longer had to go to bed with their pillows.

I managed to get on a boat for Puerto Rico: from there I took a plane to Colombia and then another boat to Venezuela.

It was only some months later that I learned what had happened. A water-main had burst in the big avenue the other side of the bank and the traffic was diverted into the streets running parallel. A huge truck loaded with iron girders took our road, passed over our tunnel and plunged its back wheels into it. Shrieks, amazement, police: they grasped the whole thing in a moment.

7: Carotte: the Pawn-Shop

IN Caracas it was Christmas. Splendid illuminations in all the big streets, cheerfulness everywhere, carols sung with the Venezuelans' marvellous sense of rhythm. For my part I was rather depressed by our failure; but I wasn't bitter. We'd gambled and we'd lost; but I was still alive and freer than ever. And then after all, as Gaston said, it was a lovely tunnel!

Gradually the atmosphere of these songs about the Child of Bethlehem seeped into me; and easy in my mind, my heart peaceful again, I sent Maria a telegram: 'Maria, may this Christmas fill the house where you gave me so much joy.'

I spent Christmas Day at the hospital with Picolino, sitting on a bench in the little hospital garden. I'd bought two *hallacas*, specialities they make only at Christmas, and they were the most expensive and the best I could find. I also had two little flat bottles of delicious Chianti in my pockets.

It was a Christmas of two men brought back to life, a Christmas ablaze with the light of friendship, a Christmas of total freedom—freedom even to splash money about as I had done. The snowless Christmas of Caracas, filled with the flowers of this little hospital garden: a Christmas of hope for Picolino, whose tongue no longer hung out now he was being treated, who no longer dribbled. Yes, a miraculous Christmas for him, since he distinctly—and happily—pronounced the word 'Yes' when I asked him if the *hallacas* were good.

But Lord above, how hard it was to make a new life! I went through some very tough weeks; yet I did not lose heart. I had two things in me: first, an unshakeable confidence in the future; and second, an unquestionable love for life. Even when it would have been more sensible for me to be worrying, a mere trifle in the street would make me laugh; and if I met a friend I might spend the evening with him, having fun like a twenty-year-old.

Dr Bougrat gave me a little job in his beauty-products laboratory. I didn't earn much, but enough for me always to be well dressed and almost elegant. I left him for a Hungarian woman who had a little yoghourt factory in her villa, and it was there that I met a pilot whose name I won't mention because at this moment he's in command of an Air France jet. I'll call him Carotte.

He was working for the Hungarian woman too, and we made enough to be able to have some fun. Every evening we'd stroll around the Caracas bars; and we often had a drink or two at the Hotel Majestic, in the Silencio district. It has vanished now, but at that time it was the only modern place in the city.

It was then, during one of those periods when you think nothing fresh can possibly turn up, that a miracle took place. One day Carotte vanished: a little while later he came back again, from the United States, with a plane—a little observation plane with two seats, one behind the other. A wonderful gadget. I asked no questions about where it came from: the only question I did ask was what was he going to do with it?

He laughed and said, 'I don't know yet. But we might be partners.'

'To do what?'

'No matter what, so long as we have fun and make a little dough.'

'OK. We'll look around.'

The sweet Hungarian woman, who couldn't have had many illusions about how long our jobs would last, wished us good luck; and then there began an utterly demented and extraordinary month.

Hey, that huge great butterfly—the things we did with her!

Carotte was an ace. During the war he used to fly French agents out of England, land them by night in fields guarded by the Resistance, and fly others back to London. He often came down with no more guidance than torches held by the men who were waiting for him. He was completely reckless, and he dearly loved a laugh. Once, without a word of warning, he banked so hard, right over, that I almost lost my pants, and all this just to frighten a fat woman who was quietly doing her business in the garden, her bottom bare to the winds.

I so loved that machine and our darting about in the air that when we had no money to buy juice, I brought up the brilliant

116

idea of turning myself into a plane-borne pedlar.

This was the only time in my life that I ever conned anyone. He was called Coriat and he owned a men's and women's clothes shop, the Almacen Rio. He was in business with his brother. Coriat was a medium-sized Jew, dark, with an intelligent head; he spoke very good French. His shop was well run and he was making money hand over fist. On the women's side he had all the newest, most fashionable dresses imported from Paris. So I had the choice of a whole range of very saleable merchandise. I persuaded him to let me have a quantity of blouses, trousers and dresses, on sale or return; they were worth a good deal of money and the idea was we would sell them in the remoter parts of the country.

We set off, going wherever we liked and coming back whenever it suited us. But although we sold our stuff pretty well, we didn't make enough to cover our expenses, and Coriat's share vanished in petrol. There was nothing left for him.

Our best customers were the whores, and of course we never failed to go round the brothels. It was a great temptation for them when I spread our things out on the dining-room table— garish blouses, the latest in the way of trousers, silk scarves, flowered skirts—and started my patter. 'And listen to what I say, ladies. This is not a useless luxury as far as you are concerned. If I may say so, it is more like a business investment, because the more attractive you are, the more the customers come crowding in. As for those ladies who just think of saving, I can tell them for sure that it's a deeply unwise economy not to buy from me. Why? Because all the really well-dressed girls are going to be dangerous competitors.'

There were some brothel-keepers who did not much care for our doing business this way; it made them feel bad to see money going into pockets other than their own. A good many of them sold 'professional equipment' to their girls—on tick, sometimes—and the bastards wanted to monopolize the profit.

We often went to Puerto La Cruz, because there was a good airfield at Barcelona, a town a short way off. The best-run, classiest brothel there had sixty women in it, but the boss was an ugly great sod of a man, vulgar, pretentious and obstinate. He was a Panamanian. His wife was a Venezuelan, and she was charming; but unfortunately he was the one who gave the orders, and there was no question of even opening our cases for a quick look, far less of spreading things out on a table.

One day he went too far. He fired a girl then and there for having bought a scarf I was wearing round my neck. The argument turned nasty and the cop on duty told us to get out and never come back.

'OK, you fat shit of a phony ponce,' said Carotte. 'We shan't come back by land but we shall by air. You can't stop us doing that.'

I didn't understand the threat until next morning, when we were taking off at dawn from Barcelona and he said to me on the intercom, 'We'll go and say hello to the Panamanian. Don't be frightened and hold on tight.'

'What are you going to do?'

He made no reply, but when we came within sight of the brothel he climbed a little and then he dived straight for it at full throttle, shot under the high-tension cable just outside and roared over the corrugated-iron roof, almost touching it. Several of the sheets of iron were loose, and they flew off, displaying the rooms, with their beds and the people in them. We banked, climbed and flew back a little higher to contemplate the sight. I've never seen anything more utterly comic than those naked women and their naked customers, hopping mad in their lidless boxes, shaking furious fists at the plane, which had cut them short either in their games or in an exhausted sleep. Carotte and I laughed until we were almost sick.

We never went back, because now there would not only be a furious boss, but a furious pack of women too. Later I did find one girl who had the good taste to laugh at the whole thing with us. Apparently it had wreaked havoc, and in his rage the fat sod of a Panamanian had insisted on fixing the corrugated sheets on all the women's rooms himself, with enormous bolts.

Carotte and I were both devoted to nature and we often flew off just to look for beautiful places. That was how we came to find one of the real wonders of the world—Los Roques, about a hundred and fifty miles out at sea, a scattering of more than three hundred and sixty little islands, close together in an oval and forming a huge lake in the ocean. A calm lake, because the islands made a barrier, and its pale-green water was so clear you could see the bottom sixty or seventy feet down. Unfortunately in those days there was no landing-strip, and we flew the whole length and breadth of the cluster ten times before pitching on another island some twenty miles to the west, called Las Aves.

Carotte really was a wonderful pilot. I've seen him land on a steeply sloping beach with one wing touching the sand and the other sweeping the sea. Isla de Aves means the island of birds. There were thousands and thousands of them, and they had grey feathers except when they were young: then they were white all over. They were called bobos, because they were rather slow-witted and perfectly trusting. It was an extraordinary feeling, being there, just the two of us, stark naked on an island as flat as a pancake and being surrounded by birds that landed on you or walked about without the least fear, never having seen a man. We spent hours browning in the sun, lying on the narrow beach that ran right round the island. We played with the birds, taking them in the hollow of our hands; some were deeply interested in our heads, and gently pecked our hair. We swam, sun-bathed again, and when we were hungry we could always find crayfish warming themselves on the surface. We'd catch a few with our hands and grill them on the spot. The only difficulty was finding enough dry stuff for the fire, because almost nothing grew on the island.

Sitting there on that untouched beach, eating those succulent crayfish and drinking a full-bodied white wine—we always had a few bottles on board—with the sea, the sky and the birds all round us and nothing else at all, gave us such a feeling of paradise that we didn't have to speak to be wholly in touch with one another.

And when we took off again, before nightfall, our hearts were filled with sun and happiness and zest for life; we did not give a damn for anything, not even for finding the money for the petrol for the trip—a trip whose only reason was to let us live in a beautiful and unexpected world.

At Las Aves we discovered a huge sea-cave: at low tide its mouth was above the surface and light and air came in. I had a passion for this splendid grotto; you could swim into it, and inside the water was clear and shallow—not more than three feet deep. When you stood up in the middle and looked around, the roof and the walls seemed to be covered with cicadas. They weren't cicadas, of course, but thousands of little crayfish clinging to the rock. We sometimes stayed there a long while, never disturbing them. The only time we interfered was when a big octopus, a great lover of baby crayfish, put out an arm to gather a few. We jumped on him right away and turned him inside-out. There he could lie and rot, if he had the time, because he was an unusual treat for the crabs.

We often went to Las Aves and spent the night there. We each had a big electric torch and we gathered crayfish, each weighing about two and a half pounds, until we had filled two sacks with them. We dumped all the finery we were meant to be selling at Carlotta, the airfield in the middle of Caracas, and that meant we could bring back close on half a ton of crayfish. It was insane to load the plane like that, but it was all part of the fun. We could just about get off the ground, and as for gaining height, the stars were in no danger! We would labour up the twelve miles of valley from the coast to Caracas, just skimming the housetops; and there we would sell our crayfish at the ridiculous price of two bolivars fifty apiece. At least it paid for the petrol and kept us going. But when you go after crayfish with your hands you often get hurt, and sometimes we'd come back without any. It didn't matter; we never gave a damn—we were living to the full.

One day as we were on our way to Puerto La Cruz and not very far from it, Carotte said to me over the intercom, 'Papi, we're short of juice. I'm going to put her down on the San Tomé oil-company's field.' We flew over the strip to show we wanted to come down on their private landing-place, and the sods instantly ran a tanker full of petrol or water, God knows which, right out into the middle of the strip. Carotte had nerves of steel, and although I told him again and again I couldn't see where we could possibly touch down, he just said, 'Hold on, Papi,' and side-slipped towards a fairly wide road. He landed without bumping too much, but the speed carried him along towards a turning, and round this turning came a trailer filled with bullocks, tearing along as fast as it could go.

The shriek of the brakes must have drowned our shrieks of horror, because if the driver hadn't lost control and run his trailer into the ditch we should certainly have been done for. We jumped out of the plane and Carotte hushed the swearing driver—he was an Italian. 'Help us push the plane and you can beef later.' The Italian was still trembling all over and as white as a sheet. We helped him catch his beasts—they had escaped when the trailer came to pieces.

This prodigious landing made such a stir that the government bought Carotte's plane and made him a civilian instructor at the Carlotta camp.

My life as an airman was over. Sad. I'd had a few hours of lessons and I was coming on well. Never mind. The only one who came out of this business a loser was Coriat. The extraordinary thing was he never sued me. Some years later I paid him back every penny; and here I should like to thank him for the generosity of his attitude.

But at that particular moment, not only had I lost the plane and not only had my job with the Hungarian woman been taken by someone else but I also had to avoid the central parts of Caracas, because Coriat's shop was there and I had no wish to bump into him. So once more the position was far from brilliant. But I didn't care: those few weeks with Carotte had been too marvellous for me to regret anything at all.

Carotte and I often saw one another after that: we used to meet in a quiet little joint run by an old Frenchman who had retired from the Compagnie Transatlantique. One night when we were playing dominoes in a corner with a Spanish republican and an ex-lag, who now made a peaceful living by selling scent on tick, two men wearing sunglasses came in—we didn't know them—and asked if it was true that a Frenchman often came here, a pilot.

Carotte stood up and said, 'That's me.'

I examined these unknown types from head to foot and straight away, in spite of his dark glasses, I recognized one of them. I felt a sudden wave of emotion. I went up to him. Before I could speak he knew me. 'Papi!'

It was Big Léon, one of my best friends in penal. A tall guy with a thin face; a real man, open-hearted. This was not the moment to seem too friendly and he just introduced me to his side-kick Pedro the Chilean and said no more. We had a drink in a corner and Léon said he was looking for a light plane with a pilot and he had been told about this Frenchman.

'The pilot's here,' said Carotte, 'and I'm him. But the plane is not. It belongs to other people now.'

'That's sad,' said Léon laconically.

Carotte returned to his game of dominoes: someone else took my place. Pedro the Chilean went and stood at the bar, so we could talk quietly.

'Well, Papi?'

'Well, Léon?'

'The last time we met was more than ten years ago.'

'Yes. You were coming out of solitary just as I was going in. How are you doing, Léon?'

'Not bad, not bad at all. And you, Papi?'

Since it was Léon, I felt I could talk. 'I'll tell you straight, Léon: I'm more or less in the shit. It's not so easy to climb up the hill. It's all very well coming out of stir stuffed with the best intentions: life's so tough when you have no trade that all you think of is going on the loose again. Léon, you're older than me and you aren't the ordinary kind of lag. I can tell *you* what's on my mind. Speaking dead serious and dead straight, as far as I'm concerned I owe this country everything. I came back to life here and I've promised myself to respect this great community—to do the least possible number of things that could be criticized. But it's not easy. Yet I'm perfectly certain that even with my love for pulling things off I could set myself up here, starting from nothing and going straight, if only I hadn't a long bill to present to some people in Paris, *and I can't wait, in case those buggers should die before I get there.*

'When I see the young people of this country, utterly care-free and full of the joy of life, then in spite of myself I look back at all those years that were stolen from me, the best years of my life. And I see the black holes of the Réclusion, and the three years of waiting before the trial and after it, and that stinking penal where I was treated far worse than a mad dog. And then for hours, sometimes for whole days on end, I walk about the streets of Caracas turning it all over in my mind. I don't thank fate for having brought me here: no, that's not what goes on in my mind at all. I feel I'm back in those places where I was buried alive; I see them, I keep seeing them, and I go back to my *one, two, three, four, five, turn,* just as I did when I was buried there and walked to and fro like a bear in a cage. It's beyond my control; it's a real obsession. I can't bear the idea that those who unjustly put me through that hell should die in peace, without having paid.

'So when I'm walking along the streets like that, I don't look around like an ordinary man. Every jeweller's shop, every place that is sure to hold the money I need—I can't help casing it and working out just how I could get my hands on everything it contains. It's not because I don't feel like it that I haven't yet pulled anything off; there are jobs here so dead easy they almost cry out to be done.

'Up until now I've managed to keep a hold on myself; I've done nothing serious against this country that trusts me. That would be vile, as odious as raping the daughters of a house that had taken you in. But I'm afraid, yes I'm afraid of myself: I'm afraid one day I may not be able to resist the temptation of pulling off a big job. Because I'll never, never be able to scrape together the huge sum I need for my revenge, not by working honestly. Between you and me, Léon, I'm at the end of my tether.'

Big Léon listened to me in silence, gazing at me attentively. We had a last drink, hardly exchanging another word. He got up and gave me a time to come and have lunch with him and Pedro the Chilean the next day.

We met in a quiet restaurant with an arbour. The sun was shining.

'I've been thinking about what you said to me, Papi. So listen, and I'll tell you why we're in Caracas.'

They were only passing through, on their way to another South American country. There they were going to pay serious attention to a pawnshop, where, according to their own inquiries and information supplied by one of the chief employees, there was enough jewellery for each of them to come out with a very elegant fortune, once the jewels were turned into dollars. That was why they were looking for Carotte. They had meant to make him a proposition for his plane and himself; but now there was no point in talking about it.

'You can come in with us, if you like, Papi,' ended Léon.

'I've no passport and nothing much in the way of savings either.'

'We'll look after the passport. Isn't that right, Pedro?'

'It's just as if you had it already,' said Pedro. 'In a phony name: that way you'll officially neither have gone out of Venezuela nor come back.'

'What'll it cost, roughly?'

'Round about a thousand dollars. You got that much dough?'

'Yes.'

'Well then, seeing how you're placed, you shouldn't hesitate.'

A fortnight later there I was some miles from a South American capital, having hired a car the day after the job, busy burying a biscuit tin with my share of the jewels in it.

The carefully programmed operation had been simple. We went in through a tie shop next door to the pawnbroker's. Léon and Pedro had been there to buy ties several times so as to get a good look at the lock and fix the exact spot where they would make the hole in the wall. There were no safes, only cupboards armoured all round. We went in at ten p.m. on Saturday and we came out at eleven on Sunday night.

A smooth, well-run job. So there I was, a dozen miles from the town, burying my tin at the foot of a huge tree. I knew I should find the place again without any difficulty, because apart from the mark I had cut with my knife, the tree was easy to spot: the forest began just after a bridge, and the first tree of this forest, right by the road, was mine. Driving back, I threw the pick away some five miles along the road.

That evening we all met in a classy restaurant. We walked in separately and behaved as if we met by chance at the bar and then decided to have dinner together. Each one of us had hidden his share, Léon with a friend and Pedro in the forest, like me.

'It's much better for each to have his own private hole,' said Léon. 'That way, no one of us knows what the others have done with theirs. It's a precaution they often take in South America, because if the pigs pull you in, what they put you through is no kind of fun at all. Then if a poor guy starts to talk, why, he can only do the Judas on himself. So that's sewn up: tell me, Papi, are you satisfied with the share-out?'

'I think our rough estimate of each piece was dead right. Everything's fine: I've not a word to say against it.'

So all was satisfactory and everyone was pleased.

'Hands up!'

'Why, what the hell?' cried Léon. 'Are you crazy?'

No time for further observations: in a flash we were clubbed, handcuffed and wheeled off to the police headquarters. We hadn't even finished the oysters.

In that country, the pigs do not coddle you at all: the party went on all night. Eight hours at the very least. First questions: 'Do you like ties?'

'You go and bugger yourself.'

And so it went. By five in the morning we were nothing but lumps of bruised flesh. The pigs were furious at not having been able to get anything out of us: they frothed with rage. 'OK. Since you're all in a sweat and your temperature's too high, we'll cool you.' We could scarcely stand, but they tossed us into a black maria and a quarter of an hour later there we were in front of a huge building. The pigs went in and then we saw workmen coming out: the pigs must have asked them to leave. Then it was our turn to go in, each propped up by two pigs and almost dragged along.

An enormous corridor; steel doors right and left, each with a kind of clock over it: a clock with only one hand. Thermometers. Straight away I grasped that we were in the corridor of the deep-freeze of a big slaughter-house. We stopped at a place where there were several tables standing in the corner. 'Well, now,' said the chief pig. 'I'll give you one last chance to think it over. These are deep-freezers for meat. You understand what that means? So for the last time, where have you put the jewels and the other things?'

'We know nothing about any jewels nor about any ties,' said Léon.

'OK, lawyer. You can go first.'

The cops unbolted a door and opened it wide. A kind of icy fog came out and wafted down the corridor. Having taken off Léon's shoes and socks they shoved him in.

'Shut it quick,' said the chief, 'or we'll be frozen too.'

'Now, Chilean. Are you going to talk, yes or no?'

'I've nothing to talk about.'

They opened another door and pushed the Chilean in.

'You're the youngest, Italian [my passport had an Italian identity]. Take a good look at these thermometers. They show minus forty. That means that if you don't talk and we stuff you in there in a sweat, after the party you've been through, it's ten to one you'll catch pneumonia and die in hospital in less than forty-eight hours. I'm giving you one last chance, you see: did you rob the pawnbroker's by going through the tie shop, yes or no?'

'I've nothing to do with those men. I only knew one of them, long ago, and I just met them by chance in the restaurant. Ask the waiters and barmen. I don't know whether they had anything to do with this job, but I'm dead certain I didn't.'

'Well, Macaroni, you can perish too. I'm sorry to think of you dying at your age; but it's your own fault. You asked for it.'

The door opened. They shot me into the darkness, and hitting my head on an iron-hard side of beef hanging from a hook I fell flat on the floor: it was covered with ice an dhoar-frost. Immediately I felt the appalling cold seize upon my flesh, pierce right through and reach my bones. With a terrible effort I got to my knees, then, clinging to a side of beef, I stood upright. Every movement hurt, after the beating they had given us, but in spite of that I thumped my arms and rubbed my neck, cheeks, nose and eyes. I tried warming my hands under my armpits. All I had on was my trousers and a torn shirt. They had taken my shoes and socks too, and the soles of my feet hurt terribly as they stuck to the ice; and I felt my toes beginning to freeze.

I said to myself, 'This can't go on for more than ten minutes —a quarter of an hour at the most. Otherwise I'll be like one of these sides of beef: a lump of deep-frozen meat. No, no, it's not possible. They can't do that to us! Surely they can't freeze us alive? Stick it, Papi. A few minutes more and the door will open. That icy corridor will seem as warm as toast.' My arms were not working any more; I could no longer close my hands nor move my fingers; my feet were sticking to the ice and I no longer had the strength to pull them away. I felt I was going to faint and in the space of a few seconds I saw my father's face, then the prosecutor's floating over it, but that was not so clear, because it merged with the faces of the cops. Three faces in one. 'How strange,' I thought. 'They are all alike, and they are laughing because they've won.' Then I passed out.

What was happening? Where was I? As I opened my eyes there was a man's face leaning over me, a handsome face. I could not speak, because my mouth was still frozen stiff with cold, but inside my head I asked myself what I was doing here, stretched out on a table.

Big, powerful, efficient hands rubbed me all over with warm grease and gradually I felt heat and suppleness coming back. The chief cop was watching, two or three yards away. He looked hot and bothered. Several times they opened my mouth to pour a drop of spirits into it. Once they poured too much; I choked and shot it out.

'There we are,' said the masseur. 'He's saved.'

They went on rubbing me for at least half an hour. I felt that I could talk if I wanted to, but I preferred keeping my mouth shut. I realized that over there on the right there was another body lying on a table the same height as mine. He was naked too, and they were rubbing and massaging him. Who was it? Léon or the Chilean? There had been three of us: but with me on this table and the guy on the other, that only made two. Where was the third? The other tables were empty.

Helped by the masseur I managed to sit up, and I saw who the other one was. Pedro the Chilean. They dressed us and put us into those padded overalls specially made for men who work inside deep-freezes.

The chief pig returned to the attack. 'Can you speak, Chilean?'

'Yes.'

'Where are the jewels?'

'I don't know anything.'

'And what about you, Spaghetti?'

'I wasn't with those men.'

'OK.'

I slipped off the table. I could only just stand, but once I was up I felt a healthy burning on the soles of my feet, and that pleased me although it hurt; and I felt the blood flowing inside me, racing round my whole body with such strength that it thumped in the farthest veins and arteries.

I thought that for one day I had gone as far in horror as possible: but I had got it wrong, quite wrong.

They put Pedro and me side by side, and the chief, who had now recovered his self-assurance, called out, 'Take off their overalls.'

They took them off, and there I was, naked to the waist: straight away I started shivering with cold again.

'And now take a good look at this, *hombres*.'

From under a table they dragged a kind of rigid parcel and stood it up on end in front of us. It was a frozen corpse, as stiff as a board. Its eyes were wide open and fixed, like two marbles: it was hideous to see, terrifying. Big Léon! They had frozen him alive!

'Take a good look, *hombres*,' said the chief again. 'Your accomplice wouldn't talk: so all right, we went all the way with him. Now it's your turn, if you're as stubborn as he was. I've been given orders to be merciless, because this job of yours is much too serious. The pawnshop is run by the state, and there's an ugly rumour in the town—people think it's a put-up job worked by some of the officials. So either you talk, or in half an hour you'll be like your mate here.'

My wits had not yet come back, and the sight so churned me up that for three long seconds I felt like talking. The only thing that prevented me was that I didn't know where the other hiding-places were. They'd never believe me and I'd be in worse danger than ever.

To my utter amazement I heard a very collected voice, Pedro's voice, say, 'Come on now; you can't frighten us with that stuff. Why, of course it was an accident—you never meant to freeze him; it was an error of judgement, that's all; but you don't want another error with us. One you can get away with; but three, three foreigners turned into blocks of ice, that mounts up. And I can't see you giving watertight explanations to two different embassies. One, OK. Three, it's too much.'

I could not help admiring Pedro's steely nerve. Very calmly the pig looked at the Chilean, not speaking. Then after a little pause, 'You're a crook, and that's for sure; but I have to admit that you've also got guts.' Turning to the others he said, 'Find them each a shirt and take them back to the prison: the judge will look after them. With brutes like this there's no point in going on with the party—it's a waste of time.' He turned his back and walked off.

A month later they let me out. The tie merchant admitted I had never been to his shop, which was true: the barmen stated that I had had two whiskies by myself, that I had already booked a table for one before the other two appeared, and that we had seemed very surprised to meet one another in this town. Still, they ordered me to leave the country in five days, because they were afraid that as Léon's so-called countryman (Léon also had an Italian passport) I would go and tell the consulate what had happened.

During the inquiries, we had been brought face to face with a guy I did not know but Pedro did—the pawnshop employee who had put him on to the job. The very evening we shared out, this silly bastard presented a girl from an all-night bar with a splendid antique ring. The pigs were tipped off, and they had no difficulty in making him talk: that was why Big Léon and Pedro were identified so quickly. Pedro the Chilean stayed there, stuck fast in this business.

I took the plane with five hundred dollars in my pocket. I never went near my hiding-place: it was too risky. I took stock, to see how things stood after the hideous nightmare I had just been through: the papers reckoned the pawnshop job at two hundred thousand dollars; even if they had exaggerated and doubled it, that still left a hundred thousand: so in my hole I had about thirty thousand. Since the value had been reckoned according to the amount lent on the jewels, that is to say half their real value, and if I sold them without going through a receiver, then by my calculations I should be the owner of more than sixty thousand dollars! So I had what I needed for my revenge, so long as I did not break into it for living. This money was sacred; it was for a sacred purpose, and I must never use it for anything else *upon any pretext whatsoever*.

In spite of the horrible way it ended for my friend Léon, this job had been a triumph for me. Unless indeed I was forced to help the Chilean; but in a few months he was sure to send a trusted friend to collect his nest-egg for paying his lawyer and maybe for organizing a break. Anyhow, that was our agreement—each with his own hiding-place so that no one of us should be connected with the fate of the others. I hadn't been in favour of that method, but it was the customary way of working in the South American underworld—once the job was done, then each for himself and God for all.

And God for all . . . If it was really Him that had saved me, then He had been more than noble; He had been magnanimous. And yet God could not possibly have been the artisan of my revenge! He did not want me to take it, and that I knew. I remembered that day in El Dorado, the day before I was to be let out for good. I had wanted to thank the God of the Catholics, and in my emotion I had said to Him, 'What can I do to prove that I am sincerely grateful for your kindness?' And it seemed to me that I heard the words, just as though a voice were speaking to me, 'Give up your revenge.'

And I'd said no; anything else, but not that. So it could not have been God who took care of me in this business. Impossible. I'd had luck, that was all, the luck of the devil. The good Lord above had nothing to do with shit of that kind.

But the result—oh the result was there all right, buried at the foot of an ancient tree. It was a huge weight off my mind, knowing I possessed what I needed to carry out the plan I had been feeding my heart with these last thirteen years.

How I hoped the war had spared the sods who sent me down! Now all I had to do, while I waited for my D-day, was to look for a job and live quietly until I could go and unbury my treasure.

The plane was flying at a great height in a brilliant sky, way above a carpet of snow-white clouds. It was purity up here, and I thought of my people, my father, my mother, my family and of my childhood bathed in light. Beneath that white cumulus there were dirty clouds, a greyish, unclean rain—a fine image of the earthly world: that desire for power, that desire to prove to others that you are better than them, that dry, heartless desire you see in the kind of people who do not give a damn if they destroy a human being so long as by doing so something is gained or something is justified.

8: The Bomb

CARACAS again. It was with real pleasure that I walked the streets of this great living city once more.

I had been free twenty months now, and yet still I had not become a member of this community. It was all very well to say 'All you have to do is get a job': but, besides not being able to find any suitable work, I had difficulty in speaking Spanish, and many doors were closed to me because of this. So I bought a grammar, shut myself in my room and determined to spend however many hours it needed to speak Spanish. I grew angrier and angrier; I could not manage to hit the pronunciation, and after a few days I flung the book to the other end of the room and went back to the streets and the cafés, looking for someone I knew who could find me something to do.

More and more Frenchmen were coming over from Europe, sickened by its wars and political upheavals. Some were on the run from an arbitrary justice that varied according to the political climate of the moment; others were looking for peace and quiet—a beach where they could breathe without someone coming up every other moment to feel their pulse and see what rhythm it was beating at.

These people were not like Frenchmen; and yet they were French. These honest citizens had nothing in common with Papa Charrière or any of the people I had known in my childhood. When I was with them, I found they had ideas so different and so twisted in comparison with those of my young days that I was quite at sea. Often I'd say to them, 'I believe that maybe you shouldn't forget the past, but that you should stop talking about it. Is it possible that even now after the war is over there are supporters of Nazism among you? I'll tell you something: when you talk about the Jews, it's like seeing one race spew out hatred against another race.

'You're living in Venezuela, in the midst of its people, and yet you aren't capable of grasping their wonderful philosophy. Here there's no discrimination, either racial or religious. If anyone should be infected with the virus of revenge against the privileged classes the poorest class should be because of their wretched conditions of life. Well now, *that virus doesn't even exist in this country.*

'You aren't even capable of settling down to living for the sake of living. Is life made up of nothing more than never-ending battles between men who don't share the same ideology?

'Please, just you shut up. Don't come here as Europeans filled with notions of the superiority of their race, like explorers. True enough, you have had more intellectual training than the majority of the people here, but what of it? What good is it to you, since you're a more stupid bunch of sods than they are? As far as you're concerned education doesn't mean intelligence, generosity, goodness and understanding, but only learning things from books. If your hearts stay dry, selfish, rancorous and fossilized, what you've learnt doesn't mean a thing.

'God made the sun, the sea, the vast prairies and the bush, but did He make them just for you?

'Do you think you're a race pre-ordained to organize the world? When I look at you and listen to you, it occurs to me that a world run by poor sods like you will mean nothing but wars and revolutions. Because although you say you long for peace and quiet, you only long for it if it agrees with your point of view.'

Every one of them had his list of people to be shot, proscribed or shoved into gaol; and although it upset me, I couldn't help laughing when I heard these people, sitting in a café or the lounge of some third-rate hotel, criticizing everything and coming to the conclusion that they were the only ones who could really run the world.

And I was afraid, yes I was afraid, because I had a very real feeling of the danger that these newcomers brought with them—the virus of the old world's fossilized ideological passions.

1947. I'd come to know an ex-con by the name of Pierre-René Deloffre: he had only one object of worship, and that was General Angarita Medina, the former president of Venezuela, who had been overthrown by the last military *coup d'état*, in 1945. Deloffre was a high-powered character. Very active, but

133

open-hearted and enthusiastic. He brought all his passion to bear to persuade me that the people who had profited by this *coup d'état* weren't worth Medina's bootlaces. To tell the truth, he did not convince me; but since I was in a tricky position I was not going to cross him.

He found me a job through a financier, a truly remarkable guy called Armando. He came from a powerful Venezuelan family; he was noble-minded, generous, intelligent, well-educated, witty and unusually brave. There was only one drawback—he was burdened with a stupid brother, Clemente. Some of this brother's recent capers have made it clear to me that he hasn't changed in these last twenty-five years. Deloffre introduced me to the financier with no beating about the bush: 'My friend Papillon, who escaped from the French penal settlement. Papillon, this is the man I was telling you about.'

Armando adopted me right away, and with the directness of a real nobleman he asked me whether I was in need of money.

'No, Monsieur Armando; I'm in need of a job.'

I wanted to see how the land lay first; it was better to take one's time. What's more, I was not really short of cash for the moment.

'Come and see me at nine tomorrow.'

The next day he took me to a garage, the Franco-Venezuelan it was called, and there he introduced me to his associates, three young men full of life, ready to break into a furious gallop at the drop of a hat. Two of them were married. One to Simone, a magnificent Parisienne of twenty-five; the other to Dédée, a twenty-year-old blue-eyed girl from Brittany, as delicate as a violet and the mother of a little boy called Cricri.

They were good-looking, open types, frank and unreserved. They welcomed me with open arms, as though they'd known me for ever. Straight away they fixed me up a bed in a corner of the big garage, more or less curtained off and close to the shower. They were my first real family for seventeen years. This team of young people liked, cherished and respected me; and it made me all the happier because although I was a few years older I had just as much zest for life, just as much joy in living without rules and without limits.

I asked no questions—I didn't really have to—but I soon saw that not one of them was a genuine mechanic. They had a faint, a very faint notion of what a motor was: but even less than a notion as far as the motors of American cars were concerned, and they were the main or indeed the only customers. One of them was a turner, and that explained the presence of a lathe in the garage—they said it was for correcting pistons. Pretty soon I found that what the machine was really used for was changing gas-bottles so they would take a detonator and a Bickford fuse.

For the swarm of newly-arrived Frenchmen, the Franco-Venezuelan garage repaired their cars, more or less; but for the Venezuelan financier it fixed bombs for a *coup d'état*, a *golpe*. I didn't altogether care for this.

'Hell,' I said. 'Who's it in favour of and who's it against? Tell me about it.' It was evening; we were sitting there under the lamp and I was questioning the three Frenchmen—their wives and the kid had gone to bed.

'That's none of our business. We just fix the pots Armando asks us for. And that's fine by us, mate.'

'Fine for you, maybe. But I have to know.'

'Why? You earn a fat living and you have fun, don't you?'

'Sure. As far as fun goes, we have fun. But I'm not like you. They've given me asylum in this country: they trust me and they let me walk about as free as air.'

Hearing me talk like this in my position struck them as very odd. Because they knew what I had in the back of my head; they knew all about my obsession—I'd told them. But one thing I hadn't told them was about the pawnshop job. So they said to me, 'If this business comes off, you can make the money you need to carry out what you have in mind. And of course we don't intend to spend the rest of our lives in this garage. Certainly we have fun, but it brings in nothing like the solid cash we'd dreamed of when we came to South America.'

'And what about your wives and the kid?'

'The women know all about it. A month before the balloon goes up, they leave for Bogota.'

'They know all about it, then. Just as I thought: so they aren't too surprised at some of the things that go on.'

135

That same evening I saw Deloffre and Armando and I had a long talk with them. Armando said to me, 'In this country of ours, it's Bétancourt and Gallegos who run everything, under the cover of the phony A.D. [*Acción Democrática*]. The power was put into their hands by simple-minded soldiers who no longer really knew why they overthrew Medina—he was a soldier too, and he was more liberal and far more human than the civilians. I see the former Medina officials being persecuted, and there's nothing I can say; and I try to understand how it comes about that men who carried out a revolution with the slogans of "social justice and respect for all without the least exception" can become worse than their predecessors once they're in power. That's why I want to help bring Medina back.'

'Fine, Armando. I quite see that what you want above all is to stop the party now in power going on with their persecution. And as for you, Deloffre, you've got just one God, and that's Medina, your protector and your friend. But you listen to me, now: the people who let me, Papillon, out of El Dorado were this very party now in power. Straight after the revolution, the minute the new chief arrived he stopped the savage reign of terror in the settlement, stopped it dead. He's still there, I believe—Don Julio Ramos, a lawyer and a distinguished writer, the guy who let me out. And you want me to join in a coup against those people? No: let me go. You know you can rely on my keeping my mouth shut.'

Armando knew the tough spot I was in, and like a real gentleman he said to me, 'Enrique, you don't make the bombs; you don't work at the lathe. All you do is look after the cars and pass the tools when the panel-beater asks for them. So stay a little longer. I ask it as a favour; and if we make a move I promise you'll know a month ahead for sure.'

So I stayed there with those three young guys: they are still alive and they would be easily recognizable, so I will use the initials P.I., B.L. and J.G. instead of their names. We made up a splendid team and we were always together, living it up at such a pitch that the French of Caracas called us the three musketeers—as everybody knows, there were four of them. Those few months were the finest, the happiest and the liveliest I ever spent in Caracas.

Life was one long laugh. On Saturdays we kept some elegant car belonging to a customer for our own use, saying it wasn't ready yet, and we drove down to one of the gorgeous beaches lined with flowers and coconut-palms to swim and have fun all day long. Sometimes, of course, we would meet the owner, far from pleased at seeing the car he thought was in the garage filled with all these people. Then gently, very gently, we would explain that we were doing this for his sake—that we could not bear the idea of giving him back a car not in perfect condition, and so it had to be tried out. It always worked, and no doubt the ravishing smiles of the girls helped a great deal.

On the other hand, we did have some bloody awkward situations. The Swiss ambassador's petrol-tank leaked: he brought the car in for us to solder the joint. I carefully emptied the tank with a rubber pipe, sucking out the very last drop. But apparently that wasn't enough, because as soon as the flame of the blowpipe touched it, the cow of a tank blew up, setting fire to the car and roasting it to a frazzle. While the other guy and I groped about, covered with black oil and smoke and just beginning to grasp that we had escaped from death, I heard B.L.'s calm voice saying, 'Don't you think we ought to tell our partners about this little mishap?'

He phoned the brothers, and the half-wit Clemente answered. 'Clemente, can you give me the number of the garage's insurance?'

'...'

'What for? Oh yes, I was forgetting. Because the Swiss ambassador's car caught fire. It's just a heap of cinders now.'

I don't have to tell you that five minutes later Clemente appeared at a brisk run, waving his arms about and hopping mad because in fact the garage was not covered in any way at all. It took three stiff whiskies and all the charm of Simone's amply-displayed legs to quieten him down. Armando only turned up the following day; he was perfectly calm, and this was his charming way of taking it—'Things happen only to people who work. Anyhow, don't let's talk about it any more: I've fixed everything with the ambassador.'

The ambassador got another car, but somehow we lost his custom.

From time to time, while we were living this zestful life, I thought about my little treasure lying there hidden at the foot of a tree in a republic well known for its frozen meat. And I put money aside for the fare there and back when the time came to go and fetch it. The knowledge that I had enough, or close on enough, to satisfy my revenge had completely transformed me. I no longer worried about making money, and I lived without care or worry of any kind; it was because of this that I could plunge so whole-heartedly into our musketeering life—plunge into it so deep that one Sunday afternoon at three o'clock there we were, all of us, bathing in a fountain in one of the Caracas squares with nothing but our drawers on. This time at least, Clemente rose to the occasion and had his brother's partners released from the police-station where they had been shut up for indecent exposure. By now a good many months had gone by, and at last it seemed to me safe to go and fetch my treasure.

So fare you well, buddies, and thanks for all your kindness: and there I was on my way to the airport. I got there at six in the morning; on arrival, I hired a car, and at nine I reached the spot.

I crossed the bridge. Christ above, what had happened? Had I gone mad, or was it a mirage? I stared around, but my tree was not there. And not only my tree but hundreds of others. The road had been made much wider, and the bridge and the stretch leading up to it had been entirely changed. Working it out from the bridge, I managed to more or less pinpoint the place where my tree and my wealth must have been. I was flabbergasted. Not a trace!

A kind of madness came over me, a stupid fury. I ground my heels into the asphalt, just as though it could feel anything. I was filled with an enormous overflowing rage and I looked around for something to destroy: all I could see was the white lines painted on the road—I kicked them, as if knocking off little bits of paint could destroy the road.

I went back to the bridge. The approach road the other side had not been altered, and judging from that I reckoned they must have shifted the earth to a depth of more than twelve feet. And since my loot had not been buried deeper than a yard, it can't have lasted long, poor thing.

I leant on the parapet and for a while I watched the water flow by. Gradually I calmed down, but still the thoughts whirled about inside my head. Was I always going to come unstuck like this? Should I give up trying to pull things off? What was I going to do now? My knees sagged. But then I got a hold on myself and I said, 'How many times did you fail before you brought off your break? Seven or eight times, right? Well, it's the same thing in life. You lose one banco, you go and win another. That's life, when you really love it.'

I didn't stay long in this country that felt itself called upon to change its roads so fast. It made me sick to think that a civilized nation didn't even respect ancient trees. And why, I ask you, why widen a road that was quite broad enough for all the traffic it had to carry?

In the plane taking me back to Caracas, I laughed to think that men can suppose they are the masters of their fate, that they imagine they can build the future and foresee what they'll be doing the next year or the year after. All so much balls, Papi! The brightest calculator, the cleverest imaginable organizer of his life is no more than a toy before fate. Only the present is certain: all the rest is something we know nothing about—something that goes by the name of luck, misfortune, destiny or indeed the mysterious and incomprehensible hand of God.

Only one thing really matters in life and that is never to admit you're beaten and to start up again after every flop. That was what I was going to do.

When I'd left, I'd said good-bye for keeps. Because once I'd dug up the loot I meant to go to other countries, not Venezuela, alter the jewels so they could not be recognized, sell them and move on to Spain. From there it would be easy to go and pay a call on Prosecuting Counsel and Co. So you can imagine the terrific uproar when the musketeers saw me turn up at the garage door. Dinner and a party-cake to celebrate my return, and Dédée put four flowers on the table. We drank to the re-formed team and life started off again at full throttle. But still, I was no longer as carefree as I had been.

I felt sure Armando and Deloffre had ideas about me that they were keeping back. It seemed to me that these must have something to do with the *coup d'état*, although both knew my position as far as that was concerned. They often asked me to come and have a drink or to eat at Deloffre's place. Wonderful food, and no witnesses. Deloffre did the cooking, and it was his faithful chauffeur, Victor, who waited at table. We talked about a great many things, but in the end the conversation always came round to the same subject—General Medina. The most liberal of all Venezuelan presidents; not a single political prisoner during his régime; no one persecuted because of his ideas; a policy of coexistence with all other states, all other régimes, even to the point of setting up diplomatic relations with the Soviet Union; he was good, he was noble, and the people so loved him for his simplicity that one day, during a celebration at El Paraiso, they carried him and his wife in triumph, like toreros.

By perpetually telling me about this wonderful Medina, who walked around Caracas with just one aide-de-camp and who went to the cinema just like an ordinary citizen, Armando and Deloffre almost persuaded me that any man with his heart in the right place would do anything to bring Medina back to power. They painted a very dark picture of the present government's injustice and its revengeful attitude towards a whole section of the population; and to make me like his marvellous president even more, Deloffre told me he lived it up with the very best of them. What was more, he was a personal friend, although he knew Deloffre had escaped from penal. I also noted the fact that Deloffre had lost everything in this last revolution. Some mysterious 'avengers' had wrecked his luxurious restaurant-cabaret where Medina and all the top people of Caracas often used to come to have dinner or sit around.

At last, almost won over—mistakenly, as I learnt afterwards —I began to think of taking part in the *coup d'état*. My hesitation vanished entirely (I have to say this because I want to be sincere) when I was promised the money and all the facilities I needed to set *my* plan of revenge in motion.

So this is how it was that one night Deloffre and I were sitting there at his place, me dressed as a captain and Deloffre as a colonel, ready to go into action.

It began badly. To recognize one another, the civilian conspirators were supposed to wear a green armband, and the password was *Aragua*. We were supposed to be at action stations at two in the morning. But then about eleven that night four guys turned up in the one horse-drawn cab left in Caracas: they were completely sozzled and they were singing at the top of their voices, to the accompaniment of a guitar. They stopped just in front of the house, and to my horror I heard them singing songs full of allusions to tonight's *coup d'état*— allusions as obvious as an elephant. One of them bawled out to Deloffre, 'Pierre! Tonight the nightmare comes to an end at last! Courage and dignity, *amigo*! Our Papa Medina must return!'

For goddamned utter foolishness you could not have asked better. The time between some lemon telling the pigs and the moment they came to call on us would be very short. I was hopping mad, and I had every reason to be: we had three bombs there in the car, two in the boot and one on the back seat, covered with a rug.

'Well, they're an elegant lot, your mates! If they're all like this, we needn't bother: we might just as well go straight to prison.'

Deloffre howled with laughter, as calm as if he were going to a ball; he was delighted with himself in his colonel's uniform and he kept admiring his reflection in the glass. 'Don't you worry, Papillon. Anyhow, we aren't going to hurt anyone. As you know, these three gas-bottles have got nothing but powder in them. Just to make a noise, that's all.'

'And what's going to be the point of this little noise of yours?'

'It's merely to give the signal to the conspirators scattered about the town. That's all. There's nothing bloody or savage about it, you see—we don't want to hurt anybody. We just insist upon them going away, that's all.'

OK. Anyhow, whether I liked it or not I was in this right up to the neck: so much the worse for me. It was not my job to quiver with alarm or be sorry: all I had to do was to wait for the given time.

I refused Deloffre's port—it was the only thing he drank: two bottles a day at least. He tossed back a few glasses.

The three musketeers arrived in a command-car transformed into a crane. It was going to be used to carry off two safes, one belonging to the airline company and the other to the Model Prison (the *Carcel Modelo*); one of the governors—or maybe the man in command of the garrison—was in the plot. I was to have fifty per cent of what was inside and I had insisted on being there when the prison safe was grabbed: they had agreed. It would be a sweet revenge on all the prisons in the world. It was a job very near to my heart.

A dispatch-rider brought the final orders: arrest no enemies; let them escape. Carlotta, the civilian airport right in the middle of the city, had already been cleared so that the chief members of the present government and their officials could get away in light planes without a hitch.

It was then that I learned where the first bomb was to be let off. Well, well, well: this Deloffre certainly went about things in style. It was to go off right in front of the presidential palace at Miraflores. The others were to explode one in the east and the other in the west of Caracas so as to give the impression that things were breaking out everywhere. I smiled to myself at the idea of the alarm and despondency we were going to cause in the palace.

This big wooden gate was not the official entrance to the palace. It was at the back of the building; the military trucks used it, and this way big shots and sometimes the president himself could come and go without being noticed.

Our watches were all set to the same time. We were to be at the gate at three minutes to two. Someone inside was going to open it a crack for just two seconds, long enough for the driver to make the noise of a toad with a little child's toy that imitated it very well. That was how they would know we were there. What was the point? I had no idea: nobody told me. Were President Gallego's guards in the plot and would they take him prisoner? Or would they be put out of action straight away by other conspirators already inside? I knew nothing about that.

One thing was certain: at two o'clock precisely I had to light the fuse leading to the detonator on the gas-bottle I had between my knees and then toss it out of the door, giving it a good shove so it should roll towards the palace gate. The fuse lasted exactly one minute thirty seconds. So I was to light it with my cigar, and the moment it started to fizz, shift my right leg and open the door, counting thirty seconds as I did so. At the thirtieth, start it rolling. We had worked out that as it rolled along, the wind would make it burn faster and that there would be only forty seconds before the explosion.

Although the bottle had no bits of iron in it, its own splinters would be extremely dangerous, so we should have to shoot straight off in the car to take shelter. That would be Victor the chauffeur's job.

I'd persuaded Deloffre that if there was a soldier or a cop near by, he, in his colonel's uniform, would order him to run to the corner of the street. He promised me he'd do just that.

We reached this famous gate at three minutes to two without any difficulty. We drew up along the opposite pavement. No sentry: no cop. Fine. Two minutes to two ... One minute to two ... Two o'clock.

The gate did not open.

I was all tensed up. I said to Deloffre, 'Pierre, it's two o'clock.'

'I know. I've got a watch too.'

'This stinks.'

'I don't understand what's going on. Let's wait another five minutes.'

'OK.'

Two minutes past two ... The gate shot open: soldiers came running out and took up their positions, weapons at the ready. It was as clear as gin: we had been betrayed.

'Get going, Pierre. We've been betrayed!'

It took more than that to knock Pierre off his perch: he seemed not to have grasped the situation at all. 'Don't talk bullshit. They're on our side.'

I brought out a forty-five and rammed it against the back of Victor's neck. 'Get going, or I kill you!'

I was certain of feeling the car leap forward as Victor stamped on the accelerator with all his force, but all I heard was this unbelievable remark: '*Hombre*, it's not you who gives orders here: it's the boss. What does the boss say?'

Hell: I'd seen some guys with guts, but never one like this half-caste Indian. Never!

There was nothing I could do because there were soldiers three yards away. They'd seen the colonel's stars on Deloffre's epaulette up against the window, so they came no closer.

'Pierre, if you don't tell Victor to get going, it's not him I'll put the chill on but you.'

'Little old Papi, I keep telling you they're on our side. Let's wait a little longer,' said Pierre, turning his head towards me. As he did so I saw his nostrils were shining with white powder stuck to them. I got it: the guy was stuffed full with cocaine. Fear came over me, yes, an appalling fear; and I was putting my gun to his neck when he said with the utmost calm, 'It's six minutes past two, Papi. We'll wait two more. We've certainly been betrayed.'

Those hundred and twenty seconds went on for ever. I had my eye on the soldiers; the nearest were watching me, but for the moment they were making no move. At last Deloffre said, '*Vamos*, Victor: let's go. Gently, naturally, not too fast.'

And by a positive miracle we came out of that man-trap alive. Phew! Some years later there was a film called *The Longest Day*. Well, you could have made one called *The Longest Eight Minutes* out of that party of ours.

Deloffre told the driver to make for the bridge that runs from El Paraiso to the Avenida San Martin. He wanted to let off his bomb under it. On the way we met two trucks filled with conspirators who didn't know what to do now, having heard no explosion at two o'clock. We told them what was going on and that we had been betrayed: saying all this made Deloffre change his mind and he ordered the chauffeur to drive back to his place, fast. A mistake the size of a house, because since we had been betrayed, the pigs might very well be there already. Still, we went: and as I was helping Victor put my bomb into the boot I noticed that it had three letters painted on it: P.R.D. I couldn't help roaring with laughter when Pierre-René Deloffre told me the reason for them: we were taking off our uniforms at the time. 'Papi, never forget that whenever the business is dangerous you must always do things in style. Those initials were my visiting card for the enemies of my friend.'

Victor went and left the car in a parking-place, forgetting, of course, to leave the keys as well. The three bombs were not found until three months later.

No question of hanging around at Deloffre's. He went his way. I went mine. No contact with Armando. I went straight to the garage, where I helped carry away the lathe and the five or six bottles of gas that were lying about. Six o'clock: the telephone rang and a mysterious voice said, '*Francès*, get out all of you. Each in a different direction. Only B.L. must stay in the garage. You get it?'

'Who's that?'

He hung up.

Dressed as a woman and driven in a jeep by a former officer of the French Resistance I'd helped a good deal since his arrival, I made my way out of Caracas with no trouble at all and reached Rio-Chico, about a hundred and twenty-five miles away on the coast. I was going to stay there for a couple of months with this ex-captain and his wife and a couple of friends from Bordeaux.

B.L. was arrested. No torture: only a stiff, thorough-going but correct interrogation. When I heard that, it seemed to me the Gallegos and Bétancourt régime was not as wicked as they said; at least not in this case. Deloffre took refuge that same night in the Nicaraguan embassy.

As for me, I was still full of confidence in life, and a week later the ex-captain and I were driving the Rio-Chico Public Works Department's truck. Through a friend we'd got ourselves taken on by the municipality. We made twenty-one bolivars a day between us, and on that we lived, all five of us.

This road-making life lasted two months, long enough for the storm raised by our plot to die down in Caracas and for the police to turn their minds to the reports about a new one that was cooking. Very wisely they concentrated on the present and left the past to itself. I asked nothing better, because I had thoroughly made up my mind not to let myself be dragged into another job of that kind. For the moment, by far the best thing to do was to live here quietly with my friends, drawing no attention to myself.

In the late afternoon I often went fishing, to add to our daily rations. That evening I had hauled out a huge *robalo*, a kind of big sea-bream, and I was sitting on the beach, scaling it in no particular hurry and admiring the wonderful sunset. A red sky means hope, Papi! And in spite of all the flops I had had since I was let out, I began to laugh. Yes, hope must make me live and win: and it was going to do just that. But exactly when was success going to come along? Let's have a look at things, Papi: let's tot up the results of two years of freedom.

I was not broke, but I didn't have much: three thousand bolivars at the outside, the sum total of two years on the loose.

What had happened during this time?

One: the heap of gold of El Callao. No point in brooding over that: it was not a flop but something you voluntarily gave up so the ex-lags there could go on living in peace. You regret it? No. OK, then forget the ton of gold.

Two: craps at the diamond-mines. You nearly got yourself killed twenty times over for the sake of ten thousand dollars you never cashed in on. Jojo died in your place: you came out alive. Without a brass farthing, true enough; but what a terrific adventure! You'll never forget all those nights, keyed-up to the breaking-point, the gamblers' faces under the carbide lamp, the unmoved Jojo. Nothing to regret there either.

Three: the tunnel under the bank. Not the same thing at all: there really was no luck about that job. Still, for three months you lived at full blast twenty-four hours out of the twenty-four, just on what each hour brought in the way of emotion. Even if you got no more out of it than that, you don't have to be sorry for yourself. Do you realize that for three months on end, even in your dreams, you felt you were a dollar-millionaire with never a doubt about getting your hands on the dough? Doesn't that mean anything? Of course, just a trifle more luck might have given you a fortune; but on the other hand you might have been much more unlucky. Suppose the tunnel had caved in while you were at the far end? You'd have died like a rat or they would have caught you like a fox in its earth.

Four: what about the pawnshop and its fridges? No complaints—except for the Public Road Works of that bleeding country.

Five: the plot. Frankly, you were never really wholehearted about that business. These political jobs and those bombs that might kill anybody—it's not your line. What it really comes to is that you were taken in first by the patter of two very nice guys and then by the promise of being able to carry out your plan. But your heart wasn't in it, because you never felt it was quite regular to attack the government that had let you out.

Still, on the credit side you had four months of fun with the musketeers, their wives and the kid; and you aren't likely to forget those days full of the joy of life.

Conclusion: I'd been unjustly imprisoned for thirteen years and almost all my youth had been stolen from me; and although I sleep, eat, drink and have fun, I never forget that one day I must have my revenge.

So, to put it in a nutshell, you've been free these last two years, and in these two years you've had countless experiences and terrific adventures. Better still, you've never even had to look for them: they came all by themselves. You've had wonderful love; you've known men of every kind who've given you their friendship—men you've risked your life with; and with all this, do you still keep moaning? You're broke, or nearly broke? What does that matter? Poverty's not a difficult disease to cure.

So glory be to God, Papi! Glory to adventure, glory to the risks that make you so vividly alive every day and every minute! You gulp it down like some marvellous drink that goes right to the bottom of your heart. And you're fit, which is the really important thing.

Let's wipe it all out and begin again, gentlemen. The chips are down! Make your last bets—this is it! Banco lost, banco again: banco again and again and again. Banco right along the line. But let your whole being thrill and quiver, singing a song of hope that one day you'll hear 'Nine on the nose! Rake it in, Monsieur Papillon! You've won!'

The sun was almost touching the horizon. Red in the evening, that meant hope. And sure enough I was crammed with hope and trust in the future. The breeze had freshened, and with a calmer mind I stood up, happy to be free and alive; my feet sank in the wet sand as I went back towards the house, where they were waiting for what I had caught for the evening meal. But all these colours, these countless touches of light and shade playing on the crests of the little waves stretching out for ever and ever stirred me so deeply, what with my remembering past dangers overcome, I couldn't help thinking of the creator of it all, of God. 'Good night, big guy, good night! In spite of all these flops, I still thank You for having given me such a beautiful day full of sun and freedom and, to finish it off, this marvellous sunset!'

ONE day, when I was making a quick trip to Caracas, a friend introduced me to a former Paris mannequin who was looking for someone to help her in a new hotel she had just opened at Maracaibo. I very willingly accepted the job of being her general-purposes man. She was called Laurence; I think she had come to Caracas to show a collection; and decided to settle in Venezuela. Six hundred miles lay between Caracas and Maracaibo, and that suited me fine; you never knew whether the police might re-open their inquiries into our *coup d'état*.

A friend gave me a lift, and after fourteen hours' driving I had my first sight of the lake of Maracaibo: they call it a lake, although in fact it is a huge lagoon nearly a hundred miles long and sixty wide at the broadest point, and it is joined to the sea by a channel about eight miles across. Maracaibo lies to the north, on the west bank of the channel, which is now linked to the east bank by a bridge; but in those days, if you came from Caracas, you had to cross on a ferry.

This lake was really extraordinary, dotted with thousands of derricks. It looked like a huge forest stretching away out of sight, a forest whose trees, all exactly lined up, allowed you to see as far as the horizon. But these trees were oil-wells, and each oil-well had an enormous pendulum that went to and fro all day and all night, never stopping, perpetually pumping up the black gold from the bowels of the earth.

A ferry-boat ran non-stop between the end of the Caracas road and Maracaibo, carrying cars, passengers and goods. During the crossing I hurried from one side to the other, absolutely fascinated by the sight of these iron pylons rising from the lake; and as I stared at them I thought that twelve hundred miles from here, down at the far end of the country in Venezuelan Guiana, the Good Lord had stuffed the ground with diamonds, gold, iron, nickel, manganese, bauxite, uranium and all the rest, while here He had filled it with oil, the motor of the world—with such enormous quantities of oil that these thousands of pumps could suck away day and night without ever sucking it dry. Venezuela, you've got no call to blame the Lord!

The Hotel Normandy was a splendid great villa surrounded by a carefully-kept garden full of flowers. The lovely Laurence welcomed me with open arms. 'This is my kingdom, Henri,' she said, laughing.

She had opened the hotel just two months before. Only sixteen rooms, but all luxurious, in the best taste, and each with a bathroom fit for the Ritz. She had designed all the décor herself, from the bedrooms to the staff lavatories, taking in the drawing-room, terrace and dining-room on her way.

I set to work: and it was no laughing matter being Laurence's right-hand man—she was under forty and she got up at six to see to her guests' breakfast or even make it herself. She was tireless, and all day long she hurried about, seeing to this and that, supervising everything, and yet still finding time to look after a rose-bush or weed a garden path. She had grasped life with both hands; she had overcome almost impossible difficulties to set this business going; and she had so much faith in its success that I was seized with a will to work almost as consuming as her own. I did everything I could to help her cope with the hundreds of difficulties that kept cropping up. Money difficulties, above all. She was in debt up to the neck, because to turn this villa into something like a luxury hotel she had borrowed every penny.

Yesterday, by a private deal I carried out without consulting her, I got something marvellous out of an oil company.

'Good evening, Laurence.'

'Good evening. It's late, Henri: eight o'clock already. I'm not blaming you, now; but I haven't seen you this whole afternoon.'

'I've been for a stroll.'

'Is this a joke?'

'Yes, I'm laughing at life. It's always good for a laugh, don't you think?'

'Not always. And at this time I should have liked your support: I'm in a bad jam.'

'Very bad?'

'Yes. I've got to pay for all these fittings and alterations, and although the place is running well, it's not easy. I owe a great deal.'

'Here comes the big surprise, Laurence: hold on. You don't owe anything any more.'

'Are you making fun of me?'

'No. Listen: you've brought me in as a kind of partner, and in fact I've noticed a good many people think I'm the boss.'

'What of it?'

'Well, one of the people who thought that way is a Canadian belonging to the Lumus Company, and a few days back he talked to me about a deal he thought we might make. I went to see him this afternoon: I've just come back.'

'Tell me quickly!' cried Laurence, her eyes wide with interest.

'The result is the Lumus Company takes your hotel, the whole of it, with full board, *for a year*!'

'It's not possible!'

'It is, I promise you.' In her emotion, Laurence kissed me on both cheeks and collapsed into a chair. 'Of course there was no question of *me* signing this terrific contract, so tomorrow they'll call you to their office.'

This contract meant that Laurence made a right little fortune out of the Hotel Normandy. The first quarter's advance alone let her pay off all her debts.

After the signing of the contract, Laurence and I drank champagne with the Lumus bosses. I was happy, very happy, as I lay there in my big bed that night. With the help of the champagne I saw life a fine rosy pink. Papi, you're no more of a fool than Laurence: so isn't it possible to get rich *by working*? And starting from almost nothing? Well, Christ above, this was a real discovery I'd made here at the Hotel Normandy. Yes, a real discovery, because in France, for the few years I'd been able to take a quick glance at life, it had always seemed to me that a working-man stayed a working-man all his life. And this completely wrong idea was even more wrong here in Venezuela, where the man who really wants to do something has every opportunity and every facility open to him.

This realization was very important for the carrying out of

my plan. It was not from love of money that I had gone for crooked jobs: I was not a thief out of a deep liking for theft. It was just that I'd never been able to believe it was possible to really get to the top in life starting from scratch—nor, as far as I was concerned, to get hold of a lump of money big enough for me to go and present my bill in Paris. But it *was* possible, and only one thing was necessary to start—a little bit of capital, a few thousand bolivars; and it would be easy to save that once I'd found a good job.

So there you are, Papi: no more crooked stuff, great or small. Let's go for plain, honest methods. Laurence succeeded that way: well then, so shall I! And if you can only bring this off, how happy your father will be!

The only snag was that if I went this way about it, I should need a good deal of time before being able to take my revenge: I could not scrape the necessary cash together in a day. 'Revenge is a dish you want to eat cold,' Miguel had said at the diamond diggings. I was certainly going to find out about that.

Maracaibo was on the boil. There was excitement in the air, and so many businesses, buildings of every kind and oil-refineries, were springing up that everthing, from beer to cement, was sold on the black market. Everything was snapped up right away—there was never enough to meet the demand. Labour was making money, jobs were well paid and every kind of business was doing well.

When there is an oil boom, a district's economy goes through two completely different phases. First comes the period before the wells begin to yield, the period of pre-exploitation. The companies turn up and settle in: they need offices, camps, roads, high-tension lines; they have to drill the wells, put up the derricks and pumps, etc. This is the golden age, golden for all the skilled workers and golden for every level of the community.

The people, the genuine horny-handed people, have bank-notes in their pockets; they begin to discover the meaning of money and of security. Families start to get themselves organized, homes grow bigger or better and the children go to school in good clothes, often taken by companies' buses.

Then comes the second phase, the one that corresponds to my first view of the Maracaibo lake, with all I could see of it turned into a forest of derricks. This is the period of exploitation. Thousands of pumps, working away there by themselves, tirelessly sucking out millions of tons of black gold every day.

But this unbelievable great mass of dough does not pass through the people's hands: it goes straight into the coffers of the state banks or the companies. Things begin to grow sticky, staff is cut down to the strict minimum, there's no more money just floating around, all the active business is over. The coming generations will only know about it when they hear their grandfathers say, 'Once upon a time, when Maracaibo was a millionaire, there was a ...'

But I was lucky. I came in for Maracaibo's second boom. It had nothing to do with the pumps on the lake, but several oil companies had just got new concessions running from the Perija mountains down to the lake and the sea, and they were wild with excitement. The moment might have been made for me.

I was going to dig in here. And I swore the hole I made would be a sizeable cavern. To succeed I'd work at anything I could lay my hands on to gather in every possible crumb of this gigantic cake. That's a sacred oath, Papi! My turn now to get to the top, taking the straight path. The straights are right after all; they manage to grow rich without ever going to gaol.

Good French cook, 39, seeks position with oil company. Minimum salary $800.

I'd learned the rudiments of cookery with Laurence and her chef, and I decided to try my luck. The advertisement came out in the local paper and a week later there I was as cook to the Richmond Exploration Co. I was sorry to leave Laurence, but she could not possibly pay me wages like that, not by a long chalk.

Now, having been through that school, I know a good deal about cooking; but when I first started my job I quaked in fear that the other guys in the kitchen would soon see the French cook knew precious little about saucepans. But to my

153

surprise I soon grasped the fact that they too were all of a tremble in case the French cook should find out that they were only dish-washers, every last one of them! I breathed again; and all the deeper because I had a great advantage over them— *I owned a cookery-book, in French.* L'Escoffier, a present from a retired whore.

The personnel manager was a Canadian, M. Blanchet. Two days later he put me in charge of the cooking for the camp executives, a dozen of them—the big chiefs!

The first morning I showed him a menu like something out of the Ritz. But I pointed out that before I could prepare the food the kitchen would have to be better stocked. It was decided that I should have a separate budget, and that I should run it myself. I don't have to tell you I greased my own palm pretty handsomely when I did my buying; but still, the executives stuffed themselves heartily, no doubt about that. This way, everybody was happy.

Every evening I stuck up tomorrow's menu in the hall: written in French, of course. These grand-sounding names out of the cookery-book made a terrific impression. What's more, in the town I'd discovered a shop that specialized in French things, so what with Potel et Rodel's tins and my recipes I managed so well that the executive guys often brought their women-folk. Twenty would turn up instead of twelve. From one point of view it was a bloody nuisance, but from another, they took less notice of what I spent; because by the rules I was supposed to feed only the people on the list.

I saw they were so pleased that I asked for a rise—1,200 dollars a month, an increase of four hundred. They said no, but they gave me a thousand; and although I kept telling them it was wretched pay for a big-time chef like me, I let myself be persuaded.

Some months went by like this, but in time these set hours of work began to irk me like a shirt-collar that's too tight. I'd had about enough of this job and I asked the chief of the geologists to take me with him when he went out on a prospecting expedition into the most interesting regions, even if they were dangerous.

The point of these expeditions was to make a geological survey of the Sierra Perija, the mountain chain to the west of

154

the lake of Maracaibo that divides Venezuela from Colombia. It is the country of a very fierce, warlike tribe of Indians, the Motilones: so much so that the Sierra Perija is often called the Sierra de los Motilones. Even now nobody knows just where this tribe came from: their language and their customs are quite unlike those of the neighbouring tribes, and they are so dangerous that even now, 'civilization' is only just beginning to make its way among them. They live in communal huts that house from fifty to a hundred people, men, women and children all mixed up together. Their only domestic animal is the dog. They are so wild that you hear of many cases where Motilones, captured by 'civilized' people, sometimes having been wounded, absolutely refuse to eat or drink; and although they may be well treated, they end up by killing themselves, biting the veins in their wrists with their front teeth, which are specially filed for tearing meat. Since the days I am talking about, the Franciscans have bravely settled on the banks of the Rio Santa Rosa, only a few miles from the nearest communal house. The Father Superior uses the most modern methods, dropping food, clothing, blankets and photographs of Franciscans over the huts from a plane. Even better, he parachutes straw figures dressed in Franciscan robes, the pockets filled with different kinds of food and even tins of milk. No fool, the good Father: the day he turns up on foot, they'll believe he's dropped from heaven.

But when I asked to take part in these expeditions it was back in 1948, a long time before those attempts at 'civilized' penetration.

As far as I was concerned, these expeditions had three positive advantages. In the first place, they meant a completely different life from the one I was leading in the kitchen of the Richmond Company's camp: and I had seen just about all I ever wanted to see of that. It would be an adventure starting again, but adventure on the level this time. There was real danger, of course, as there is in any adventure: quite often an expedition would come back short of one or two of its members, because the Motilones were highly skilled at archery: where a Motilone sets his eye, there he sets his arrow, as they say in those parts. But if you were killed, at least you were not eaten, because they were not cannibals. There was always that to be thankful for.

Second advantage: these three-week tours in the deep, unexplored, dangerous bush were very well paid. I'd make more than twice what I earned at my kitchen stove.

Third: I liked being with the geologists. They knew a great deal. Although I was well aware it was too late for me to learn enough to make me a different man, I had the feeling that I would not be wasting my time, going about with these scientists.

So, as a member of their expedition, I set off full of confidence and enthusiasm. No need for any cookery-books; I just had to know how to open tins and make bread and pancakes.

My new friend, the geologist in charge of the expedition, was called Crichet. He had been lent to the Richmond by the California Exploration Co. He knew absolutely everything about the oil side of geology, but he wasn't quite sure whether Alexander the Great came before Napoleon or after. In any case, he didn't give a damn in hell, one way or the other; he didn't need to know history to be very fit, to have a splendid wife, to give her babies and to provide his company with the geological information they needed. Still, I dare say he did know more than he let on—in time I learned to watch out for his sort of half-English humour, quite unlike what we were used to in my native Ardèche. We got along very well.

An expedition of this kind lasted between twenty and twenty-five days, with a week's leave when you got back. It was made up of a geologist in charge, two other geologists, and from twelve to eighteen porters and helpers—strength and discipline was all that was asked of them. They had their own tents and their own cook. I only looked after the three geologists. The men were not fools in any way, and among them there was a militant member of the left-wing *Acción Democrática* who saw the union laws were obeyed. His name was Carlos. There was a good over-all understanding, and I was the one who kept count of the overtime, which they always put down with absolute precision.

This first expedition fascinated me. Getting hold of geological intelligence about oil-fields is a very interesting business: the idea is to follow the rivers up into the mountains as far as possible, keeping to the passage they have cut through the rock. You go as far as you can in trucks, and then you take to jeeps. When there is no path any more, you paddle up the river in canoes; and when the river is too shallow you get out and shove, still going up as far as you can towards the source. The equipment is carried by the porters, about a hundred pounds a man; but the three geologists and the cooks don't carry anything.

Why go so far into the mountains? Because you see all the successive geological formations, just like in a school-book, along the course the river has dug out. You cut samples from the banks, sort them, label them, and pack them away in little bags. The geologists note the direction of the different layers sloping towards the plain. And so with these hundreds of geological samples taken from different places they draw up a map of the strata that should be found in the plain at a depth of say between three thousand and six thousand feet. And by working it out very carefully from all this information, one day they hit oil perhaps fifty miles away in some place where nobody has ever been, because they know in advance that the oil will be there at a given depth. Talk about the wonders of science—I was filled with admiration.

All this would have been fine if it hadn't been for the Motilones. Often members of the expeditions were killed or wounded by their arrows. This did not make recruiting any easier, and it cost the companies a great deal of money.

I went on several expeditions, and I had some marvellous experiences. One of the geologists was a Dutchman named Lapp. One day he was gathering alligators' eggs—they are very good, once they are dried in the sun. You can easily find them by following the track the alligator leaves as it crawls on its belly from the river to the dry place where it lays its eggs: it broods them for hours and hours. Taking advantage of the alligator's absence, Lapp dug up the eggs and calmly carried them back to the camp. He had scarcely reached our clearing before the alligator appeared, tearing along like a racing-car and coming straight for him. It had followed the robber's trail and was going to punish him. About ten feet long, it gasped hoarsely as it came, as if it had laryngitis. Lapp started to run, darting round and round a big tree; and I howled with laughter at the sight of this big guy in shorts bounding about and bawling for help. Crichet and his men came running: two explosive bullets stopped the alligator dead. As for Lapp, he fell on his arse, as pale as death. Everybody was shocked by my behaviour. I told them there was nothing I could have done in any case, because I never carried a rifle—it got in the way.

That evening, while we ate my tinned dinner in the tent, Crichet said to me, in his sort of French, 'You not so young; at least thirty-four, eh?'

'Rather more. Why?'

'You living, you behaving like man of twenty.'

'Well, you know, I'm not much more. I'm twenty-six.'

'Not true.'

'Yes it is, and I'll tell you why. For thirteen years I was stuffed into a cupboard. So as I did not live those thirteen years then, I have to live them now. And since thirteen from thirty-nine makes twenty-six, I'm twenty-six years old.'

'Don't follow.'

'It doesn't matter.'

Yet it was true enough: my heart was that of a boy of twenty. I had to live it—those thirteen years that had been stolen from me; I needed them and I had to get them back. I had to burn them up, not giving a damn for anything at all, the way you do when you are twenty and your heart is filled with a crazy love for life.

One day, just before dawn, a scream jerked us all awake. As he was hanging up the hurricane-lamp he had lit before making the coffee, the men's cook had been struck by two arrows—one in his side, the other in his buttock. He had to be taken straight back to Maracaibo. Four men carried him as far as the canoe on a kind of litter; the canoe took him down to the jeep, the jeep to the truck and the truck to Maracaibo.

The day went by in a heavy, brooding atmosphere. We could sense the Indians all around us in the bush, though we never heard or saw them. The farther we went, the more we had the feeling we were right in their hunting-grounds. There was a fair amount of game, and as all the men had a rifle, every now and then they shot a bird or a kind of hare. Everyone was serious, nobody sang; and when they had fired a shot they stupidly talked very low, as though they were afraid someone might hear them.

Gradually a general fear came over the men. They wanted to cut the expedition short and go back to Maracaibo. Our leader, Crichet, kept on up the river. The union man, Carlos, was a brave guy, but he too felt uneasy. He took me aside.

'Enrique, what do you say to turning back?'

'What for, Carlos?'

'The Indians.'

'True enough, there are Indians: but they might just as easily attack us on the way back as if we go on.'

'I'm not so sure about that, Enrique. Maybe we're close to their village. Look at that stone there: they've been crushing grain.'

'There's something in what you say, Carlos. Let's see Crichet.'

The American had been through the Normandy landings; it took a lot to shake him, and he was completely in love with his job. When all the men were gathered together, he said we were in one of the richest districts for geological information. He lost his temper, and in his anger he said the one thing he never should have said—'If you're afraid, all right, go back. I'm staying.'

They all went off, except for Carlos, Lapp and me. But I stayed only on the condition that when we left we'd bury the equipment, because I did not want to carry anything heavy. Ever since I had broken both my feet in one of my unsuccessful breaks from Baranquilla, walking with a load made me tire very quickly. Carlos would see to the samples.

Crichet, Lapp, Carlos and I went on for five days without anyone else at all. Nothing happened, but I've never had a more thrilling and stirring time than those five days when we knew we were being watched twenty-four hours out of the twenty-four by God knows how many pairs of unseen eyes. We gave up when Crichet, who had gone down to the edge of the river to relieve himself, saw the reeds move and then two hands gently parting them. That wrecked his urge; but with his usual calmness he turned his back on the reeds as though nothing had occurred and came back to the camp.

He said to Lapp, 'I believe the moment has come for us to return to Maracaibo. We've got enough samples of rocks, and

I'm not sure it's scientifically necessary to leave the Indians four interesting samples of the white race.'

We reached La Burra, a hamlet of some fifteen houses, without trouble. We were having a drink, waiting for the truck to come and fetch us, when a drunken half-caste Indian of those parts took me aside and said, 'You're French, aren't you? Well, it's not worth being French if you're as ignorant as all that.'

'Ah? How come?'

'I'll tell you. You make your way into the Motilones' country, and what do you do? You blaze away right and left at everything that flies or runs or swims. All the men carry guns. It's not a scientific exploration: it's an enormous great hunting-party.'

'What are you getting at?'

'If you carry on that way, you'll destroy what the Indians look upon as their food reserve. They haven't got much. They just kill what they need for a day or two. Not more. Then again, their arrows kill with no noise—they don't make the other animals run away. Whereas you kill everything and you frighten away all the game with your shooting.'

It was not so foolish, what this guy said. I was interested. 'What'll you drink? It's on me.'

'A double rum, Frenchman. Thanks.' And he went on, 'It's because of this that the Motilones shoot their arrows at you. They say that because of you it's going to be hard for them to eat.'

'So we are robbing their larder?'

'You're dead right, Frenchman. Then again, when you go up a stream, have you never noticed that where it's narrow or where there's so little water you have to get out of the canoe and shove—have you never noticed that when you do so you destroy a kind of dam made of branches and bamboos?'

'Yes I have. Often.'

'Well, the things you destroy like that, never thinking twice, are fish-traps built by the Motilones; so there again you do them harm. Because there's a great deal of work in these traps. They are a kind of maze, and the fish that are running up the stream pass through zig-zag after zig-zag until they reach a big trap at the end, and then they can't escape. There's a wall of bamboos in front, and they can't find the entrance again, because it's made of little creepers that the fish pushed aside to get in. The current pushes them back against the gate once the fish has passed. I've seen traps more than fifty yards long from one end to the other. Beautiful work.'

'You're right, absolutely right. You have to be vandals like us to smash work of that kind.'

As we travelled back I thought about what the rum-soaked half-breed had told me, and I made up my mind to try something. As soon as we reached Maracaibo, even before I went home for my week's leave, I left a letter for M. Blanchet, the personnel manager, asking him to see me next day.

He called me in, and there with him I saw the top geologist. I told them there would be no more killed or wounded in the expeditions if they would leave the management to me. Crichet would still be the official boss, of course, but I would be the one who saw to the discipline. They decided to have a try; Crichet had put in a report saying that if they could get higher up than the last expedition, that is to say into an even more dangerous region, they would find a real treasure-house of information. As to the pay for my new job, which would be in addition to being cook (I was still to be the geologists' chef), that would be settled when I came back. Of course I said nothing about the reasons why I could guarantee the expedition's safety, and since the Yankees are practical people they asked me no questions either—it was the result that mattered.

Crichet was the only one who knew about the arrangement. It suited him, so he fell in with the scheme and relied on me. He was sure I had found some certain way of avoiding trouble: and then the fact that I had been one of the three who stayed when all the others left had made a good impression.

I went to see the governor of the province and explained my business. He was friendly and understanding, and thanks to his letter of recommendation, I got the National Guard to give orders that the last post before the Motilones' territory should take all the weapons carried by the men on my list before letting the expedition through. They would think up some likely, comforting excuse. Because if the men knew back in Maracaibo that they were going into Motilone country un-armed, they wouldn't even start. I'd have to catch them short and con them on the spot.

It all passed off perfectly. At La Burra, the last post, their weapons were taken away from all the men except two, and I told those two never to fire except in immediate danger— never for hunting or for fun. I had a revolver, and that was all.

From that day on, there was no trouble whatsoever in any of our expeditions. The Americans got the message, and being for efficiency above all, they never asked me the reason why.

I got on well with the men and they obeyed me. My job fascinated me. Now, instead of smashing the fish-traps with our canoes, we worked round them, destroying nothing. Another thing: since I knew the Motilones' chief problem was hunger, every time we struck camp I left old tins filled with salt or sugar; and according to what we could spare, we'd also leave a machête or a knife or a little axe. When we came back through these camping-places we never found a thing. Everything had vanished, even the old cans themselves. So my tactics worked, and since nobody in Maracaibo knew what it was all about, there was a rumour that I was a *brujo*, a wizard, or that I had a secret understanding with the Motilones.

It was during one of these expeditions that I had an extraordinary lesson in how to fish—in how to catch a fish without bait, hook or line, just quietly picking it up on the surface. My teacher was a *danta*, a tapir, an animal bigger than a large pig. Sometimes they'll be more than six feet long. It was one afternoon, when I was near the stream, that I saw one for the first time. It came out of the water, and I watched, keeping perfectly still so as not to frighten it. Its skin was rather like that of a rhinoceros; its front legs were shorter than its back ones; and over its mouth it had a short but distinct trunk. It went over to a creeper and ate a good deal of it: so it was a herbivore. Then I saw it go down to the stream again, walk in and go towards a stretch of slack water. There it stopped, and began to sort of belch, like a cow: so it was a ruminant. Then it brought up a green liquid through its trunk. Very cleverly it mixed this stuff with the water, stirring with its big head. I was still wondering about the reason for all this when a few minutes later, to my astonishment I saw fish come to the surface, belly uppermost, moving slowly as though they had been drugged or put to sleep. And then there was my *danta* taking the fish one by one, not hurrying at all; and calmly he ate them up. I was absolutely amazed.

After that, I had a try. I carefully marked down the creeper I had seen the *danta* eating, gathered an armful and crushed it between two stones, collecting the juice in a calabash. Then I poured it into a part of the river where there was no current. Victory! A few minutes later I saw the fish come to the top, knocked out. Just as they had done for the *danta*. There's only one precaution you have to take: if they are edible fish, you must gut them right away, otherwise they go bad in two hours. After this experiment, the geologists' table often had splendid fish dishes. There was one order I gave the men—never, in any circumstances, kill such a charming fisherman. Particularly as tapirs are perfectly harmless.

Sometimes, in these expeditions, I took a family of alligator-hunters along as guides, the Fuenmayors, a father and his two sons. This suited everybody, because the Fuenmayors knew the region very well; but if they were alone they would be an easy prey for the Motilones. Going along with the expedition, they guided us by day in exchange for their keep, and at night they hunted alligators.

They were people from Maracaibo, Maracuchos, very sociable souls. They spoke in a musical way; and they had a very high notion of friendship. There was a great deal of Indian blood in their veins and they had all the Indian qualities; very knowing and intelligent.

I had some wonderful, indestructible friendships with the Maracuchos, and I have them still. Both with the men and the women, because the women are beautiful and they know how to love and how to make themselves loved.

Hunting alligators, creatures seven to ten feet long, is a very dangerous business. One night I went along with Fuenmayor and his eldest son. The father sat at the back of this very narrow, very light canoe, steering, me in the middle and his son in front. It was pitch dark; all you could hear were the noises of the bush, and very faintly the lapping of the water against the canoe. We didn't smoke; we didn't make the slightest sound. The paddle that moved the canoe and at the same time steered it was never allowed to scrape against the side.

Every now and then we sent the beam of a huge electric torch sweeping the surface, and pairs of red dots appeared. Two red points: one alligator. In front of these eyes there would be the nostrils, because the eyes and the nose are the only two parts of an alligator that show when it is resting on the surface. The victim was chosen according to the shortest distance between the hunters and the red dots. Once it was selected we felt our way towards it with the light out. Old Fuenmayor was wonderfully skilful at fixing the alligator's exact position, just by one flash of the torch lasting no more than a second. We paddled quickly towards it, aimed the beam, and almost always the brute just lay there, dazzled. The beam stayed on the alligator until we were two or three yards away. In the front of the canoe young Fuenmayor kept his torch aimed with his left hand and with all the strength of his right arm he threw a harpoon weighted with twenty pounds of lead —the only thing that could pierce a hide as tough as that and go through to the flesh.

Now we had to get moving, because the second the alligator was harpooned it dived: we took our three paddles and rapidly made for the shore. You really have to jump to it, because if you give the alligator time it comes to the surface again, rushes for you and with one sweep of its tail capsizes the canoe, turning the hunters into a quarry for the other alligators, who've been warned by the turmoil. You have scarcely reached the bank before you jump out, rush for a tree and take a turn round it with the rope. He comes along, you feel him coming along to see what's holding him. He can't tell what's happening to him, apart from the pain in his back. So he comes to find out. Gently, without pulling, you take in the slack and pass it round the tree. He's going to come out—he's almost at the edge. Just as he emerges, young Fuenmayor, holding a thin, razor-sharp American axe, gives his head a tremendous crack. Sometimes it needs three to finish the alligator off. At each blow it gives a sweep with its tail that would send the axeman to heaven if it touched him. It may happen that the axe does not kill the alligator, and in that case you have to give slack right away so the brute can go off into deep water. Because it is so strong it would wrench out even a deeply planted harpoon: you wait a minute and then start heaving again.

That was a wonderful night: we killed several alligators, leaving them on the bank. At daybreak, the Fuenmayors returned and took the skin of the belly and the underside of the tail. The skin of the back is too hard to be of any use. Then they buried each huge creature—if they were thrown back they would poison the river. Alligators don't eat other alligators, not even dead ones.

I made several of these expeditions, making a good living and managing to save a fair amount: and then there occurred the most extraordinary event in my life.

WHEN I was in the solitary confinement cells at Saint-Joseph I used to take off for the stars and invent wonderful castles in Spain so as to people the loneliness and the terrible silence: often I would imagine myself free, a man who had conquered 'the road down the drain' and who had begun a new life in some big city. Yes, it was a genuine resurrection: I pushed back the tombstone that crushed me down in the darkness and I came back into the daylight, into real life; and among the pictures my mind thought up, there would appear a girl as good as she was beautiful. Neither tall nor short; blonde; hazel eyes with jet-black pupils sparkling with life and intelligence. She had a wonderfully drawn mouth, and her laugh showed brilliantly white and pearly teeth. A lovely, perfectly proportioned figure: and this woman, just as I saw her then, was one day to be mine for life.

I invented a heart for this goddess—the finest, the noblest, the most sincere of hearts, the richest in all the qualities that make a woman both one you love and one who is your friend. Without doubt, some day I should meet her, and then, joined to her for ever, I should be loved, wealthy, respected and happy for life.

Yes: there in the stifling damp heat that deprived the unhappy prisoners of the Réclusion of the least waft of living air, when, half smothered, I breathed in that unbearable steam that hurt my lungs—gasping in the hope of finding some hint of freshness—and when in spite of my weakness, my unquenchable thirst and the anxiety that wrung my heart, I took off for the stars where the air was cool and the trees had fresh green leaves, and where the cares of everyday life did not exist because I had grown rich, there, in every vision, appeared the one I called my *belle princesse*. She was always the same, down to the very last detail. Nothing ever varied, and I knew her so well that every time she stepped into these different scenes it seemed to me quite natural—wasn't it she who was to be my wife and my good angel?

Coming back from one of these geological trips, I decided to quit my room in the Richmond Company's camp and live right in Maracaibo. So one day a company truck set me down in a shady little square somewhere in the city centre, with a small suitcase in my hand. I knew there were several hotels or *pensions* thereabouts and I took the Calle Venezuela, a street in a very good position, running between the two main squares of Maracaibo, the Bolivar and the Baralt. It was one of those narrow colonial streets lined with low houses—one storey or at the most two. The heat was shattering, and I walked in their shade.

Hotel Vera Cruz. A pretty colonial house dating from the conquest: painted a pale blue. I liked its clean, welcoming look and I walked into a cool passage that gave on to a patio. And there, in this airy, shaded courtyard I saw a woman; and this woman was *her*.

It was her: I could not be wrong—I had seen her thousands of times in my dreams when I was a wretched prisoner. There she was; there was my *belle princesse* before me, sitting in a rocking-chair. I was certain that if I went closer I should see her hazel-coloured eyes and even the minute beauty-spot on her lovely oval face. And these surroundings— I had seen them too, thousands of times. So it was impossible that I should be wrong: the princess of my dreams was there before me; she was waiting for me.

'*Buenas dias, Señora.* Have you a room to let?' I put my bag down. I was certain she was going to say yes. I did not just look at her: I ate her up with my eyes. She stood up, rather surprised at being stared at so hard by someone she did not know, and came towards me.

'Yes, Monsieur, I have a room for you,' said my princess, in French.

'How did you know I was French?'

'From your way of speaking Spanish. Come with me, please.'

I picked up my bag and, following her, I walked into a clean, cool, well-furnished room giving straight on to the patio.

I cooled myself down with a shower, washed, shaved and smoked a cigarette; and it was only after that, as I sat on the edge of the bed in this hotel room, that I really came to believe

I was not dreaming. 'She's here, man, here, just a few yards away! But don't go and lose your head. Don't let this stab in the heart make you do or say anything bloody foolish.' My heart was beating violently and I tried to calm myself. 'Above all, Papillon, don't tell anyone this crazy story, not even her. Who could possibly believe you? Unless you want to get yourself laughed at, how can you possibly tell anyone that you knew this woman, touched her, kissed her, had her, years ago, when you were rotting in the cells of an abominable prison? Keep your trap shut tight. The princess is here: that's what matters. Don't worry: now you've found her, she won't escape you. But you must go about it gently, step by step. Just from looking at her, you can see she must be the boss of this little hotel.'

It was in the patio, a garden in miniature, that one splendid tropical night I said my first words of love. She was so completely the angel I had dreamt of so often that it was as though she had been waiting for me for years. Rita, my princess was called: she came from Tangier, and she had no ties at all to hamper me. Her brilliant eyes gazed at me, shining like the stars in the sky over our heads. I was frank: I told her I had been married in France, that I did not know just how things were at present, and that there were serious reasons why I could not find out. And that was true: I could not write to the *mairie* of my village for a statement of my position—there was no telling how the law might react to a request like that: maybe by a demand for extradition. But I said nothing about my past as a crook and a convict. I devoted all my strength and all the resources of my mind into persuading her. I felt this was the greatest chance in my life, and I could not let it go by.

'You are beautiful, Rita, wonderfully beautiful. Let yourself be loved, deeply loved for ever, by a man who has nobody in his life either, but who needs to love and be loved. I haven't much money, it's true, and with your little hotel you are almost rich; but believe me, I want our two hearts to be just one, for ever, until death. Say yes, Rita. Rita as beautiful as the loveliest flowers of this country, as lovely as the orchids. I can't tell you when or how, but although it may seem impossible to you, I've known you and loved you for years and years.

You must be mine, just as I swear I'll be yours, wholly and for ever.' But Rita was not an easy girl; and that did not surprise me. It was only after three days that she agreed to be mine. She was very shy, and she asked me to hide when I came to her room. Then one fine morning, without making any sort of announcement, we quite naturally made our love obvious and official; and quite naturally I stepped into the role of the hotel's boss.

Our happiness was whole and entire, and a new life opened before me, a family life. Now that I, the pariah, the fugitive from the French penal settlement, had succeeded in overcoming that 'road down the drain', *I had a home*, and a girl as lovely in her body as she was in her soul. There was only one little cloud in our happiness—the fact that having a wife in France, I could not marry her.

Loving, being loved, having a home of my own—God, how great You are to have given me all this!

Wanderers on the roads, wanderers on the seas, men on the loose who need adventure as ordinary people need water and bread, men who fly through life as migrating birds fly through the sky, wanderers of the cities who search the streets of the slums night and day, ransack the parks and hang around the wealthy districts, their angry hearts watching for a job to pull off, wandering anarchists, liberated prisoners, servicemen on leave, soldiers back from the front, fugitives hunted by an organization that wants to catch them and put them in a cell to wipe them out—all, all without exception suffer from not having had a home at one moment or another; and when Providence gives them one, they step into it as I stepped into mine, with a new heart, full of love to give and burning to receive it.

So I too, like ordinary people, like my father, like my mother, like my sisters, like all my family, I too had *my home* at last, with a girl who loved me inside it.

For this meeting with Rita to make me change my whole way of living, and for me to feel that this was the turning-point of my life, she had to be someone quite exceptional.

In the first place, like me she had reached Venezuela when she was making a break. Not a break from a penal settlement, of course, nor from prison, but still a break.

She had arrived from Tangier some six months before with her husband; he had left her about three months back to go and try some kind of adventure two hundred miles from Maracaibo—she didn't want to go with him. He left her with the hotel. She had a brother in Maracaibo, a commercial traveller who moved around a great deal.

She told me about her life, and I listened intently: my princess was born in a poor part of Tangier; her widowed mother bravely raised six children, three boys and three girls. Rita was the youngest. When she was a little girl, the street was her field of action. She did not spend her days in the two rooms where the seven members of the family had their being. Her real home was the town with its parks and its *souks*, among the dense crowds of people who filled them, eating, singing, drinking, talking in every conceivable language. She went barefoot. To the kids of her age and to the people of her quarter she was Riquita. She and her friends, a lively flock of sparrows, spent more time on the beach than at school; but she knew how to look after herself and keep her place in the long queue at the pump when she went to fetch a bucket of water for her mother. It was only when she was ten that she consented to put on a pair of shoes.

Everything interested her lively, inquisitive mind. She spent hours sitting in the circle round an Arab teller of tales. So much so that one story-teller, tired of seeing this child who never gave him anything always there in the front row, butted her with his head. Ever after, she sat in the second row.

She did not know much, but that did not stop her dreaming vividly about the great mysterious world where all those huge ships with strange names came from. To travel, to go far away —that was her great desire, her great ambition, and one that never left her. But little Riquita's idea of the world was rather special. North America was top America and South America bottom America: top America, that meant New York, which covered it completely. All the people there were rich and they were all film actors. In bottom America lived the Indians, who gave you flowers and who played the flute: there was no need to work there, because the blacks did everything that had to be done.

But apart from the *souks*, the camel-drivers, the mysterious veiled women and the swarming life of the port, what she liked most was the circus. She went twice—once by slipping under the edge of the tent, and once thanks to an old clown who was touched at the sight of the pretty barefoot kid; he let her in and gave her a good seat. She longed to go off with the circus; it drew her like a magnet. One day she would be the one who danced on the tightrope, making pirouettes and receiving all the applause. The circus was to leave for bottom America, and she yearned with all her heart to go with it—to go, go far off and come back rich, bringing money for her family.

Yet it was not the circus she went off with, but her family. Oh, not very far, but still it was a voyage. They went and settled at Casablanca. The port was bigger and the liners longer. Now she was sixteen. She was always dressed in pretty little dresses she made herself, because she worked in a shop, Aux Tissus de France, and the boss often gave her short lengths of cloth. Her dream of travelling could not fail to grow stronger, because the shop, in the rue de l'Horloge, was very close to the offices of the Latécoère airline. The pilots often dropped in. And what pilots! Mermoz, Saint-Exupéry, Mimile the writer, Delaunay, Didier. They were handsome, and what's more they were the greatest and the bravest travellers in the world. She knew them all and they all made passes at her; now and then she would accept a kiss, but that was all, because she was a good girl. But what voyages through the sky she made with them, listening to the stories of their adventures as she ate an ice in the next-door cake-shop! They liked her; they thought of her as their little protégée; they gave her small but highly valued presents; and they wrote her poems, some of which were published in the local paper.

When she was nineteen she married a man who exported fruit to Europe. They worked hard, they had a little daughter, and they were happy. They had two cars, they lived very comfortably, and Rita could easily help her mother and her relations.

Then in quick succession two ships loaded with oranges reached port with damaged cargoes. Two whole cargoes completely lost, that meant ruin. Her husband was deeply in debt, and if he set about working to pay his creditors, it would take him years and years. So he decided to slip off to South

America. It was not hard for him to persuade Rita to go with him, to make this wonderful voyage to a land of milk and honey where you could just shovel up the diamonds, gold and oil. They entrusted their little girl to Rita's mother, and Rita, full of adventurous dreams, waited impatiently to go aboard the big ship her husband had told her about.

The 'big ship' was a fishing-boat thirty-six feet long and sixteen wide. The captain, a somewhat piratical Estonian, had agreed to ship them to Venezuela without papers, along with a dozen other irregulars. Price: five hundred pounds. And it was in the crew's quarters of this old fishing-boat that Rita made the voyage, packed in with ten Spanish republicans escaping from Franco, one Portuguese escaping from Salazar, and two women, one a twenty-five-year-old German, the captain's mistress, and the other a fat Spanish woman, the wife of Antonio the cook.

A hundred and twelve days to reach Venezuela! With a long stop at the Cape Verde islands, because the boat leaked and during one spell of rough weather it very nearly sank.

While it was being repaired in a dry-dock, the passengers slept ashore. Rita's husband no longer trusted the boat. He said it was madness to launch out into the Atlantic in a rotten tub like that. Rita put courage into him: the captain was a Viking, she said, and the Vikings were the best seamen in the world; they could have total confidence in him.

Then an incredible piece of news. The Spaniards told Rita that the captain was a double-crosser, that he had made a deal with another group of passengers and that he was going to take advantage of their being ashore to set off for Dakar by night, leaving them there. Instant turmoil! They warned the authorities and went to the ship in a body. The captain was surrounded and threatened: the Spaniards had knives. Calm returned when the captain promised they should go to Venezuela. In view of what had happened, he agreed to remain under the constant supervision of one of the passengers. The next day they left Cape Verde and faced the Atlantic.

Twenty-five days later they came in sight of the Testigos islands, the most outlying point of Venezuela. They forgot everything, the storms, the sharks' fins, the backs of the playful dolphins rushing at the boat, the weevils in the flour and the business at Cape Verde. Rita was so happy she forgot the captain had meant to betray them and she hugged him, kissing him on both cheeks. And once again they heard the song the Spaniards had made up during the crossing; because wherever there are Spaniards there is always a guitar and a singer:

> A Venezuela nos vamos
> Aunque no hay carretera.
> A Venezuela nos vamos
> En un barquito de vela.

(We're going to Venezuela, although there is no road. We're going to Venezuela, in a little boat with a sail.)

On 16 April 1948, after a voyage of 4,900 miles, they reached La Guaira, the port of Caracas, fifteen miles from the city.

To call the health authorities aboard, the captain used a flag made out of a petticoat belonging to Zenda, the German girl; and when they saw the Venezuelan tender, all their sun-cooked faces beamed with joy. This was Venezuela: they had won!

Rita had held out splendidly, although she lost twenty pounds in weight. Never a complaint nor a sign of fear. Yet from time to time there had been plenty to worry about in that cockleshell right out in the full Atlantic! She had only faltered once, and even then no one had known about it. When she left Tangier, among the books she took along to amuse herself she had packed the one tale she should have left behind—Jules Verne's *Twenty Thousand Leagues under the Sea*. One day, in really rough weather, she had not been able to bear it any more and she tossed it overboard: night after night she had been dreaming that a giant octopus was dragging their boat, like the *Nautilus*, down to the bottom.

A few hours after their arrival, the Venezuelan authorities agreed to allow them into the country, although not one of them had any papers. 'We'll give you identity-cards later on.' They sent two who were ill to hospital, and they clothed, housed and fed the others for several weeks. Then each found himself a job.

That was Rita's story.

*

Wasn't it strange that I should have met the woman who had filled my horrible solitude in the Réclusion for two years, and then that this woman should have come here just as I did, making a break—although indeed a very different kind of break? Without papers too, and, just like me, generously treated by this nation?

Nothing came to disturb our happiness for more than three months. Then one fine day, unknown hands opened the safe of the Richmond Company, for which I was still organizing and running the geological expeditions. How the local pigs found out about my past I never did discover. But what is certain is that I was pulled in as suspect number one and shut up in the Maracaibo prison.

Naturally enough, Rita was questioned about me and that was how she suddenly learned everything I had hidden from her—and learned it from the pigs. Interpol had given them all the information. But still she did not leave me in the lurch and while I was in prison she helped me as much as she possibly could. She paid for a lawyer, he defended me, and in less than a fortnight got me out—charge dismissed. My complete innocence was established; but the damage had been done.

When she came to fetch me from the prison, Rita was deeply moved; but she was very sad, too. She did not look at me the same way as before. I sensed that she was really frightened—that she was hesitating about taking up with me again. I had the feeling that everything was lost. And I wasn't wrong, because straight away she said, 'Why did you lie to me?'

No, I must not, must not lose her. I'd never have another chance like this. Once again I had to fight, and fight with all my strength. 'Rita, you've just got to believe me. When I met you, I liked you so much, I loved you so much straight away, that I was afraid you wouldn't want to see me any more if I told you the truth about my past. You remember what I said about myself? Of course I made it up, but that was because I wanted to say only what I thought you would like to hear.'

'You lied to me ... you lied to me ...' she kept repeating, over and over again. 'And I who thought you were a decent man.'

She was crazy with fear, as though she were living in a nightmare. Yes, she's afraid, man, *she's afraid of you.*

174

'And who's to say I can't be a decent guy? I believe that like everybody else I deserve a chance of becoming good, honest and happy. Don't forget, Rita, that for thirteen years I had to fight against the most horrible prison system in the world. I love you with all my heart, Rita; and I love you not with my past but with my present. You must believe me: the reason why I didn't tell you the story of my life was just that I was afraid of losing you. I said to myself that although I'd lived crooked before, my future with you would be the complete opposite. I saw the whole of the road we were to travel together, hand in hand, and I saw it all clean and straightforward, all in lovely colours. I swear it's true, Rita, I swear by the head of my father, whom I've made to suffer so much.' Then I cracked, and I began to weep.

'Is it true, Henri? Is that really how you saw things? Is that really how you saw our future?'

I got a hold on myself; my voice was hoarse and broken as I replied, 'It has to be like that, because now in our hearts that's the way it is. Besides, you feel it in yourself. You and me—we have no past. All that matters is the present and the future.'

Rita took me in her arms. 'Henri, don't cry any more. Listen to the breeze—it's our future that is beginning. But swear to me that you'll never do another dishonest thing. Promise me you'll never hide anything from me any more and that there'll be nothing dirty in our lives to be kept hidden.'

We held one another tight, and I made my oath. I felt that my life's greatest chance was at stake. I saw that I should never have hidden from this brave, honest woman, that I was a man with a life-sentence, a fugitive from the penal settlement.

So I told her everything, absolutely everything. It was all on the move inside me, even the thing that had been gnawing at me for eighteen years and more—the fixed idea that had turned into an obsession: my revenge. I decided to lay it at her feet—to give it up as a proof of my sincerity. I could not make a greater sacrifice, a sacrifice of which she could not in any case grasp the importance; I heard myself doing it as if, by a miracle—as though someone else were speaking. 'To prove how much I love you, Rita, I offer you the greatest sacrifice I can make. From this very moment on, I give up my revenge. The prosecutor, the pigs, the false witness, all those people who made me suffer so—let them just die in their beds. Yes, you are right. To fully deserve a woman like you, I must—not forgive, because that's impossible—but put out of my mind this desire to punish mercilessly the men who tossed me into the penal cells. Here before you there is a completely new man: the old one is dead.'

Rita must have thought over this conversation all day, because that evening, after work, she said to me, 'And what about your father? Since you're now worthy of him, write to him as soon as you can.'

'Since 1933 neither he nor I have heard from one another. Since October 1933, to be exact. I used to see the convicts being given their letters, those wretched letters opened by the screws, those letters in which you could say nothing. I used to see the despair on the faces of the poor guys who had no mail at all, and I could make out the disappointment of the ones who read a longed-for letter and didn't find what they had hoped for in it. I've seen them tear letters to pieces and stamp on them; and I've seen tears fall on the ink and blur the writing. And I could imagine just what those damned letters from the penal settlement might mean when they got there—the Guiana stamp that would make the postman and the neighbours and the people in the village café say "The gaol-bird has written. There's a letter, so he's still alive." I could guess the shame of taking it from the postman and the pain when the postman said "Is your son getting along all right?" So I wrote my sister Yvonne just one letter, the only letter I wrote from penal, saying "Never expect to hear from me, and never write. Like Alfred de Vigny's wolf, I shall know how to die without howling."'

'All that belongs to the past, Henri. You'll write to your father?'

'Yes. Tomorrow.'

'No. Now—at once.'

A long letter set off for France, just telling my father what could be told without wounding him. I described no part of my sufferings; only my resurrection and my life at present. The letter came back: 'Gone away without leaving an address.'

Dear Lord above: who could tell where my father had gone

to hide his shame because of me? People were so evil they might have made life impossible for him.

Rita's reaction came at once. 'I'll go to France and look for your father.' I stared at her. She went on, 'Give up your exploring job; it's too dangerous in any case. While I'm away, you'll see to the running of the hotel.'

I had not got my Rita wrong. Not only was she ready to plunge unhesitatingly into the dangers of this long journey all by herself, but she had so much trust in me—in me, the ex-convict—that she would leave everything in my hands. She knew she could rely on me.

Rita had only rented the hotel, with an option to purchase. So in order to prevent it slipping out of our hands, the first thing to do was to buy it. Now I really learnt what it meant, struggling to make one's place in life by honest means.

I got the Richmond Company to let me go, and with the six thousand bolivars I received and Rita's savings we gave the owner fifty per cent of the price. And then began a positive battle day by day, and night by night, to make money and meet our instalments. Both she and I worked like crazy eighteen hours and sometimes nineteen hours a day. We were united by a wonderful will to win at all costs and in the shortest possible time. Neither she nor I ever mentioned our weariness. I did the buying and I helped with the cooking and I received the guests. We were everywhere at once, always smiling. We died on our feet and then we began again the next morning.

To make a little more money, I had a two-wheeled cart that I filled with jackets and trousers to sell in the Plaza Baralt market. These clothes were manufacturer's rejects, which meant I could buy them very cheaply at the works. Under the blazing sun I reeled off my patter, bawling like a jack-ass and putting so much energy into it that one day, tweaking a jacket to show how strong it was, I split it from top to bottom. It was all very well explaining that I was the strongest man in Maracaibo, but I sold precious few that morning. I was in the market from eight until noon. At half past twelve I hurried to the hotel to help at waiting in the restaurant.

The Plaza Baralt was the commercial heart of Maracaibo, one of the liveliest places in the town. At the far end, the church; at the other, one of the most picturesque markets in the world, a market where you would find anything you could possibly think of in the way of meat, game, sea-food and shell-fish, not forgetting big green iguanas—a lovely dish—with their claws twined so they could not escape; and there were alligator's, tortoise's and turtle's eggs, armadillos and *moro-coys*, a kind of land-tortoise, all sorts of fruit and fresh palm-hearts. The market of this ebullient town swarmed with people in the scorching sun—skins of every colour, eyes of every shape, from the Chinese slit to the Negro's round.

Rita and I loved Maracaibo, although it was one of the hottest places in Venezuela. This colonial town had a lovable, warm-hearted population that lived happily. They had a musical way of speaking; they were fine, generous people with a little Spanish blood and all the best qualities of the Indians. The men were fiery creatures; they had a very strong sense of friendship, and to those they liked they could be real brothers. The Maracucho—the inhabitant of Maracaibo—did not much care for anything that came from Caracas. He complained that they provided the whole of Venezuela with gold by means of their oil, and that the people of the capital always overlooked him: the Maracucho felt like a wealthy man who was being treated as a poor relation by the very people he had enriched. The women were pretty and rather small: faithful, good daughters and good mothers. The whole town seethed with life and the noise of living, and everywhere there was brilliant colour—the clothes, the houses, the fruit, everything. And everywhere movement, business, activity. The Plaza Baralt was full of street-traders and small-time smugglers who scarcely bothered to hide the liquers, spirits or cigarettes they were selling. It was all more or less among friends: the police-man was only a few yards away, but he would turn his back just long enough for the bottles of whisky, the French cognac or the American cigarettes to pass from one basket to another.

Running a hotel was no trifle. When Rita first came, she took a decision completely opposed to the customs of the country. The Venezuelan customers were used to eating a sub-stantial breakfast—maize cakes (*arepas*), ham and eggs, bacon, cream cheese. And as the guests were there on full board, the day's menu was written up on a slate. The first day she wiped the whole lot out and in her pointed hand she wrote 'Breakfast: black coffee or café au lait, bread and butter.' 'Well, what do you think of that?' the guests must have said: by the end of the week half of them had changed their quarters.

I turned up. Rita had made some alterations, but with my arrival it was a downright revolution.

First decree: double the prices.

Second decree: French cooking.

Third decree: air-conditioning throughout.

People were astonished to find air-conditioning in all the rooms and in the restaurant of a colonial house turned into a hotel. The clientele changed. First came commercial travellers; then a Basque settled in: he sold 'Swiss' watches entirely manufactured in Peru, and he ran his business from his room, selling only to retailers, who hawked them from door to door and all through the oil-fields. Although the hotel was safe, he was so suspicious that he had three big locks put on his door at his own expense. But in spite of the locks he noticed that from time to time a watch disappeared. He thought his room was haunted until the day he found that in fact there was a female thief, our bitch Bouclette. She was a poodle, and she was so cunning she would creep in without a sound, and right under his nose would knock off a strap for pure fun, whether it had a watch attached or not. So here he was, shrieking and bawling, saying it was me who had trained Bouclette to steal his things. I laughed till I could laugh no more, and after two or three rums I managed to convince him that I had nothing to do with his lousy watches and that I would really be ashamed of selling such phony stuff. Comforted and easy in his mind, he shut himself up in his room again.

Among our guests there were people of every possible kind. Maracaibo was full to overflowing, and it was almost impossible to find a room. A flock of Neapolitans went from house to house, swindling the citizens by selling them lengths of cloth folded in such a way that there seemed to be enough for four suits while in fact it would only run to two. They were dressed as sailors and they carried a big bag on their shoulder; they combed the town and the country round, above all the oil-fields. I don't know how these sharp-witted creatures discovered our hotel. As all the rooms were full, there was only one solution—for them to sleep in the patio. They agreed. Every evening they came back about seven and had a shower. They had dinner at the hotel, so we learned to make spaghetti à la napolitaine. They spent their money freely and they were good customers.

At night, we brought out iron bedsteads and the two little maids helped Rita make them up in the patio. As I made the Neapolitans pay in advance, every night there was the same argument—paying the price of a room for sleeping in the open was too much. And every night I told them that on the contrary it was perfectly logical and completely fair. To bring out the beds, put on the sheets, the blankets and the pillows and then take them all in again in the morning was a huge amount of work—beyond price. 'And don't you go on beefing too much, or I'll put up your rent. Because here am I, literally slaying myself shifting things in and out—all I make you pay is the cost-price of moving.'

They would pay up and we would all have a laugh. But although they were making a lot of money, the next evening the whole thing would start all over again. They beefed even more one night when it rained and they had to run in with all their clothes and their mattresses and sleep in the restaurant.

A woman who kept a brothel came to see me. She had a very big house two or three miles from Maracaibo, at the place called La Cabeza de Toro: the brothel was the Tibiri-Tabara. Eléonore was her name, and she was an enormous mass of flesh: intelligent; very fine eyes. More than a hundred and twenty women worked at her place—only at night.

'There are some French girls who want to get out,' she told me. 'They don't like spending twenty-four hours out of the twenty-four in the brothel. Working from nine in the evening until four the next morning, that's fine. But they want to be able to eat well and sleep in peace in comfortable rooms away from the noise.'

I made a deal with Eléonore: the French and Italian girls could come to our hotel. We could raise the price by ten bolivars a day without worrying: they would be only too happy to be able to stay at the Vera Cruz, with French people. We were supposed to take six; but after a month, I don't quite know how, we had twice as many.

Rita laid down iron-hard rules. They were all young and all lovely. It was absolutely forbidden to receive any male at the hotel, even in the courtyard or the dining-room. But in any case, there was no trouble at all: in the hotel these girls were like real ladies. In everyday life they were proper, respectable women who knew how to behave. In the evening, taxis came for them. They were transformed—gorgeously dressed and made-up. Discreet, without any noise, they went off to the 'factory', as they called it. Now and then a ponce would come from Paris or Caracas, drawing as little attention to himself as possible. His girl could see him at the hotel, of course. Once he had made his haul, collected his money and made his girl happy he would go off again as quietly as he had come.

There were often little things that were good for a laugh. A visiting ponce took me aside one day and asked to have his room changed. His woman had already found another girl who was willing to switch. Reason: his neighbour was a full-blooded, well-equipped Italian, and every night, when his girl came back, he made love to her at least once and sometimes twice. My ponce was not yet forty and the Italian must have been fifty-five.

'Man, I just can't keep up the pace with Rital, if you follow me. There's no getting anywhere near that kind of a performance. And my chick and me being next door, we hear the lot—groans, shrieks, the whole works. And as I can scarcely manage to stir my baby once a week, I ask you to imagine what I look like. She doesn't believe in the headache stuff any more; and of course she makes comparisons. So if it doesn't put you out, do this for me.'

I kept my laughter inside me, and moved by such an unanswerable argument, I switched his room.

Another time, at two o'clock in the morning, Eléonore called me up. The cop on duty had found a Frenchman who could not speak a word of Spanish perched in a tree opposite the brothel. The cop asked him how he came to be in that curious position—was he there to steal or what?—and all he answered was, 'Enrique of the Vera Cruz.' I jumped into my car and darted out to the Tibiri-Tabara.

I recognized the fellow right away. He was from Lyons and he had already been to the hotel. He was sitting there, and the madam too: standing in front of them, two grim-faced cops. I translated what he told me—he put it very briefly. 'No, the gentleman wasn't in the tree with the idea of doing anything wrong. It's just that he is in love with one of the women, but he won't say which. He climbed up to admire her in secret, because she won't have anything to do with him. It's nothing serious, as you see. Anyhow, I know him, and he's a good citizen.'

We drank a bottle of champagne: he paid, and I told him to leave the change on the table—someone would surely pick it up. Then I drove him back in my car. 'But what the hell were you doing, perched up in that tree? Have you gone crazy, or are you jealous of your girl?'

'It's not that. The trouble is the takings have dropped off without any reason for it. She's one of the prettiest there and she earns more than the others. So I thought I'd come and watch how often she went to work without her knowing. That way, it seemed to me, I'd soon find out if she was holding out on me and keeping back my money.'

Although I was sore at having been pulled out of bed in the middle of the night on account of a ponce, I roared with laughter at his explanation. This 'tree-perched pimp', as I called him from that time on, left for Caracas the next day. It was no longer worth his while keeping a check. The whole business had made a lot of noise in the brothel; like everybody else his woman knew all about it, but she was the only one who knew why her fancy-man had chosen just that tree—it was dead opposite her room.

We worked hard, but the hotel was a cheerful place, and we had fun all the time. There were some evenings, after the girls had gone off to their factory, when we made the dead speak. We all sat at a round table with our hands flat on the top, and each one called up the spirit he wanted to question. It was a good-looking woman of about thirty, a painter, who started these seances—she was a Hungarian, I think. She called up her husband every evening, and of course with my foot under the table I helped his spirit to reply: otherwise we'd be there yet.

She said her husband was tormenting her. Why? She could

not tell. At last one night the spirit came through by means of the table, and after that he never left it quiet. He accused her of having round heels. We all exclaimed that that was very serious, and that this jealous spirit might take a horrible revenge; all the more so as she was perfectly willing to admit that in fact her heels were quite round. What was to be done about it? We discussed it very gravely and we told her there was only one thing to do: at full moon she was to provide herself with a brand-new machête, stand stark naked in the middle of the patio with her hair down and no make-up on, having washed all over with yellow soap, but with no trace of scent and no jewels, clean from head to foot. Nothing but the machête in her hand. When the moon was right over the patio, casting no shadow except directly beneath her, she was to slash the air exactly twenty-one times.

It worked perfectly, and the night after the exorcism (we had laughed fit to burst, hidden behind the shutters) Rita said the joke had lasted long enough; so the table replied that from now on her late husband would leave her in peace and her heels could be as round as she liked, always provided she never slashed the air with a sword at full moon any more, because it hurt him too much.

We had a poodle called Minou, quite a big poodle, that had been given to us by a French guest who was passing through Maracaibo. He was always perfectly clipped and brushed, and the stiff, thick hair on the top of his head was cut in the shape of a tall, impressive fez. He had puffed-out thighs, shaved legs, a Chaplin moustache and a little pointed beard. The Venezuelans were astonished at the spectacle, and often one of them would overcome his shyness and ask what kind of an animal this strange beast might be.

Minou very nearly brought about a serious clash with the Church. The Vera Cruz stood in the Calle Venezuela; our street led to a church and processions often went along it. Now Minou loved sitting at the hotel door to watch the people walking about. He never barked, whatever happened in the street. But although he did not bark, he did cause a sensation; and one day the priest and the choir-boys belonging to a procession found themselves all alone, while fifty yards behind the faithful of Maracaibo stood massed in front of the hotel, gazing at this extraordinary object. They had forgotten to follow the procession. Questions ran through the group, and they jostled to see Minou close to; some were of the opinion that the unknown creature might very well be the soul of a repentant sinner, since it had sat there so quietly, watching a priest and his choir-boys all dressed in red go by singing heartily. At last the priest realized that things were very silent behind, and turning round he saw there was no one left. He came striding back, crimson with fury and bawling out his parishioners for their lack of respect for the ceremony. Alarmed, they fell back into line and marched off. But I noticed that some who had been most struck by the sight walked backwards so as not to lose a minute of Minou. After that we kept an eye on the Maracaibo paper, *Panorama*, for the date and the time when a procession should come along our street, so that we could tie him up in the patio.

It seems this was the season for incidents with the clergy. Two French girls left Eléonore's brothel and the hotel; they had made up their minds to be independent and to set up a little 'house' in the centre of the town where they would just work by themselves, the two of them. It was quite a good scheme, because like this the customers would not have to get their cars and drive six miles there and back to see them. To get themselves known, they had cards printed, saying 'Julie and Nana: conscientious work' and the address. They handed them out in the town; but instead of giving them directly to the men, they often slipped them under the windscreen-wipers of parked cars.

They had the bad luck to put two, one under each wiper, on the car belonging to the bishop of Maracaibo. This set off a hell of an explosion. To show the profane nature of their action, the paper *La Religion* published a picture of the card. But the bishop and the clergy were indulgent: the little brothel was not closed, and the ladies were only begged to be more discreet. Anyhow, there was no point in going on handing out the cards: after the free publicity in *La Religion* a very considerable number of customers hurried to the given address. Indeed, the crowd was so great that to provide a reasonable excuse for this troop of men at their door, the girls asked a hot-dog seller to wheel his barrow quite close, so it would look as if the queue was standing there to buy a *perro caliente*.

That was the picturesque side of life at the hotel. But we were not living our life on a planet far out in space: we were living it in Venezuela, and we were mixed up with the country's economic and political ups and downs. And in 1948 politics were not so peaceful. Gallegos and Bétancourt had been governing the country since 1945, in the first attempt at a democratic régime in the history of Venezuela. On 13 November 1948, scarcely three months after I had set to work with Rita to buy the hotel, there came the first shot directed against the régime. A major called Thomas Mendoza had the nerve to try a rising all by himself. He failed.

On the twenty-fourth of the same month the soldiers seized power in a *coup d'état* run with clockwork precision: there were almost no victims. Gallegos, the president of the republic and a distinguished writer, was forced to resign. Bétancourt, a real political lion, took refuge in the Colombian embassy.

In Maracaibo we lived through hours of very tense anxiety. There was one moment when all at once we heard a passionate voice on the radio crying 'Workers, come out into the streets! They want to steal your freedom from you, close down your unions and impose a military dictatorship by force! Everybody occupy the squares, the...' Click, and it was cut off dead, the mike snatched from the brave militant's hands. Then a calm, grave voice: 'Citizens! The army has withdrawn the power from the men to whom they entrusted it after having dismissed General Medina, because they made an unworthy use of their authority. Do not be afraid: we guarantee the life and property of one and all, without exception. Long live the army! Long live the revolution!'

That was all I saw of a revolution which caused no blood to flow at all; and when we woke up next day, there was the composition of the military junta in the papers: three colonels —Delgado-Chalbaud as president, Perez Jimenez and Llovera Paez.

To begin with, we were afraid this new régime would mean the suppression of the rights given by the former one. But nothing of the kind. Life went on just the same, and we scarcely noticed the change of government, apart from the fact that the key-posts were taken over by soldiers.

Then two years later came the assassination of Delgado-Chalbaud. A very ugly business with two conflicting explanations. First theory: they meant to murder all three and he was the first to be killed. Second theory: one of the other colonels or both had him put out of the way. The truth was never known. The murderer was arrested, and he was shot and killed while he was being transferred to prison—a lucky shot that prevented any embarrassing statement. From that day on Perez Jimenez was the strong man of the régime; and he officially became dictator in 1952.

So our life went on; and although we never went out for any fun or entertainment or even a drive, this life and our eagerness to work filled us with a wonderful joy. For what we were building up by our labours was to be our home, the home in which we should live happily, having earned it ourselves, united as only two people can be when they love one another as we did.

And into this home would come Clotilde, Rita's daughter, who would be mine, and my father, who would be theirs. And to this house there would come my friends, to draw breath a while when they were in need. And in this home filled with happiness we would be so thoroughly contented that never again should I think of taking my revenge upon those who had caused so much suffering to me and my people.

At last the day came—we had won. December 1950: a beautiful document was drawn up at the lawyer's, and we were the owners of the hotel for good and all.

11: My Father

TODAY Rita set off on her journey, her heart filled with hope. She was going to find out the place where my father had retired—where he had hidden himself.

'Rely on me, Henri. I'll bring you back your father.'

I was alone in the running of the hotel. I gave up selling trousers and shirts, although I could make quite a packet out of it in a few hours. But Rita had gone to look for my father, so I was going to look after everything not only as though she were there, but even better, twice as well.

To look for my father: *to look for my father*! My father, the schoolmaster of a village in the Ardèche; my father, who twenty years ago, *twenty years ago*, could not embrace his son, a convict with a life-sentence, when he came to see him in prison for the last time, because of the bars in the visiting-room. My father, to whom my wife Rita would be able to say, 'I have come as your daughter to tell you that by his own efforts your son has regained his freedom, that he has made himself a life as a good and honest man, and that he and I have built up a home that is waiting for you.'

I got up at five o'clock and went shopping with Minou and a twelve-year-old boy called Carlitos I had taken in when he came out of prison. He carried the baskets. In an hour and a half I'd done the buying for the whole day—meat, fish and vegetables. We came back both loaded like mules. Two women in the kitchen: the one twenty-four, the other eighteen. I dumped everything we had brought on the table and they sorted it out.

For me, the best moment in this simple life was at half past six in the morning, the time when I ate my breakfast in the dining-room with the cook's daughter on my knee. She was four; she was coal-black, and she would not eat unless she had her breakfast with me. All these things—her little naked body, still cool from the shower her mother gave her when she got up, her little girl's piping voice, her lovely shining eyes that looked at me so trustingly, the jealous barking of my dog, cross at being neglected, Rita's parrot pecking at its bread and milk by my coffee-cup—yes, all this really made breakfast the top moment of my day.

Rita? No letter. Why? It was more than a month now that she'd been gone. The voyage took sixteen days, true enough; but after all she'd been in France a fortnight now—had she still found nothing, or did she not want to tell me? All I asked for was a cable, a very short cable just to say 'Your father is well and he loves you still'.

I watched for the postman. I never left the hotel unless I had to in order to keep it running smoothly and I hurried over the shopping and the other business so as to be on the spot all the time. In Venezuela the people who bring telegrams have no uniform, but they are all young; so the moment any boy walked into the patio I hurried towards him, my eyes fixed on his hands to see if he was carrying a green paper. Not a thing. Most of the time they weren't even telegraph-boys, except on two or three occasions when some young fellow did appear with a green slip in his hand: I'd rush out, snatch the telegram and then see with a sinking heart that it was addressed to someone staying at the hotel.

This waiting and this lack of news made me all on edge and anxious. I worked till I dropped; I always had to be busy because I felt that otherwise I should not be able to hold out. I helped in the kitchen, I worked out extraordinary menus, I checked the rooms twice a day, I talked to the guests about no matter what and listened to them whatever they had to say. The only thing that mattered was filling up these hours and days so as to be able to endure the want of news and the waiting. There was only one thing I couldn't do—take a hand in the poker-game that started up about two o'clock every night.

There was only one really serious calamity. Carlitos got things wrong. Instead of buying paraffin for cleaning the kitchen, he bought petrol. The cooks swilled the concrete floor with a good deal of it and then, never suspecting a thing, they lit the stove. The whole kitchen blazed up with a vivid burst of flame, and the two sisters were burnt from foot to belly. I just had time to wrap a tablecloth round Rosa's little black girl and save her—not a second to spare. She was almost unhurt, but the other two were badly burned. I had them looked after in their room in the hotel and engaged a Panamanian cook.

Life in the hotel carried on as usual, but I began to be seriously worried about Rita's silence and her not being there.

Fifty-seven days she had been gone. But now in ten or twenty minutes she'd be back. There I was waiting for her at the airport. Why just that simple telegram—'Arrive Tuesday 15.30 flight 705. Love Rita'? Why nothing more? Has she not found anyone? I couldn't tell what to think any more, and I didn't want to make any more guesses.

Here she was, my Rita. Now at last I'd know. She was the fifth coming down the gangway. She saw me right away and we both waved at the same moment. She came towards me, just as usual. From forty yards I searched her face: she was not laughing, just smiling. No, she was not coming with a triumphant air: no, she hadn't waved as a sign of joy and victory but just naturally, to show she'd seen me. At ten yards I saw she'd come back beaten.

'Did you find my father?'

The question hit her point-blank, after no more than just a kiss, a single kiss after two months of separation. I couldn't wait any longer.

Yes, she had found him. He was lying in the graveyard of a little village in the Ardèche.

She showed me a photograph. A well-made cement tomb with J. Charrière on it. He had died four months before she got there. And all Rita brought me back was this picture of his grave.

My heart, which had seen my wife go off so full of hope, almost stopped at this appalling news. I felt a deep, wrenching pain inside me, the collapse of all those illusions I had had as a man who still sees himself as a little boy for his father. God, not only have You struck the whole of my youth but You have also refused to let me embrace my father and to hear his voice, which would have said, I am certain of it, 'Come to my arms, my little Riri. Fate has been unmerciful to you; the law and its penitentiary system have treated you abominably; but I love you still, I have never renounced you, and I am proud that you have had the strength to win in spite of everything and to become what you are.' Over and over again Rita told me the small amount of information she had been able to get almost by begging, the little she had been able to find out about my father's life after I was sentenced. I said nothing; I could not speak; something inside me was tied into a furious knot. And then all at once, as though a sluice had burst open, the idea of revenge came over me again. 'Pigs, I'll set off that trunk of dynamite at 36, quai des Orfèvres, not just to kill a few but as many as possible—a hundred, two hundred, three hundred, a thousand! And you, Goldstein, you perjurer, believe you me, you'll get what's coming to you, every last bit of it. As for you, prosecuting counsel, so eager to send me down, it won't take long for me to find a way of getting hold of your tongue and tearing it out with as much agony as you can suffer!

'Rita, we must part. Try to understand: they've utterly wrecked my life. They prevented me from embracing my father and having his forgiveness. I must have my revenge: they can't get away with this. This is our last night: tomorrow I go. I know where to find the money for the journey and to carry out my plan. The only thing I ask you is to let me take five thousand bolivars out of our savings for my first expenses.'

An interminable silence settled; I no longer saw Rita; her face disappeared behind the unfolding vision of the plan I had worked out so often.

What did I need to put it into action? Less than two hundred thousand bolivars, in fact. I'd asked too much before. I'd have plenty to spare with these sixty thousand dollars. There were two jobs I'd left alone so as to respect this country. First, El Callao with its heap of gold guarded by ex-lags. Then right in the middle of Caracas, the cashier of a big firm. He was a push-over: he carried large sums of money without an escort. The entrance to the building was perfect; so was the fourth-floor corridor: both were badly lit. I could work alone, unarmed, with chloroform. The only bloody inconvenience was that when the sums were very large three men carried them. Holding them up all by myself was not a hundred per cent safe. The easiest was El Callao, of course. There I could take just what I needed, half a hundredweight of gold, not more, and bury it. A simple job: I could go to bed with Maria, and when she was asleep I'd chloroform her so she would not wake up when I got up to do the job. I could come back to her bed without having been seen by anyone. Getting close to the guard would be easy, naked, painted black and on a pitch-dark night.

As for the getaway, that would have to be through British Guiana. I'd get to Georgetown with just a little gold melted down into nuggets—easy enough with a blow-lamp. I'd be certain of finding a buyer for the lot. The fence and I would carry out the deal on the basis of notes cut in two: he'd keep one half and only give it me when I delivered the goods on the British side of the Caroni, where I would have the stuff hidden. That way, there would be confidence all round.

It would be all right for me to show up in Georgetown, because when I left some years back I'd done so secretly. Coming back secretly too, if I was ever asked what I was doing— always a possibility—I could say I had spent those years way out in the bush looking for balata or gold, and that was why no one had seen me for so long.

I knew Little Julot was still there. He was a regular guy and he would put me up. Just one risk: Indara and her sister. I'd only go out at night; or better still not go out at all, but get Julot to do the deal for me. And I thought Big André was in Georgetown too, on a Canadian passport. Switching the photo, changing the stamp—nothing to it. If he wasn't there, then I'd buy papers from anyone who was broke or from a seaman at the Mariners' Club.

Transfer the dough to Buenos Aires through a bank; carry a certain amount in notes; take a plane from Trinidad to Rio de Janeiro. At Rio, change passports and get into the Argentine.

Once there, no problem. I had friends in Rio, ex-lags; and it must be easy to find former Nazis with their trunks full of papers. Leave for Portugal from Buenos Aires with four sets of passports and identity papers—different nationalities but all in the same name so as not to get muddled up.

From Lisbon, take the road into Spain and reach Barcelona; still travelling by road, into France on a Paraguayan passport. I spoke Spanish well enough by now for an inquisitive French gendarme to take me for a South American.

Half the money would have been transferred to the Crédit Lyonnais, the other half kept in reserve at Buenos Aires.

Every single person I contacted in Georgetown, Brazil and the Argentine would have to believe I was going to Italy, where my wife was waiting for me to start a business in some seaside resort.

In Paris I'd stay at the Georges V. Never go out at night: have dinner at the hotel and send for tea in my suite at ten. The same thing every day of the week. That's the hallmark of a serious type leading an exactly regulated life. In a hotel this kind of thing gets known right away.

I'd have a moustache, of course, and hair cut *en brosse*, like an officer. Only say what was strictly necessary and use a Spanish sort of French to say it. Have Spanish newspapers put in my pigeon-hole at the reception every day.

Thousands and thousands of times I'd turned over the questions of which man or which men to begin with, so that the three jobs would never be connected with Papillon.

The first to get their deserts would be the pigs, with the trunk stuffed with explosives at 36, quai des Orfèvres. There would be no reason to think of me if I did it cleverly. To begin with I'd have a look at the premises and check the exact time it took to go up the stairs to the report-room and then get back to the entrance. I didn't need anyone to work out the fuse for the detonator: I'd made all the necessary experiments at the Franco-Venezuelan garage.

I'd turn up in a van with *Maison So-and-so: Office Equipment* painted on it. With me dressed as a delivery-man and with my little crate on my shoulder, it should work easily. But when I first went over the place I'd have either to find some inspector's card on a door or manage to get hold of the name of an important character with his office on that floor. Like that I could say the name to the pigs on duty at the door; or indeed I could show them the invoice, as if I didn't remember who the trunk was for. And then all aboard for the fireworks. It would need diabolical bad luck for anyone to connect the explosion—a sort of anarchist's job, after all—with Papillon.

In that way Pradel would not be warned. To cope with him, and to prepare the trunk, the fuse, the explosives and the bits of old iron, I'd have taken a villa, using my Paraguayan passport if I hadn't managed to get hold of a French identity-card. I was afraid it might be too dangerous to get into contact with the underworld again. Better not risk it: I'd make out with the passport.

The villa would be near Paris, somewhere along the Seine, because I'd have to be able to get there by water and by road. I'd buy a light, fast little boat with a cabin, and it would have moorings right by the villa and on the banks of the Seine in the middle of Paris, too. For the road, I'd have a small, high-powered car. It was only when I got there and when I knew where Pradel lived and worked and where he spent his week-ends and whether he took the métro, the bus, a taxi or his own car that I'd take the necessary steps to kidnap him and shut him up in the villa.

The main thing was to make dead sure of the times and the places where he was alone. Once he was in my cellar, I had him on toast. This prosecutor who, way back in 1931, at the trial, had seemed to say to me, with his vulture-look, 'You won't escape from me, young cock; I'm going to make use of everything that can look bad for you, all this ugly muck in your file, to make you seem disgusting, so that the jury will turn you out of society for good and all'—this prosecutor, who had brought all his abilities and all his education to bear to paint the vilest and most hopeless picture of a boy of twenty-four, and with such success that the twelve incompetent bastards of jurymen sent me to penal servitude for life—this prosecutor, I'd have to torture him for at least a week before he died. And at that he wouldn't have paid too dear.

The last to pay the bill would be Goldstein, the perjurer. I'd take him last, since he was the most dangerous for me. Because once I'd killed him, they'd look back over his life, and the pigs were not always half-wits—they'd soon see the part he had played in my trial. And as they'd know right away that I was on the run, it wouldn't take them long to figure out there might be a Papillon fluttering about in the Paris air. At that point everything, hotels, streets, stations, ports and airfields, would become extremely dangerous for me. I'd have to make my getaway quickly.

It would not be hard to pinpoint him and follow him, because of his father's fur shop. There were several ways of killing him, but whichever way I chose, I wanted him to recognize me before he died. If possible, I'd do what I had so often dreamed of doing—strangle him slowly with my bare hands, saying, 'Sometimes the dead come to life again. You didn't expect that, brother? You didn't expect my hands to kill you? Still, you win, because you're going to die in a few minutes, whereas you sent me down to rot slowly all my life until I died of it.'

I couldn't tell whether I'd manage to get out of France, because once Goldstein was dead things would be very dangerous. It was almost certain they would identify me. I didn't give a damn. Even if I had to die for it, they must pay for my father's death. I'd have forgiven them for my suffering. But the fact that my father should have died without my being able to tell him his boy was alive and had gone straight; the fact that maybe he had died of shame, hiding from all his old friends, and that he should have lain down in his grave without knowing what I was now—that, no, no, no! That I could never forgive!

During the very long silence while I went through every step of the action again to see there was no hitch anywhere, Rita had been sitting at my feet, with her head leaning against my knee. Not a word, not a sound; almost seemed to be holding her breath.

'Rita, sweetheart, I leave tomorrow.'

'You shan't go.' She stood up, put her hands on my shoulders and looked me straight in the eye. She went on, '*You must not go:* you can't go. There's something new for me too. I took advantage of my journey to send for my daughter. She'll be here in a few days. You know perfectly well the reason why I didn't have her with me was I needed a settled place for her. Now I've got one, and she'll have a father too—you. Are you going to run away from your responsibilities? Are you going to spoil everything we've built up with the love and trust between us? Do you think killing the men who were responsible for your sufferings and perhaps for your father's death is really the only thing to do when you compare it with what we have? Is that the only answer you can find?

'Henri, our fates are linked for ever. For my sake and for the sake of this girl who is coming to you and who I am sure will love you, I ask you to give up your idea of revenge for ever. Why, you'd made up your mind to do so. And now here's your father's death throwing you back down the road to ruin.

Just you listen to me: if your father, that upright, kind village schoolmaster who spent his life teaching thousands of children to be good, straight, industrious and charitable, and to respect the law—if your father could speak, do you think he would accept your idea of revenge and approve of it? No. He'd tell you that neither the cops nor the false witness nor the prosecutor nor the jurymen nor the warders were worth your sacrificing a wife who loves you and whom you love, and my daughter who hopes to find a father in you, and your good, comfortable home, and your honest life.

'I'll tell you how I see your revenge: it's this—that our family should be a symbol of happiness for everybody; that with your intelligence and my help, we should succeed in life by honest means; and that when the people of this country talk about you not one would say anything but this—the Frenchman is straight and honest, a good man whose word is his bond. That's what your revenge ought to be; and that revenge would be the best kind—the revenge of proving to them all that they were terribly mistaken about you; the revenge of proving that you managed to come through the horrors of prison unspoilt and become a fine character. That is the only revenge worthy of the love and the trust I have placed in you.'

She had won. All night we talked, and I learned to drain the cup to the dregs. But I could not resist the temptation of knowing every last detail of Rita's journey. She lay on a big sofa, exhausted by the failure of this long voyage and by her struggle with me. Sitting there on the edge of it I leant over her, questioning her again and again and again, and little by little I dragged out everything she had meant to hide.

At the very beginning, after she left Maracaibo for the port of Caracas where she was to take the boat, she had a foreboding that she was going to fail: everything seemed to combine to prevent her from leaving for France. Just as she was going aboard the *Colombie* she noticed that she lacked one of the necessary visas. A race against time to get it in Caracas, tearing along that dangerous little road I knew so well. Back to the port with the paper in her bag and her heart beating for fear the boat should leave before she got there. Then a terrible storm broke out, bringing landslides down over the road. It became so dangerous that the driver lost his head and turned back, leaving Rita there alone in the storm by the side of the road, among the landslides. She walked nearly two miles in the downpour and then by a miracle she found a taxi that was returning to Caracas: but at the sight of the landslides it turned back for the port. And from the port she could hear ships' sirens. In her panic she was sure it was the *Colombie* leaving.

Then when she reached her cabin at last, weeping with joy, there was some accident aboard and the ship could not leave for several hours. All this gave her a very uneasy feeling, as if it was the finger of fate.

Then the ocean: Le Havre, Paris, and without a stop, Marseilles. Marseilles, where she stayed with a woman she knew, and there the woman introduced her to a municipal councillor; straight away he wrote her a cordial letter to a friend of his called Henri Champel, who lived at Vals-les-Bains in the Ardèche.

Then the train and the bus again, and it was not until she reached these wonderfully kind Champels that Rita could draw breath and begin to organize her search, but she was not at the end of her difficulties.

Henri Champel took her to Aubenas, in the Ardèche, where Maître Testud, the family lawyer, lived. Ah, that Testud! A heartless bourgeois. In the first place he told her my father was dead—just straight out, like that. Then on his own initiative, without consulting anyone, he forbade her to go and see my father's sister and her husband, my uncle and aunt Dumarche, retired teachers who lived in Aubenas. Many years later they welcomed us with open arms, indignant at the thought that because of this wretched Testud they had not been able to have Rita to stay and to get in touch with me again. The same thing with my sisters: he refused to give their address. Still, she did manage to get this stony heart to tell her where my father had died—Saint-Peray.

The journey to Saint-Peray. There Henri Champel and Rita found my father's grave; and they learnt something else. After having been a widower for twenty years he had married again—a retired schoolmistress; this was when I was still in the penal settlement. They found her. The family called her Tante Ju, or sometimes Tata Ju.

A fine woman, said Rita, and with such a noble character that she had kept the memory of my mother alive in this new home. In the dining-room Rita had seen big photographs of my mother, whom I worshipped, and of my father. She had been able to touch and fondle objects that had belonged to her. Tante Ju, who now suddenly came into my life—although at the same time I felt I already knew her—had done all she could to let Rita feel the atmosphere she and my father had wanted to keep alive—the memory of my mother and the continual presence of that vanished little boy who was still Riri to my father.

November the 16th was my birthday, and every 16 November my father used to weep. Every Christmas there was a chair left empty. When the gendarmes came to tell them their son had escaped again, they almost kissed them for having brought such wonderful news. Because although Tante Ju did not know me, she had already adopted me in her heart as though I were her own son, and both she and my father shed tears of joy at hearing what was for them news of hope.

So she had received Rita more than kindly. Only one shadow: Tante Ju had not given her the address of my two sisters. Why not? I thought quickly. No doubt about it: she wasn't sure how they would take the news of my reappearance. Since she did not say to Rita, 'Hurry over and see them at such-and-such a place; they'll be wild with delight to know their brother's still alive and doing well, and to meet his wife' she must have had her reasons. Maybe Tante Ju knew that neither my sister Yvonne nor my sister Hélène, nor my brothers-in-law, would care to be visited by the wife of their brother, the escaped gaol-bird sentenced to life for murder. No doubt she did not want to take the responsibility of disturbing their peace.

They were married and they had children, and probably these children did not even know of my existence. Take care, she must have said to herself. It seemed to me that although throughout my thirteen years of penal I had lived with them and through them, they, on the other hand, must have spent those thirteen years doing their best to forget me or at least trying to blot me out from their daily life. So all my wife brought back was a little earth from my father's grave and a photograph of the tomb where just four months before her coming my father had been laid to rest for ever.

Still, through Rita's eyes (for Champel had driven her everywhere) I did see the bridge of Ucel once more, the bridge of my childhood. I listened as she told me every detail about the big primary school where we had lived in the flat over the classrooms. Once again I could see the war memorial opposite our garden, and the garden itself, where a splendid flowering mimosa seemed to have kept itself in full bloom so that Rita, whose eyes drank in the garden, the memorial and the house, should be able to say to me 'Nothing, or almost nothing, has changed; and you've so often described the scenes of your childhood that I did not feel I was seeing something new but rather coming back to a place I already knew.'

Often in the evenings I would ask Rita to tell me some part of her journey all over again. At the hotel life went back to what it had been before. But deep inside me something inexplicable had happened. I had not felt this death as a forty-year-old man in the prime of life feels when he hears of the death of a father he has not seen for twenty years, but like a boy of ten—one who lives with his father, disobeys him, plays truant, and then on coming home, hears of his death.

Rita's daughter Clotilde arrived. She was over fifteen, but she was so frail and slight you would have said she was twelve. Long, thick, black, curling hair down to her shoulders. Her small jet-black eyes sparkled with intelligence and curiosity. Her little face was not that of a girl but of a child that might still be playing at hopscotch or with a doll. There was immediate sympathy between us. Right away she felt that this man who lived with her mother was going to be her best friend and that he would always love and protect her.

Since she had appeared, something new had come over me —the protective instinct, the wish that she should be happy and that she should look upon me if not as her father then at least as her surest support.

Now that Rita was back again, I did the shopping later, at seven. I took Clotilde with me, and we walked hand in hand.

with her leading Minou and Carlitos carrying the baskets. Everything was new for her, and she wanted to see it all at once. When she found something unexpected she piped up loud and clear to know what it was. What struck her most was the Indian women with their long shimmering robes, painted cheeks and shoes decorated with huge, many-coloured woollen pompons.

Having a child beside me, a child that trustingly grasped my hand whenever there was an imaginary danger, a little creature that leaned on my arm to make me understand that in the midst of this hurrying and shouting crowd, she felt completely protected, moved me deeply and filled me with a hitherto unknown feeling—the feeling of a father's love. 'Yes, little Clotilde, go forward into life with a trusting, easy mind; you can be sure that until the end I shall do everything I can to keep your path clear of thorns.'

And we would go happily back to the hotel, always with something amusing to tell Rita about what had happened to us or what we had seen.

12 : I become a Venezuelan

I KNOW perfectly well that what the reader expects is my own personal adventures and not a history of Venezuela. Forgive me if I feel I should mention certain important political events that happened during the time I am writing about, because they had a direct influence on my life and on the decisions I took.

For many people Venezuela is just a country in South America (most aren't quite sure just where) that produces oil, a country exploited by the Americans as though it were a kind of American colony. This is far from true.

To be sure, the oil companies did have very great weight; but little by little the Venezuelan intellectuals have set the country almost entirely free from the influence of American policy.

At present Venezuela is completely independent politically, as it has proved by the attitude it has adopted at the United Nations and elsewhere. One thing all the political parties have in common is a great zeal for Venezuela's freedom of action with respect to all foreign countries. Thus, ever since Caldera came to power we have had diplomatic relations with every country in the world, whatever their political régimes.

It is true that economically Venezuela depends on its oil, but it has succeeded in selling it at a very high price and making the oil companies hand over as much as eighty-five per cent of their profits.

Venezuela has other things besides oil, such as iron and other raw materials; and Venezuela has men, a whole mass of men whose aim is to free their country entirely from all forms of economic pressure, wherever they come from. Men who have begun to prove and who will prove more and more that in Venezuela a democracy as good as any other can be set up, respected and preserved.

The young people in the universities long for nothing but social justice and the radical transformation of their country. They are full of faith, and confident of succeeding without doing away with the foundations of real freedom—confident of bringing happiness to the whole nation without falling into a dictatorship either of the extreme right or of the extreme left. I believe in the young people of this country: they will help to make it a nation that can be held up as an example, both for its truly democratic régime and for its economy, because it must not be forgotten that its huge resources of raw materials will soon be completely industrialized. When that happens, Venezuela will have won a great battle: and Venezuela *will* win it.

Venezuela is also an ideal country for the kind of tourism that must develop in the coming years. Everything is in its favour—its beaches of coral sand, shaded by coconut-palms; its sunshine, which beats all other countries; its fishing of every kind in a sea that is always warm; a cheaper cost of living than other countries; islands by the hundred; a welcoming, hospitable people without the least trace of a colour problem. At one hour's flying distance from Caracas you find the Indians, the lake villages of Maracaibo or the Andes with their everlasting snow.

In short, Venezuela is so rich in resources that the country scarcely needs a politician at the helm but rather a good accountant with a dynamic team who would use the currency provided by the oil for building factories to exploit this wealth and to increase the labour market for all who need work and who want it.

1951: once again, as I reach this date, I have the same feeling that I had then—the feeling of having nothing more to tell. You tell about storms and shooting the rapids of a swollen river; but when the water is calm and peaceful you feel like closing your eyes and resting on the placid current. But the rain comes pouring down again, the streams rise, the quiet water grows rough, the flood carries you away, and even if you longed to live in peace from everything, outside events have such an effect on your life that they force you to follow the current, avoiding the reefs and shooting the rapids in the hope of finding a quiet harbour at last.

After the mysterious killing of Chabaud at the end of 1950, Perez Jimenez seized power, although he hid behind Flamerich, the figure-head president of the junta. The dictatorship began. First sign: the suppression of the freedom of speech. The press and the radio were throttled. The opposition went underground and the terrible police, the *Seguridad Nacional*, went into action. The Communists and the *Adecos* (the members of the *Acción Democrática*, Bétancourt's party) were hunted down.

Several times we hid them at the Vera Cruz. Never did we close our doors to anyone at all; never did we ask for any man's identity. I was only too glad to pay my tribute to these followers of Bétancourt, whose régime had set me free and given me asylum. By doing this we ran the danger of losing everything, but Rita saw that we could not behave otherwise.

Then again, the hotel had become something of a refuge for Frenchmen in a jam—for Frenchmen who had reached Venezuela with little in their pockets and who did not know where to go. They could eat and sleep at our place without paying while they were looking for a job. This reached such a point that in Maracaibo they called me the Frenchmen's consul.

But in the course of these years there happened something very important for me, almost as important as my meeting with Rita—I renewed my ties with my family. As soon as Rita left, Tante Ju wrote to my two sisters. And all of them, both my sisters and Tante Ju, wrote to me. Twenty years had gone by, and the great silence was coming to an end. I trembled as I opened the first letter. What would there be in it? I dared not read. Would they reject me for ever, or would they . . .

Victory! These letters were a cry of joy—joy at knowing I was alive, earning an honest living, and married to a woman Tante Ju described with all the kindness she had felt. Not only had I found my sisters once again, but I had also found their families, who now became *my* family.

My elder sister had four fine children, three girls and a boy. Her husband wrote himself to say that his affection had remained unaltered and that he was more than happy to know I was free and doing well. And photos and still more photos, and pages and still more pages—the story of their lives and of the war and of what they had had to go through to bring up their children. I read every word, weighing and analysing to understand it thoroughly and savour all its charm.

And my childhood came to the surface after the great black

hole of the prisons and the penal settlement: 'My dear Riri,' wrote my sister. Riri ... I could hear my mother calling me and see her lovely smile. It seemed that judging from a photo I had sent them I was the image of my father. My sister was convinced that if I was like him physically I must be like him in personality. Her husband and she were not afraid of my turning up again. The gendarmes must have heard about Rita's journey in the Ardèche, because they came to ask them about me, and my brother-in-law replied, 'Yes indeed, we have news of him. He's very happy and he's doing fine, thank you very much.'

My other sister was in Paris, married to a Corsican lawyer. They had two sons and a daughter, and he had a good job. The same cry: 'You are free, you are loved, you have a home, a good position and you are living like everybody else. Well done, little brother! My children, my husband and I bless God for having helped you to come out a winner from that terrible prison into which they threw you.'

My elder sister suggested having our daughter so that she could go on with her studies in France. But what warmed our hearts most was the fact that not one of them seemed to be ashamed of having a brother who was an ex-convict who had escaped from the penal settlement.

To round off this influx of wonderful news, I managed to get hold of the address of my friend Dr Guibert-Germain, the former doctor of the settlement, who treated me as one of his family when I was on Royale, inviting me to his house, and protecting me from the screws. It was thanks to Dr Guibert-Germain that the solitary confinement at Saint-Joseph was done away with; and it was thanks to him that I was able to get myself transferred to Devil's Island and escape. I wrote to him, and one day I had the immense happiness of receiving this letter:

Lyons, 21 February 1952

My dear Papillon,

We are very glad to have news of you at last. For a long while now I have felt sure you were trying to get in touch with me. When I was in Jibuti my mother told me she had received a letter from Venezuela, although she could not say exactly who had sent it. Then, very recently, she sent me the letter you wrote through Mme Roesberg. So after a fair amount of trials we have managed to find you again. Since September 1945, when I left Royale, a good many things have happened.

... And then in October 1951 I was posted to Indo-China; I am to stay there for two years, and I leave very soon, that is to say on 6 March. This time I am going by myself. Perhaps when I am there, and according to where they send me, I may be able to arrange for my wife to come out and join me.

So you see that since the last time we met I have travelled a fair number of miles! I retain some pleasant memories of those days; but alas I have not been able to get in touch with any of the men I used to like asking to the house. For quite a long while I did hear from my cook (Ruche), who settled at Saint-Laurent; but since leaving Jibuti I have had no word. Still, we were very pleased to know that you were happy, in good health and comfortably established at last. Life is a strange thing; but I remember you never gave up hope, and indeed you were quite right.

We were delighted with the photograph of you and your wife—it shows that you have been really successful. Who knows, perhaps one day we may come and see you! Events move faster than we do. We see from the photograph that you have excellent taste : Madame seems charming, and the hotel has a very agreeable look. My dear Papillon, you must forgive me for still using this nickname; but it brings back so many memories for us!

... So there you have some idea of our doings, old fellow. We often talk about you, you may be sure, and we still remember that stirring day when Mandolini poked his nose into a place he should have left alone.*

My dear Papillon, I enclose a photograph of both of us; it was taken at Marseilles, on the Canebière, about two months ago.

And so I leave you, with all kinds of good wishes and hoping to hear from you now and then.

---

* This was Bruet, the warder who found the raft in the grave in *Papillon*.

My wife and I send our kind regards to your wife and our best wishes to you.

A. Guibert-Germain

And following that, a few lines from Madame Guibert-Germain: 'With my best compliments on your success and kindest wishes to you both for the New Year. Greetings to my protégé.'

Madame Guibert-Germain never did join her husband in Indo-China. He was killed in 1952, so I never saw him again, that self-effacing medico who, together with Major Péan of the Salvation Army and a handful of others, was one of the very few men at the penal settlement who had the courage to stand up for humane ideas in favour of the convicts; and in his case, to succeed in getting some results while he was serving there. There are no words fine enough to express the respect due to people like him and his wife. In opposition to one and all and at the risk of his career, he maintained that a convict was still a man, and that even if he had committed a serious crime he was not lost for ever.

There were also the letters from Tante Ju. These were not the letters of a stepmother who has never known you, but real motherly letters, saying things that only a mother's heart could think of. Letters in which she told me about my father's life up until the time he died, the life of that law-abiding schoolmaster, full of respect for the legal authorities, who nevertheless cried out, 'My boy was innocent, I know it; and these swine have had him found guilty! Where can he be, now that he has escaped? Is he dead or alive?' Every time the members of the Resistance in the Ardèche brought off an operation against the Germans, he would say, 'If Henri were here, he would be with them.' Then the months of silence during which he no longer pronounced his son's name. It was as though he had transferred his affection for me to his grandchildren, whom he spoiled more than most grandfathers.

I devoured all this like a starving man. Rita and I read all these precious letters that renewed the links with my family over and over again and kept them like positive relics. Truly I was blessed by the gods—all my people without exception had enough love for me and enough courage not to give a damn for what people might say and to tell me of their joy that I was alive, free and happy. And indeed courage was necessary, because society has a hard heart and it does not easily forgive a family for having had a delinquent belonging to it.

1953: we sold the hotel. In time the shattering heat had got us down; and in any case Rita and I loved adventure, and we did not mean to spend the rest of our days in Maracaibo. All the more so as I'd heard of a tremendous boom in Venezuelan Guiana, where a mountain of almost pure iron had been discovered. It was at the other end of the country, so we were up and away for Caracas, meaning to stop there a while and look into the situation.

One fine morning we set off in my huge green De Soto brake, crammed with baggage, leaving behind us five years of quiet happiness and many friends.

And once again I saw Caracas. But was this really Caracas? Hadn't we hit on the wrong town?

At the end of Flamerich's term Perez Jimenez had himself named president of the republic; but even before that he had set about turning the colonial town of Caracas into a typical ultra-modern capital. All this during a period of unheard-of cruelty, both on the side of the government and the underground opposition. Caldera (who has been president since 1970) escaped from a shocking attempt on his life: a powerful bomb was thrown into the room where he was sleeping with his wife and a child. By an absolute miracle not one of them was killed; and with wonderful coolness—no shrieks, no panic —he and his wife just went down on their knees to thank God for having saved their lives.

But in spite of all the difficulties he had to deal with during his dictatorship, Perez Jimenez entirely transformed Caracas, and a good many other things too.

The old road from Caracas to the Maiquetia airfield and the port of La Guaira was still there. But Perez Jimenez had built a magnificent and technically outstanding motorway that meant you could get from the town to the sea in less than a quarter of an hour, whereas it had taken two hours by the old road. In the Silencio district Perez Jimenez ran up enormous buildings the size of those in New York. And he built an astonishing six-lane motorway right through the city from one end to the other—not to mention the building of working- and middle-class complexes that were models of urbanism, and many other changes. All this meant millions and millions of dollars swirling about; and it meant that a great deal of energy burst out in this country that had been dozing for hundreds of years. Foreign capital came flowing in, together with specialists of every kind. Life changed completely; immigration was wide open, and fresh blood came in giving a positive beat to the country's new rhythm.

I took the opportunity of our stop in Caracas to get in touch with friends and to find out what had happened to Picolino. These last years I had regularly sent people to visit him and take him a little money. I saw a friend who had given him a small sum from me in 1952, a sum he had asked for so as to go and settle in La Guaira, near the port. I'd often suggested that he should come and live with us at Maracaibo, but every time he replied through his friends that Caracas was the only place with doctors. It seemed that he had almost recovered his speech and that his right arm more or less worked. But now nobody knew what had become of him. He had been seen creeping about the port of La Guaira and then he had completely disappeared. Perhaps he had taken a ship back to France. I never knew; and I have always kicked myself for not having gone to Caracas earlier to persuade him to come to me in Maracaibo.

Everything was clear: if we couldn't find what we wanted in Venezuelan Guiana where there was this terrific boom and where General Ravard had just set about the overflowing virgin forest and its enormous rivers with dynamite to show they could be tamed, we would come back and settle in Caracas.

With the De Soto full of luggage, Rita and I drove to the capital of the state, Ciudad Bolivar, on the banks of the Orinoco. After eight years and more I found myself once more in that charming provincial town with its kindly, welcoming people.

We spent the night at a hotel, and we had scarcely sat down on the terrace for our morning coffee when a man stopped in front of us. A man of about fifty, tall, thin and sun-dried; he had a little straw hat on his head and he screwed up his small eyes until they almost disappeared.

'Either I'm crazy or you're a Frenchman called Papillon,' he said.

'You're not very discreet, mate. Suppose this lady here didn't know?'

'Excuse me. I was so surprised I didn't even notice I was talking like a fool.'

'Say no more about it: sit down here, with us.'

He was an old friend, Marcel B. We talked. He was quite amazed to see me in such good form; he felt I had succeeded in doing well for myself. I told him it had mostly been luck, a great deal of luck; he didn't have to tell me, poor soul, that he had not made a go of it—his clothes did the telling. I asked him to lunch.

After a few glasses of Chilean wine he said, 'Yes, Madame, although you see me like this, I was a fine upstanding type when I was young—afraid of nothing. Why, after my first break from penal I reached Canada, and there I joined the Canadian Mounted Police, no less! I might have stayed there all my life, but one day I had a fight, and the other guy fell right on to my knife. It's God's truth, Madame Papillon. This Canadian fell right on to my knife. You don't believe me, do you? Well, I knew the Canadian police wouldn't believe me either, so I made my getaway that very minute, and going by way of the United States, I reached Paris. I must have been sold by some sod or other, because they picked me up and sent me back to penal. That's where I knew your husband: we were good friends.'

'And what are you doing now, Marcel?'

'I grow tomatoes at Los Morichales.'

'Do they do well?'

'Not very. Sometimes the clouds don't let the sun come through properly. You know it's there, but you can't see it. But it sends down invisible rays that slay your tomatoes for you in a few hours.'

'Christ! How come?'

'One of the mysteries of nature, mate. I don't know anything about the cause, but the result, I know that all right.'

'Are there many ex-lags here?'

'About twenty.'

'Happy?'

'More or less.'

'Is there anything you need?'

'Papi, I swear if you hadn't said that I wouldn't have asked for a thing. But I can tell you're not doing so badly—so excuse me, Madame, but I'm going to ask for something very important.'

The thought flashed through my mind, 'God, don't let it cost too much,' and then I said, 'What do you need? Speak up, Marcel.'

'A pair of trousers, a pair of shoes, a shirt and a tie.'

'Come on: let's get into the car.'

'That's yours? Well, my cock, you have had luck.'

'Yes, plenty of luck.'

'When are you leaving?'

'Tonight.'

'Pity. Otherwise you could have driven the bridal pair in your bus.'

'What bridal pair?'

'Of course! I never told you the clothes were to go to the marriage of an ex-lag.'

'Do I know him?'

'Don't know. He's called Maturette.'

'What did you say? Maturette?'

'Right. What's so extraordinary about that? Is he an enemy of yours?'

'Not at all, a great friend.'

I couldn't get over it! Maturette! The little fairy who not only made it possible for us to escape from the Saint-Laurent-du-Maroni hospital but who also travelled fifteen hundred miles with us in a boat on the open sea.

No question of leaving now. The next day there we were at the wedding, when Maturette and a sweet little coloured girl were married. We could not do less than pay the bill and buy clothes for the three children they had produced before going to the altar. This was one of the few times when I was sorry I had not been christened, because that stopped me being his best man.

Maturette lived in a poor district where the De Soto made a

sensation, but still he did own a clean little brick house with a kitchen, a shower and a dining-room. He did not tell me about his second break and I did not tell him about mine. Just one reference to the past: 'With a little more luck, we'd have been free ten years earlier.'

'Yes, but our fates would have been different. I'm happy, Maturette; and you look pretty happy too.'

We parted, our throats tight with emotion, saying 'Au revoir,' and 'See you soon.'

As Rita and I drove on towards Ciudad Piar, a town springing up by a deposit of iron they were getting ready to exploit, I spoke about Maturette and the extraordinary ups and downs in life. He and I had been on the brink of death at sea a score of times; we had been captured and taken back to prison; and, like me, he had copped two years of solitary. And now, as she and I were driving in search of some new adventure, not only did I find him, but I found him on the eve of his marriage. And to both of us at the same moment there came this thought: 'The past doesn't mean a thing; all that matters is what you have made of yourself.'

At Ciudad Piar we found nothing suitable and we went back to Caracas to look for some business that was doing well.

Very soon we found one that answered both to our abilities and our purse. It was a restaurant called the Aragon, right next to the Carbobo park, a very beautiful spot, and it was changing hands: it suited us perfectly. The beginning was tough, because the former owners came from the Canaries and we had to change everything from top to bottom. We adopted half-French, half-Venezuelan menus and our customers increased in number every day. Among them were plenty of professional men, doctors, dentists, chemists and barristers. Some manufacturers, too. And in this pleasant atmosphere the months went by without incident.

It was on a Monday, at nine in the morning, that the wonderful news reached us: on 6 June 1956 to be exact. The Ministry of the Interior informed me that my request for naturalization had been granted.

Now came the great day: it was my reward for having spent ten years in Venezuela without the authorities finding anything to criticize in the life I had led as a future citizen. It was 5 July 1956, the national holiday. I was to go and swear loyalty to the flag of my new country, the country that accepted me knowing my past. There were three hundred of us there in front of the flag. Rita and Clotilde sat in the audience. Hard to say what I felt, there were so many ideas milling about in my head and so many emotions in my heart. I remembered what the Venezuelan nation had given me—both material and spiritual help, with never a word about my past. I remembered the legend of the Iano-Mamos, Indians who live on the Brazilian frontier, the legend that says they are the sons of Peribo, the moon. The great warrior Peribo was in danger of being killed by his enemies' arrows, and he leapt so high to escape from death that he rose far into the air, although he had been hit several times. He kept on rising, and from his wounds there fell drops of blood that turned into Iano-Mamos when they touched the ground. Yes, I thought about that legend, and I wondered whether Simon Bolivar, the liberator of Venezuela, had not also scattered his blood to give rise to a race of generous, open-hearted men, bequeathing to them the best of himself.

They played the national anthem. Everybody stood up. I stared hard at the starry flag as it rose and tears flowed down my cheeks.

I, who had thought I should never sing another national anthem in my life, I roared out the words of the anthem of my new country with the others, at the top of my voice—'*Abajo cadenas . . .*'—Down with the chains.

Yes, it was today and for ever that I really felt them drop off, the chains I had been loaded with. For ever.

'Swear loyalty to this flag, which is now your own.'

Solemnly all three hundred of us swore it; but I am very sure that the one who did so with most sincerity was myself, Papillon, the man his mother-country had condemned to a fate worse than death for a crime he did not commit. Yes, although France was the land that bore me, Venezuela was my haven.

Now events moved very rapidly. As a Venezuelan I could have a passport, and I got one right away. I trembled with emotion when they handed it to me. I trembled again when I fetched it from the Spanish embassy with an elegant three months' visa. I trembled when they stamped it as I went aboard the *Napoli*, the splendid liner that was taking Rita and me to Europe, to Barcelona. I trembled when the Guardia Civil gave it back to me in Spain, with the entrance visa. This passport, which had made me the citizen of a country once more, was so precious that Rita had sewn a zip-fastener on each of my inside coat pockets so that I could not lose it whatever happened.

Everything was beautiful during this voyage, even the sea when it was rough, even the rain when it came driving across the deck, even the ill-tempered guy in charge of the hold who unwillingly let me go below to make sure the big Lincoln we had just bought was properly stowed. Everything was beautiful because our hearts were on holiday. Whether we were in the dining-room, at the bar, in the saloon, and whether there were people around us or not, our eyes kept meeting so we could speak without anyone hearing. Because we were going to Spain, right up by the French border, and we were going for a reason I had not dared to hope for these many years. And my eyes said to Rita, 'Thank you, Minouche. It's thanks to you that I'm going to see *my people* again. And it's you who are taking me to them.'

And her eyes said, 'I promised you that if you trusted me, one day you would be able to go and embrace your family wherever you liked and whenever you liked, without having anything to fear.'

For the purpose of this hurriedly prepared voyage was to see my family once more, on Spanish territory out of reach of the French police. It was twenty-six years since I had seen them. We were going to spend a whole month together, and they were coming as my guests.

Day after day went by, and I often went into the bows,

spending a long time there, as though this part of the ship were closer to our destination. We had passed Gibraltar; we had lost sight of land again; we were getting very near.

I settled myself comfortably in a deckchair and my eyes tried to pierce the horizon where any minute now the land of Europe would appear. The land of Spain, joined to that of France.

1930-1956: twenty-six years. I was twenty-four then; I was fifty now. A whole lifetime. My heart beat violently when at last I made out the coast. The liner ran on fast, carving a huge V in the sea, a V whose far ends spread and spread until gradually they vanished and melted into the ocean.

When I left France aboard *La Martinière*, that accursed ship which was taking us to Guiana—yes, when she steamed away from the coast I did not see it: I did not see the land, *my land*, drawing gradually away from me and for ever (as I thought then), because we were in iron cages at the bottom of the hold.

And now today here was my new passport in the pocket of my yachtsman's blazer, well protected by Rita's zip—the passport of my new country, my other identity. 'Venezuelan? You, a Frenchman, born of French parents—of schoolteachers, and from the Ardèche into the bargain?'

I was perhaps five—when my grandfather Thierry bought me a beautiful mechanical horse. How splendid he was, my lovely stallion! Almost red; and such a mane! It was black, real horsehair, and it always hung down on the right-hand side. I pedalled so hard that, on the flat, our maid had to run to keep up with me; then she would push me up the little slope I called the hill; and so, after another stretch of flat, I reached the nursery school.

Mme Bonnot, the headmistress and a friend of Mama's, welcomed me in front of the school; she stroked the long curly hair that came down to my shoulders like a girl's and said to Louis, the caretaker, 'Open the door as wide as it will go so that Riri can ride in on his splendid horse.'

I pedalled with all my strength and flew into the playground. First I made a great sweep right round it and then I gently dismounted, holding the bridle so it would not roll away. I kissed Thérèse, the maid, who handed Mme Bonnot my sandwiches. And all the other boys and girls, my friends, came to admire and stroke this wonder, the one and only mechanical horse in these two little villages, Pont-d'Ucel and Pont-d'Aubenas.

Every day before I set out, Mama told me to lend it to each one in turn: this I found rather hard, but still I did it. When the bell rang, Louis the caretaker put the horse away under the lean-to, and once we were in line we marched into school, singing 'Nous n'irons plus au bois'.

I know my way of telling my story will make some people smile; but you have to understand that when I am talking about my childhood it is not a man of sixty-five who is writing but a kid—it is Riri of Pont-d'Ucel who writes, so deeply is that childhood imprinted on his mind, and he writes with the words he used then.

My childhood ... A garden with gooseberries that my sisters and I ate before they were ripe, and pears that we were forbidden to pick before Papa said we could; but by crawling like a Red Indian so that no one could see me from a window in the flat I had my fill from the pear tree, and a belly-ache afterwards.

I was eight, but still I would often go to sleep on my father's lap or in my mother's arms. Sometimes, when she tucked me into my little bed, I would half wake up, put my arms around her neck and hold her tight, and we would stay like that for what seemed to me a long, long time, our breath mingling; and at last I would go to sleep without knowing when she left me.

How beautiful Mama was! Tall, slim, always elegant. You ought to have seen how she played the piano, even when I knelt on a chair behind her music-stool and closed her eyes with my little hands. Wasn't it wonderful to have a Mama who could play the piano without seeing either the music or the keys? Besides, Mama was never meant to be a schoolmistress. My grandfather was very rich and Mama and her sister Léontine had been to the most expensive schools in Avignon. It was not Mama's fault that my grandfather Thierry had liked living high; her father was very kind, but because he had loved living so well, giving splendid parties in Avignon and meeting too many pretty farmers' wives, Mama had no dowry, and she was forced to earn her own living.

My grandfather was terrific. He had a little goatee and a snow-white moustache. Hand in hand we went round the farms in the morning, and as he was secretary of the *mairie* ('He has to earn his tobacco-money,' said Tante Léontine), he always had papers to take to the peasants or to fetch from their homes. I noticed how right my aunt was when she said he always lingered at a certain farm where the woman of the house was good-looking. I was delighted, because it was the only farm where they let me ride the little donkey and where I could meet Mireille, a girl of my age who was much better at playing papa and mama than the girl next door at Pont-d'Ucel.

Eight, and already I was beginning to play the fool. Secretly I went to swim in the Ardèche. I had learnt by myself in the canal; it was deep, but it was only five yards across. We had no bathing things, of course, so we bathed naked, seven or eight of us, all boys together. Oh, those sunny days in the water of my Ardèche! The trout we caught with our hands! I never went home until I was quite dry.

1914. The war, and Papa was called up. We went with him as far as the train. He was going with the *Chasseurs Alpins*, and he would soon be back. He said to us, 'Be good children and always obey your mother. And you girls must help with the housework, because she is going to look after both classes, mine and hers, all by herself. This war won't last long; everybody says so.' And standing there on the platform the four of us watched the train go, with my father leaning half out of the window to wave and to gaze at us a little longer. Those four years of war had no influence on our happiness at home. We drew a little closer to each other. I slept in the big bed with Mama; I took the place of my father, who was fighting at the front.

Four years in the history of the world is nothing. Four years for a kid of eight was an eternity.

I was growing fast; we played at soldiers and at battles. I would come home covered with bruises and my clothes torn, but whether I had won or lost I always came home happy, never crying. Mama bandaged the grazes and put raw meat on

215

a black eye. She would scold me a little, but gently, never shouting. Her reproaches were more like a whisper. 'Be kind, little Riri, your mama is tired. This class of sixty children is utterly exhausting. I am completely worn out, you see; it's more than I can manage. Darling, you must help me by being good and obedient.' It always ended with kisses and a promise to behave well.

Somebody was stealing our wood, stacked under the lean-to in the playground; and at night Mama was frightened. I cuddled close, putting my child's arm round her to make her feel that I was a protection. 'Don't be afraid, Mama; I'm the man of the house and I'm big enough to defend you.' I took down Papa's gun and slipped two buck-shot cartridges into it—he used them for wild boar. One night Mama woke up, shook me, and whispered in my ear, 'I heard the thieves. They made a noise, pulling out a log.' She was sweating.

'Don't be afraid, Mama.'

I got up very quietly, with the gun in my hands. With infinite care I opened the window; it squeaked a little and I held my breath. Then, pulling the shutter towards me with one hand, I unhooked it with the barrel; holding the butt against my shoulder, ready to fire on the thieves, I pushed the shutter. It opened without a sound. The moon lit up the courtyard as though it were day and I saw perfectly well that there was nobody at all in the playground. The heap of wood was still neatly arranged. 'There's no one, Mama; come and see.' And, clinging to one another, we both stayed at the window for some time, comforted by seeing there were no thieves and Mama happy at finding that her little boy was brave.

In spite of all this happiness, sometimes I would behave badly, although I did not want to hurt my adored mother; but I always believed, I always hoped, she would not know. A cat tied by the tail to a front-door bell; the water-bailiff's bicycle that we threw over the bridge into the Ardèche—he had gone down to the river to catch poachers fishing with a net. And other things ... Hunting birds with slings; and twice, when I was between ten and eleven, little Riquet Debannes and I went off into the country with Papa's gun to shoot a rabbit he had seen skipping about in a field. Getting the gun in and out of the house without my mother noticing, and twice at that, was a tremendous feat.

1917. Papa was wounded. He had many little shell-splinters in his head, but his life was not in danger. The news came by the Red Cross: a terrible shock. But no outcry; almost no tears. Twenty-four hours passed, Mama taught her class as usual—nobody knew a thing. I watched my mother, and I admired her. Normally I was in the front row in class; that day I sat at the back to keep an eye on all the pupils, determined to step in if any of them fooled about during lessons. By half past three Mama was at the end of her tether; I knew it, because we should have had natural science, but she went out, writing an arithmetic problem on the blackboard and saying, 'I must go out for a few minutes: do this sum in your arithmetic books.'

I went out after her; she was leaning against the mimosa just to the right of the gate. She was crying: my poor dear mama had given in.

I hugged her tight: and of course *I* did not cry. I tried to comfort her, and when she said to me, sobbing, 'Your poor papa is wounded,' just as if I did not know, my kid's heart found this reply, 'So much the better, Mama. This way the war is over for him and we can be sure he'll come back alive.' And all at once Mama realized that I was right.

'Why, that's perfectly true! You're quite right, darling; Papa will come back to us alive!'

A kiss on my forehead, a kiss on my cheek, and we went back to the classroom hand in hand.

The Spanish coast was quite visible, and I could make out the specks of white that must be houses. The coast was becoming more distinct, just like those holidays in 1917 that we spent at Saint-Chamas, where Papa had been sent to guard the powder-works. His wounds were not very serious, but the minute splinters could not be removed yet. He was classed as an auxiliary: no more front line for him.

We were all together again, full of happiness.

Mama was radiant: we had got right out of this horrible war; but for other people it was still going on, and she said to us, 'Darlings, you must not be selfish and spend all your days running about and picking jujubes; you must set aside three hours a day for thinking of others.'

So we went with her to the hospital, where every morning she looked after the patients and cheered them up. Each of us had to do something useful—push a badly-wounded man in his wheel-chair, lead a blind patient about, make lint, write letters or listen to what the men confined to bed had to say about their families.

It was when we were going home in the train that Mama felt so ill at Vogué. We went to my father's sister at Lanas, about twenty miles from Aubenas—to Tante Antoinette, who was a schoolmistress too. We were kept away from Mama, because the doctor's diagnosis was some unknown infectious disease, presumably caught when she was looking after the Indochinese at Saint-Chamas. My sisters went to the Aubenas high school as boarders and I to the boys' high school.

It seemed that Mama was getting better. But in spite of everything I was sad, and that Sunday I refused to go out for a walk with the others. I was alone, and I threw a knife at a plane tree; almost every time it stuck there in the bark.

That was how I was spending my time, in the road almost opposite the school, low-spirited and depressed. The road came up from the Aubenas station, some five hundred yards away. I heard a train whistle as it came in, and then again as it pulled out. I was not expecting anyone, so there was no point in looking down the road to see the people who had got out.

Tirelessly I threw my knife, on and on. My steel watch showed that it was five o'clock. The sun was low now, and it was getting in my eyes; so I changed sides. And it was then that I saw death coming silently towards me.

Death's messengers, their heads bowed, their faces hidden behind black crêpe veils almost down to the ground: I knew them well in spite of their funeral trappings—Tante Ontine, Tante Antoinette, my father's mother, and then behind them the men, as though they were using the women as a screen. My father, bent almost double, and my two grandfathers, all of them in black.

I did not go towards them; I did not stir; how could I have done so? My blood was all gone, my heart had stopped, my eyes so longed to weep they could not bring out a single tear. The group stopped more than ten yards from me. They were afraid—or rather they were ashamed: I knew it, I was certain of it, they would sooner be dead than face me and tell me what I already knew, because without having to utter a sound their black clothes told me 'Your mother has died.'

Who was with her? Nobody, since I, her greatest love, was not there. Dead and buried without my having seen her, dead without giving me a kiss. Papa was the first to come forward; he managed to stand almost straight. His poor face was a picture of the most desperate suffering and his tears fell without ceasing; still I did not move. He did not open his arms to me: he knew very well I could not stir. At last he reached me and embraced me without a word. Then at last I burst into tears as I heard the words, 'She died saying your name.' I fainted.

The war was over: Papa came home. A man called to see him; and they ate cheese and drank a few glasses of red wine. They numbered the dead of our region, and then the visitor said a dreadful thing: 'As for us, we came out of this war all right, eh, Monsieur Charrière? And your brother-in-law too. We may have won nothing, but at least we lost nothing either.'

I went out before he left. Night had fallen. I waited for him to go by and then I threw a stone with my sling, hitting him full on the back of the head. He went bellowing into a neighbour's house to have his wound dressed —it was bleeding. He did not understand who could have flung the stone at him, nor why. He had no idea that he had been struck for having forgotten the most important victim, the one whose loss could least be mended, in his list of the war-dead. My mother.

No, we had not come out of this accursed war all right: far from it.

And every year when term began again, I went back as a boarder to the high school at Crest, in the Drôme, where I was preparing for the entrance exam to the Aix-en-Provence *Arts et Métiers.**

At school I grew very tough and violent. At rugby I played scrum-half and I tackled hard: I asked no favours and I certainly gave none either.

* Roughly equivalent to a college of industrial design and engineering.

Six years now I had been a boarder at Crest, six years of being an excellent pupil, particularly in mathematics; but also six years with no marks for good behaviour. I was in all the roughest stuff that went on. Once or twice a month, always on Thursdays, I had a fight: but Thursday was the day the boys' parents came to see them.

The mothers came to take their sons out to lunch, and then if it was a fine afternoon, they would stroll about with their boys under the chestnut trees in our playground. Every week I swore I would not watch the sight from the library window; but it was no good, I just had to settle down in a place from where I could see everything. And from my window I discovered that there were two sorts of attitudes, both of which made me furiously angry.

There were some boys whose mothers were plain or badly dressed or who looked like peasants. Those fellows had the air of being ashamed of them, the swine, the dirty little sods! It was perfectly obvious. Instead of going right round the courtyard or walking from one end to the other, they would sit there on a bench in the corner and never move. They didn't want anyone to see their mother and they were hiding her; the sods had already got some idea of what educated, distinguished people were like, and they wanted to forget their origins before they were *Arts et Métiers* engineers.

It was not hard to pick a quarrel with that type. If I saw one send his embarrassing mother away early and come into the library, I would go for him at once. 'Say, Pierrot, why did you make your mother go so soon?'

'She was in a hurry.'

'That's not true. You're a liar: your mother takes the train for Gap at seven. I'll tell you why you sent her off: it's because you're ashamed of her. And don't you dare tell me that's not true, you sod!'

In these fights I nearly always came out on top. I fought so often that I became very good with my fists. Even when I got more than I gave, I didn't give a damn—I almost liked it. But I never went for a weaker boy.

The other kind that sent me into a rage, the kind I fought most savagely, were the ones I called the swaggerers. These were the fellows with pretty, well-dressed, distinguished mothers. When you are sixteen or seventeen you are proud of showing off a mother like that, and they would strut about the yard, holding her arm and mincing and simpering until it drove me mad.

Each time one of them had swaggered too much for my liking, or if his mother had a way of walking that reminded me of my own, or if she wore gloves and took them off and held them gracefully in one hand, then I could not bear it: I went out of my mind with fury.

The minute the culprit came in I went for him. 'You don't have to parade about like that, you big ape; not with a mother dressed in last year's fashions. Mine was better looking, brighter and more distinguished than yours. Her jewels were real, not phony like your mother's. Such trash! Even a guy who knows nothing about it can see that right away.'

Naturally, most of the types I spoke to like this didn't even wait for me to finish before hitting me in the face. Sometimes this first swipe would go right to my head. I fought rough: butting, cow-kicks, using my elbows in the in-fighting; and joy welled up inside me, as though I were smashing all the mothers who dared to be as pretty and fine-looking as my mama.

I really could not control it; ever since my mother's death when I was nearly eleven, I'd had this red-hot iron inside me. You can't understand death when you are eleven: you can't accept it. The very old might die, maybe. But your mother, an angel full of youth and beauty and health, how can she conceivably die?

It was because of a fight of this kind that my life changed completely.

This guy was a pretentious type, proud of being nineteen, proud of his success in maths. Tall, very tall; no good at games because he swotted all the time, but very strong. One day, when we were going for a walk, he lifted a massive tree-trunk all by himself so that we could get at the hole where a fieldmouse was hiding.

And this fellow had really let himself go that particular Thursday. A tall, slim mother, in a white dress with blue spots. If she had been trying to imitate one of Mama's dresses she couldn't have done better. Big black eyes; a pretty little hat with a white tulle veil.

And this engineer-to-be swaggered about the courtyard the whole of that afternoon, up and down, to and fro, round and round. Often they kissed; they were almost like lovers.

As soon as he was alone I started on him. 'Well, you're the wonder of the world, all right. You're as good at putting on a circus act as you are at maths. I didn't know you were such a ...'

'What's wrong with you, Henri?'

'What's wrong with me is that I just have to tell you that you show your mother like they show a bear in a circus, to amaze your buddies. Well, get this: I'm not amazed. Because your mother is just nothing at all compared with mine: she merely takes after the showy tarts I've seen during the season at Vals-les-Bains.'

'Take that back, or I'll spoil your face for you; and you know I hit hard. You know I'm stronger than you.'

'Trying to get out of it, eh? Listen: I know you're stronger than me. So to balance things, we'll have a duel. Each with compasses. Go and fetch yours and I'll fetch mine. If you're not a shit and if you can stand up for yourself, I'll be waiting for you behind the lavatories in five minutes.'

'I'll be there.'

A few minutes later he went down, my compass-point buried deep just under his heart.

I was seventeen when my father and I came out of the office of the examining magistrate in charge of my case. He had told my father that if he wanted to stop the proceedings he should make me join the navy. At the gendarmerie of Aubenas I signed on for three years.

My father did not really reproach me for the serious thing I had done. 'If I understand rightly, Henri,' he said—he called me Henri when he meant to be severe, 'and I believe what you say, you suggested fighting with a weapon because your opponent was stronger than you?'

'Yes, Papa.'

'Well, you did wrong. That is the way ruffians fight. And you are not a ruffian, my boy.'

'No.'

'Look at the mess you have got yourself into. Think of how you must have hurt your mother.'

'I don't think I hurt her.'

'Why not, Henri?'

'It was her I was fighting for.'

'What do you mean?'

'I mean I can't bear seeing other boys flaunt their mothers at me.'

'I will tell you something, Henri; it was not for your mama that this fight and all the others before it came about. It was not out of real love for her. The reason is that you are selfish; because fate had taken your mother from you, you would like it to be the same for all the other boys. I suffer too when another teacher comes to see me, arm in arm with his wife. I can't prevent myself from thinking of their happiness, of that happiness I too ought to have had. Only I am not jealous of them: on the contrary, I hope that nothing as horrible as what happened to me will happen to them.

'If you were really a reflection of your mother's heart, you would be happy at the happiness of others. Now, do you see, in order to get out of this you have to join the navy: three years at least, and they are not going to be easy ones. And I am going to be punished too, since for three years my son is going to be far away from me.' And then he said something that has always remained engraved on my heart: 'You know, my dear boy, you can become an orphan at any age. Remember that all your life.'

The *Napoli*'s siren made me jump. It wiped out that remote past, those pictures of my eighteenth year, when my father and I walked out of the gendarmerie where I had just enlisted. But immediately afterwards there rose up the unhappiest memory of them all, the moment when I saw him for the very last time.

It was in one of those grim visiting-rooms at the Santé prison—each in a barred box separated by a corridor a yard wide. I was racked by shame and disgust for what my life had been and for what had brought my father here into this wild-beast cage.

He had not come to reproach me for being suspect number

one in a dirty underworld job. He had the same ravaged face I had seen the day he told me of my mother's death, and he had come into this prison of his own accord to see his boy for half an hour, not to blame his bad behaviour nor to make him understand what this business meant for his family's honour and peace of mind, nor yet to say 'You are a bad son', but to beg my forgiveness for not having succeeded in bringing me up properly. What he said was the last thing I should ever have expected, the one thing that could touch my heart more deeply than all the reproaches in the world: 'I believe, Riri, that it is through my fault that you are here. Forgive me for having spoilt you too much.'

Nothing could have been more hostile than the iron discipline of the navy in 1923. The ratings were classed in six categories, according to their level of education. I was in the top, the sixth. And this seventeen-year-old boy, just out of the class preparing for the *Arts et Métiers*, could not understand or adapt himself to blind, instant obedience to orders given by quartermasters belonging to the lowest intellectual level.

I was in trouble right away. I could not obey orders that had no rhyme or reason. I refused to go on any specialized course, the normal thing for a man with my education, and I was at once classed among the *estrasses*, the undisciplined, the no-good 'unspecialized' types.

We were the ones who had all the nastiest, dullest, stupidest jobs. The potato-peeling fatigues, the heads, brass to polish all day long, the coaling, washing the decks: all for us.

'What the hell are you doing there, hiding behind the funnel?'

'We have finished washing the deck, quartermaster.'

'Is that right? Well, just you start again, and this time wash it from aft forward. And if it's not cleaner this go, you'll hear from me.'

A sailor is a fine sight, with his pompon, his jersey with its wide blue collar, his slightly tilted cap as flat as a pancake and his uniform made to fit properly. But we good-for-nothings were not allowed to have our things re-cut. The worse we were dressed and the drearier we looked, the better the quartermasters were pleased. In an atmosphere like this the awkward types never stopped thinking up quite serious offences. Every time we were alongside a quay, for example, we stole ashore and spent the night in the town. Where did we go? To the brothels, of course. With a friend or two I would fix things in no time at all. Right away we each had our tart: we not only made love for free, but she would also give us a note or two for a drink or a meal.

The punishments became more frequent. Fifteen days' detention; then thirty. To get our own back on a cook who refused us a bit of meat and a crust after the potatoes fatigue, we stole a whole leg of mutton, done to a turn, fishing it out with a hook we slid down a ventilator over the stove when he had his back turned: we ate it in the coal-bunker. Result: forty-five days in the naval prison; and there I was without a stitch in the Toulon prison-yard in midwinter opposite the wash-house with its huge basin of icy water into which we had to plunge.

It was a seaman's cap not worth ten francs that brought me up before the disciplinary board. Charge: destruction of naval property.

In the navy, everybody changed the shape of his cap. Not to destroy it—it was a question of being well turned out. You first wetted it, and then three of you would pull as hard as possible, so that when you put a piece of whalebone round inside it was as flat as a pancake. 'It's smashing, a right flat cap,' said the girls. Particularly a cap with a pretty carrot-coloured pompon on it, carefully trimmed with scissors. All the girls in the town knew it brought good luck to touch a pompon, and that you had to pay for touching it with a kiss.

The master-at-arms was a thick-headed brute—I became his pet aversion. He never left me in peace; he kept after me night and day. So much so that three times I went absent without leave. But never more than five days and twenty-three hours, because at six days you were put down as a deserter. And a deserter I very nearly was at Nice. I'd spent the night with a terrific girl and woke up late. One more hour and I should have been on the list. I scrambled into my clothes and left at a run, looking for a cop to get myself arrested. I caught sight of one, hurried over to him and asked him to arrest me. He was a fat, kindly old soul. 'Come now, boy, don't fly into a panic. Just you go back quietly to your ship and tell them all about it. We've all been young once.'

I told him one hour more and I was a deserter; but it was no good, he wouldn't listen. So I picked up a stone, turned to a shop window and said to the cop, 'If you don't arrest me, I'll smash this window in one second flat.'

'The boy's crazy. Come along, young fellow; the station for you.'

But it was for having stretched a cap to make it prettier that they sent me to the disciplinary sections at Calvi, in Corsica. No one can doubt that this was the first step towards the penal settlement.

They called the disciplinary section *la camise*, and you had a special uniform. As soon as you got there you went in front of a reception committee, and they decided whether you were to be rated a genuine *camisard*. You had to prove you were a man by fighting two or three seniors one after another. With my training at the Crest high school, it passed off pretty well. During the second fight, when my lip was split and my nose a bleeding mess, the seniors stopped the test. I was rated genuine *camisard*.

La camise. I worked in a Corsican senator's vineyards. From sunrise to sunset: no break, no little presents; the difficult types had to be brought to heel. We weren't even sailors any more: we belonged to the 173 Infantry Regiment at Bastia. I can still see that citadel at Calvi, our three-mile walk, pick or shovel on our shoulder, to Calenzana, where we worked, and our quick-march back to the prison. It was unendurable, we rebelled, and as I was one of the ringleaders, I was sent, along with a dozen others, to a still tougher disciplinary camp at Corte.

A citadel right up on top of the mountain: six hundred steps to go up and down twice a day to work at making a sports ground for the enlisted men near the station.

It was when I was in that hell, with that herd of brutes, that a civilian from Corte secretly passed me a note: 'Darling, if you want to get out of that horrible place, cut off your thumb. The law is that the loss of a thumb, with or without preservation of the metacarpal, automatically brings about transfer to the auxiliaries; but if this injury is caused by an accident in the course of duty, it brings about permanent incapacity for armed service and therefore discharge. Law of 1831, circular of 23 July 1883. I am waiting for you. Clara. Address, Le Moulin Rouge, Quartier Réservé, Toulon.'

I did not delay. Our work consisted of digging about two cubic yards of earth out of the mountain every day and wheeling it off in barrows for fifty yards to a place where trucks took away everything that was not needed for levelling the ground. We worked in teams of two. I must not cut off my thumb with an edged tool, or I should be accused of self-mutilation, and that would cost me another five years of *camise*.

My Corsican mate, Franqui, and I started on the mountain at the bottom, and we dug a fair-sized cave into it. One more blow with the pick and everything above would fall in on me. The supervising NCOs were tough: Sergeant Albertini was always there, just two or three yards behind us. This made the job tricky, but there was this advantage—if all went well, he would be an impartial witness.

Franqui put a big stone with a fairly sharp edge under an overhanging piece; I laid my thumb on it and stuffed my handkerchief into my mouth so as not to let out the least sound. There would be five or six seconds for us to bring the whole mass of earth down on me. Franqui was going to smash my thumb with another stone weighing about twenty pounds: it could not fail. They would be forced to amputate it even if the blow did not take it off entirely.

The sergeant was three yards away from us, scraping earth off his boots. Franqui grasped the stone, lifted it up as high as it would go and brought it down. My thumb was a shattered mess. The sound of the blow mingled with the noise of the pickaxes all round and the sergeant saw nothing. Two swings with the pick and the earth came down all over me. I let myself be buried. Bellowing, shouts for help: they dug for me and at last I appeared, covered with earth and my thumb destroyed. And I was suffering like a soul in hell. Still, I did manage to say to the sergeant, 'They'll say I did it on purpose: you see.'

'No, Charrière. I saw the accident: I'm a witness. I'm tough but I'm fair. I'll tell them what I saw, never you fear.'

Two months later, discharged with a pension and with my thumb buried at Calvi, I was transferred to the No. 5 Depot at

Toulon, and there they let me go.

I went to say thank you to Clara at the Moulin Rouge. She was of the opinion that nobody would even notice the missing thumb on my left hand, and that I could make love as well with four fingers as with five. That's what really mattered.

'You've changed in some way, Riri. I can't quite tell how. I hope your three months with those undesirables have not left too many traces.'

There I was with my father in my childhood home: I had hurried back after my discharge. Was there some deep change in me? 'I can't tell you, Papa: I don't know. I think I'm more violent and less willing to obey the rules of life you taught me when I was a little boy. You must be right: something has changed in me. I feel it, being here in this house where we were so happy with Mama and my sisters. It doesn't hurt as much as it used to. I must have grown harder.'

'What are you going to do?'

'What do you advise?'

'Find a position as soon as possible. You're twenty now, my boy.'

Two exams. One at Privas for the post office; the other at Avignon for a civilian job in the military administration. Grandfather Thierry went with me.

Both the written and the oral parts went very well. I was playing the game: I had no objection to following my father's advice—I'd be a civil servant. It would be a proper, honourable life. But I can't help wondering how long the young Charrière would have stayed a civil servant with everything that was boiling up inside him.

When the morning post brought the results of the exam, my delighted papa decided to have a little party in my honour. A huge cake, a bottle of real champagne and a colleague's daughter invited to the feast. 'She would make a fine wife for my boy.' For the first time for ten years, the house bubbled with joy.

I walked round the garden with the girl Papa dreamed of as a daughter-in-law, a girl who might make his little boy happy. She was pretty, well brought up and very intelligent.

Two months later, the bombshell! 'Since you have not been

able to provide our central office with a good-conduct certificate from the navy, we regret to inform you that you cannot enter our service.'

After the letter came, shattering all his illusions, Papa was sad, saying very little. He was suffering.

Why go on like this? Quick, a suitcase and a few clothes: let's take advantage of the teachers' meeting at Aubenas and get out.

My grandmother caught me on the stairs. 'Where are you going, Henri?'

'I'm going somewhere where they won't ask me for a good-conduct certificate from the navy. I'm going to see one of the men I knew in the disciplinary sections at Calvi, and he will teach me how to live outside this society I was still stupid enough to believe in—a society that knows very well I can expect nothing from it. I'm going to Paris, to Montmartre, Grandmother.'

'What are you going to do?'

'I don't know yet, but certainly no good. Good-bye, Grandmother. Give Papa a big kiss from me.'

The land was coming very close, and now we could even see the windows of the houses. I was coming back to it after a very, very long journey to see my people: to see them after twenty-six years.

What were they like? For them, I was dead; for their children, I had never existed—my name had never been pronounced. Or perhaps just a few times, when they were alone with Papa. It was only during these last five years that they must gradually have given their kids some idea of Uncle Henri, who lived in Venezuela.

We had corresponded for five years; letters are all very well, but won't they be afraid of what people might say? Won't they feel rather nervous about meeting an escaped ex-convict of a brother at a rendezvous in Spain?

I did not want them to come out of duty; I wanted them to come with their hearts full of genuine feeling for me.

Ah, but if they only knew ... If they only knew—the coast was coming nearer slowly now, but how it had raced away from me twenty-six years ago—if they only knew how I had been with them all the time during those thirteen years of prison!

If only my sisters could see all the visions of our childhood I had made for myself in the cells and the wild-beast cages of the Réclusion!

If only they knew how I kept myself going with them and with all those who made up our family, drawing from them the strength to beat the unbeatable, to find peace in the midst of despair, to forget being a prisoner, to reject suicide—if they only knew how the months, days, hours, minutes and seconds of those years of total solitude and utter silence had been filled to overflowing with the smallest events of our wonderful childhood!

The coast drew nearer and nearer; we saw Barcelona; we were about to enter its harbour. I had a wild desire to cup my hands and shout, with all my strength, 'Hey there! I'm coming! Come as fast as you can!' just as I used to call out to them when we were children in the fields of Fabras and I had found a great patch of violets.

'What are you doing here, darling? I've been looking for you this last hour. I even went down to the car.'

Without getting up I put my arm round Rita's waist; she bent down and gave me a little kiss on the cheek. It was only then that I realized that although I was going to meet my people full of self-questioning and full of questions to ask as well, there in my arms was my own private family, the family that I had founded and that had brought me to this point. I said, 'Darling, I was living over the past again as I watched the land come closer, the land that holds my people, the living and the dead.'

Barcelona: our gleaming car on the quay with all the baggage neatly in the boot. We did not stay the night in the great city; we were impatient to drive on through the sunlit countryside towards the French frontier. But after two hours my feelings overcame me so that I had to pull in to the side of the road—I could not go on.

I got out of the car: my eyes were dazzled with looking at this landscape, these ploughed fields, huge plane trees, trembling reeds, the thatched or tiled roofs of the farms and cottages, the poplars singing in the wind, the meadows with every possible shade of green, the cows with the bells tinkling as they grazed, the vines—ah, the vines with their leaves that could not hide all the grapes. This piece of Catalonia was exactly the same as all my French garden-like landscapes: all this was mine and always had been ever since I was born; it was among these same colours, these same growing things, these same crops that I had wandered hand in hand with my grandfather; it was through fields like these that I had carried my father's game-bag the days when he went shooting and when we urged on our bitch Clara to start a rabbit or flush a covey of partridges. Even the fences round the farms were the same as they were at home! And the little irrigation canals with their planks set across here and there to guide the water into one field or another: I did not have to go up to them to know there were frogs that I could bring out, as many as I wanted, with a hook baited with a piece of red cloth, as I had done so often as a child.

And I quite forgot that this vast plain was Spanish, so exactly was it like the valley of the Ardèche or the Rhône.

So there on the road between Barcelona and Figueras I began to sob. For a long time my tears flowed, until gently, very gently, Rita's hand stroked my neck and she said to me, 'Let us thank God for having brought us this far, so near to your France and only two or three days from meeting your own people.'

We stopped at the hotel nearest the French frontier. The next day Rita took the train to fetch Tànte Ju from Saint-Peray. I should have gone myself, but for the French police I was still a man who had escaped from Guiana. While Rita was away I found a very fine house at Rosas, right on the edge of the beach.

A few more minutes of waiting, Papi, and then you will see Tante Ju step out of the train, the woman who loved your father, and who wrote you such beautiful letters, bringing back to life your memories of those who loved you and whom you loved so much.

It was Rita who got out first. As carefully as a daughter, she helped her tall companion to climb down to the platform. And then two big arms enfolded me, two big arms pressed me to her bosom, two big arms conveying the warmth of life and a thousand things that cannot be expressed in words. And it was with one arm round Rita and the other round my second mother that we walked out of the station, quite forgetting that suitcases do not come with their owners unless they are carried.

It was eleven in the morning when Rita and Tante Ju arrived, and it was three the next morning when Tante Ju went to her bedroom, worn out by the journey, by her age, by emotion and by sixteen hours of uninterrupted exchange of memories; and it was there, when I went to say good-night, that she fell asleep in the hollow of my arm, her face as peaceful as a child's.

I fell into my bed and went straight to sleep, exhausted, without a breath of energy to keep me awake. The outburst of too great happiness is as shattering as the worst disaster.

My two women were up before me, and it was they who pulled me out of my deep sleep to tell me it was eleven in the morning, that the sun was shining, the sky blue, the sand warm, that breakfast was waiting for me and that I should eat it quickly so as to go to the frontier to fetch my sister and her tribe, who were to be there in two hours' time. 'Rather earlier,' said Tante Ju, 'because your brother-in-law will have been forced to drive fast, to prevent the family bullying him, they are so eager to see you.'

I parked the Lincoln right next to the Spanish frontier post.

Here they were! They were on foot, running—they had abandoned my brother-in-law back there in the queue by the French customs in his Citroën.

First came my sister Hélène, her arms out. She ran across the stretch of no-man's-land from the one post to the other, from France to Spain. I went towards her, my guts tied up with emotion. At four yards we stopped to look one another right in the face. Our tear-dimmed eyes said 'It is really her, my childhood Nène,' and 'It is really him, my little brother Riri from long ago.' And we flung ourselves into each other's arms. Strange. For me this fifty-year-old sister was as she had always been. I did not see her aging face; I saw nothing except that the brilliant animation of her eyes was still the same and that for me her features had not altered.

Our embrace lasted so long we forgot all about the others. Rita had already kissed the children. I heard, 'How pretty you are, Aunt!' and I turned, left my Nène and thrust Rita into her arms, saying, 'Love her dearly, because it is she who has brought me to you all.'

My three nieces were splendid and my brother-in-law was in great form. The only one missing was his eldest boy, Jacques, who had been called up for the war in Algeria.

We left for Rosas, the Lincoln in front, with my sister at my side. I shall never forget that first meal, with us all sitting at a round table. There were times when my legs trembled so that I had to take hold of them under the cloth.

1930–1956. So many, many things had happened, both for them and for me. Such a length of road, such a struggle to reach this point, and so many obstacles to overcome! I did not talk about the penal settlement during the meal. I just asked my brother-in-law whether my being found guilty had caused them a great deal of trouble and unpleasantness. He reassured me kindly, but I could feel how much they must have suffered, having a convict as brother and brother-in-law. 'We never doubted you, and you can be quite certain that even if you had been guilty we should only have been sorry for you; we would never have renounced you.'

No, I said nothing about penal, and I said nothing about my trial. For them and, I sincerely believe, for me too, my life began the day when, thanks to Rita, I buried my old self, the man out on the loose, to bring Henri Charrière back to life, the son of the Ardèche schoolteachers.

That August on the sands of Rosas beach went by too fast. I rediscovered the cries of my childhood, the laughter with no cause, the outbursts of joy of my young days on the beach of Palavas, where we used to go with my parents.

One month: thirty days. How long it is in a cell alone with oneself, and how terribly short it is with one's own people. I was literally drunk with happiness. Not only had I my sister and my brother-in-law again, but I had also discovered new people to love—my nieces, unknown only the other day, and now almost daughters to me.

Rita was radiant with joy at seeing me so happy. Bringing

us together at last, out of reach of the French police, was the finest present she could have given either them or me. I lay on the beach; it was very late—midnight, perhaps. Rita was stretched out on the sand too, with her head against my thigh; I stroked her hair. 'They all fly away tomorrow. How quickly it has passed; but how wonderful it was! One must not ask too much, darling, I know; but still, I'm sad at having to part from them. God knows when we'll see one another again. A journey like this costs so much.'

'Trust in the future: I'm sure we'll see them again one day.'

We went with them as far as the frontier. They were taking Tante Ju in their car. A hundred yards from the French border we parted. There were no tears, because I told them of my faith in the future—in a couple of years we should spend not one month of holiday together but two.

'Is it true, what you say, Uncle?'

'Of course, darlings, of course.'

A week later my other sister landed at Barcelona airport, by herself. She had not been able to bring her family. Among the forty-odd passengers coming out of the plane I recognized her at once, and after she had passed through the customs she came straight towards me without the least hesitation.

Three days and three nights—she could spend only a little while with us, so since we did not want to lose a minute, it was three days and three nights of memories almost without a pause. She and Rita liked one another at once, so we could tell one another everything—she her whole life-story and me all that could be told.

Two days later Rita's mother arrived from Tangiers. With her two fine, gentle hands on my cheeks she kissed me tirelessly, saying, 'My son, I am so happy that you love Rita and that she loves you.' Her face shone with a serene beauty in its halo of white hair.

We stayed in Spain too long, our happiness hiding the days that passed. We could not go back by boat—sixteen days was more than we could spare—so we flew (the Lincoln coming later by ship), because our business was waiting.

Still, we did make a little tour of Spain, and there in the hanging gardens of Granada, that wonder of the Arab civilization, I read these words of a poet, cut into the stone at the foot of the Marador tower: *Dale limosna, mujer, que no hay en la vida nada como la pena de ser ciego en Granada.* Give him alms, woman, because there is no greater sadness in life than being blind in Granada.

Yes, there is something worse than being blind in Granada, and that is being twenty-four, full of health and trust in life, undisciplined maybe and even not very honest, but not really corrupted through and through or at least not a killer, and to hear yourself condemned to a life-sentence for another man's crime: a sentence that means vanishing for ever without appeal, without hope, condemned to rot bodily and mentally, without having one chance in a hundred thousand of ever raising your head and of being a man again some day.

How many men whom a pitiless justice and an inhuman penitentiary system have crushed and destroyed inch by inch would have preferred to be blind in Granada! *I am one of those men.*

14: The Revolution

THE plane we had boarded at Madrid came down gently at Maiquetia, the Caracas airport, and there was our daughter waiting for us, together with some friends. Twenty minutes later we were back home. The dogs welcomed us enthusiastically, and our Indian maid, who was one of the family, never stopped asking, 'And how are Henri's people, Señora? And Henri, what did you think of Rita's mama? I was afraid you would never come back, with all those people over there to love you. Thanks be to God, here you are, all in one piece.'

The struggle for life went on. We sold the restaurant: I had begun to have enough of steak and chips, *canard à l'orange* and *coq au vin*. We bought an all-night joint, the Caty-Bar.

In Caracas an all-night bar is a place where the customers are all men, because it has its own girls to keep them company, talk to them and even more listen to them, drink with them, and if they are not very thirsty, help them on a little. It's quite a different kind of life from that of the day, much more intense and not in the least peaceful; but it is one where every night you discover something new and interesting.

Senators, deputies, bankers, lawyers, officers and high officials hurried in at night to let off the steam that had piled up during the day, when they had to keep a hold on themselves and put out an image of perfectly virtuous behaviour in their various jobs. And at the Caty-Bar each one showed himself as he really was. It was a bursting out, a throwing off of the social hypocrisy they were forced to observe, a refuge from business or family worries.

For these few hours every single one of them grew young again. With alcohol lending them a hand, they threw off their social chains and started right in on a life that left them free to shout and argue and play the Don Juan with the prettiest girls in the bar. In our place things never went farther than that, because Rita ran the bar very strictly and no woman was allowed out during working hours. But all the men enjoyed the presence of these girls who were kind enough to listen when they talked (they loved that) and to fill their hours of freedom with their beauty and their youth.

How often I have seen them at daybreak, all alone (because the girls left by another door), but nevertheless happy and easier in their minds. One was an important businessman and he was always at his desk by nine; he was a regular customer, and I used to walk to his car with him. He would put his hand on my shoulder, and waving the other arm towards the mountains of Caracas, sharp against the early-morning sky, he would say, 'The night is over, Enrique; the sun is going to rise behind the Avila. No hope of going anywhere else—everything is shut; and with the daylight we come face to face with our responsibilities. Work, the office, the slavery of every day is waiting for me; but how could we go on without these nights?'

Very soon I had another place, the Madrigal, and then a third, the Normandy. Together with Gonzalo Durand, a Socialist and an opponent of the régime who was ready night and day to defend the interests of night-club, bar and restaurant owners, we formed an association for the protection of places of this kind. Some time later I was made president, and we defended our members as well as we could against the abuses of certain officials.

I turned the Madrigal into a Russian joint, calling it the Ninoska; and by way of adding to the local colour I dressed a Spaniard from the Canaries as a Cossack and perched him on a horse, a peaceful horse, because of its great age. The two of them were to act as porters. But the customers started giving the Cossack drinks—he was bored stiff at half a dollar an hour—and, what was worse, they did not forget the horse either. Naturally, the horse didn't knock back glasses of whisky, but it dearly loved sugar dipped in spirits, particularly kummel. Result: when the old horse was drunk and the Cossack tight as a drum, they would tear off down our street, the Avenida Miranda, an important artery crammed with traffic, galloping right and left, the Spaniard shrieking 'Charge! Charge!' You can just imagine the scene: brakes jammed on so hard they almost tore up the asphalt, cars banging into one another, drivers bawling, windows opening and angry voices shouting about the din at that time of night.

To top it all, although I had only a single musician, he was not one of the ordinary kind. He was a German called Kurt Lowendal; he had a boxer's hands and he played the cha-cha on his organ with such zeal that the walls trembled even up to the ninth floor. I could hardly believe it, but the concierge and the owner took me up with them one evening to see: and it was no exaggeration.

My other joint, the Normandy, was really beautifully placed —right opposite the police headquarters. On one side of the street, terror and grilling, and on the other the gaiety of life. For once I was on the right side. Not that that prevented me from making things tricky for myself: I did the most dangerous thing I could—I acted as a secret letter-box for the prisoners, both political and criminal.

1958. For some months now things had been on the move in Venezuela: Perez Jimenez's dictatorship was limping badly. Even the privileged classes were dropping away from him, and the only supporters he had left were the army and the *Seguridad Nacional*, the terrible political police, who were making more and more arrests.

Meanwhile in New York the three most important political leaders, all in exile, had worked out their plan for seizing power. These were Raphael Caldera, Jovito Vilalba and Romulo Bétancourt. On 1 January an airforce general, Castro Leon, tried to get his men to rise, and a small group of pilots dropped a few bombs on Caracas, particularly on Perez Jimenez's presidential palace. The operation failed, and Castro Leon fled to Colombia.

But at two o'clock in the morning of 23 January a plane flew over Caracas. It was Perez Jimenez going off with his family, his closest associates and part of his fortune—a cargo of such value in people and wealth that the Venezuelans christened the plane 'the holy cow'. Perez Jimenez knew he had lost the game —the army had abandoned him, after ten years of dictatorship. His plane flew straight to San Domingo, where another dictator, General Trujillo, could only welcome his colleague.

For close on three weeks there were no police in the streets. Of course, there was pillaging and scenes of violence, but only against Perez Jimenez's supporters. It was a nation bursting out after having been muzzled for ten years. The *Seguridad Nacional*'s headquarters, opposite the Normandy, was attacked and most of its members killed.

During the three days that followed the departure of Perez Jimenez I very nearly lost the result of twelve years' work. Several people telephoned to tell me that all the bars, night-clubs, luxury restaurants and places frequented by the top sup-porters of Perez Jimenez were being broken into and sacked. We had our flat on the floor above the Caty-Bar. It was a little villa at the bottom of a blind alley, with the bar at street-level, then our living-quarters and then a flat roof over that.

I was determined to defend my house, my business and my people. I got hold of twenty bottles of petrol, made them into Molotov cocktails and lined them up neatly on the roof. Rita would not leave me: she was at my side with a lighter in her hand.

Here they came! A crowd of men, pillagers: more than a hundred of them. Since the Caty-Bar was in a blind alley, if anyone came along it, it meant they were coming to us.

They came closer and among the shouts I heard 'This is one of the Perezjimenists' places! Sack it!' They broke into a run, waving iron bars and shovels. I lit the lighter.

Suddenly the crowd halted. Four men with their arms stretched out were strung across the alley: they stopped the over-excited mob. I heard, 'We are workers, we belong to the people, and we are revolutionaries too. We've known these people for years. Enrique, the boss, is a Frenchman, and he's a friend of the people—he's proved it to us hundreds of times. Get out, there's nothing for you to do here.'

And they began to argue, but more quietly; and I heard these splendid men explain why they were defending us. It lasted a good twenty minutes, with Rita and me still on the roof, holding the lighter. The four must have persuaded them to leave us in peace, because the mob withdrew without any threats.

Lord, that was a close one! A close one for a good many of them, too, I may say. None of them ever came back.

These four men of the people, our defenders, worked for the Caracas Water Company. And it so happened that the side door of the Caty-Bar, down at the bottom of the alley, was right next to the entrance to the company's depot, the gate the tankers used when they went to supply places that were short of water. We often gave the men who worked there something to eat, and if they came for a bottle of Coke we said there was nothing to pay. Because of the dictatorship they almost never talked politics, but sometimes, when they had had a drink, a few would let out an incautious word—it was overheard and reported. Then they were either imprisoned or sacked.

Often either Rita or I had been able to get one of our customers to have the culprit let out or given back his job. In any case, among the senators, deputies and officers belonging to the régime, a good many were very kind and obliging. There were few who would not do a favour.

On that day the Water Company's men paid their debt to us, and they paid it with very great courage, because the mob was in no laughing mood. And the most extraordinary thing was that the same miracle happened for our two other places. Not a pane of glass smashed at the Ninoska. Nothing, absolutely nothing destroyed and nothing stolen at the Normandy, right opposite the terrible *Seguridad Nacional*, the hottest spot of the whole revolution, with machine guns firing in all directions and revolutionaries burning and pillaging the shops right, left and centre all along the Avenida Mejico.

Under Perez Jimenez, nobody had argued; nobody had done anything but obey. The press was muzzled.

Under his successor Admiral Larrazabal, everybody danced, sang, disobeyed to their heart's content, spoke or wrote anything that came into their heads, drunk with joy at being able to talk balls in total freedom with the accelerator right down.

The sailor was a poet into the bargain, an artist at heart, sensitive to the wretched position and the poverty of the thousands of people who came flooding into Caracas, wave after wave of them, as soon as the dictator had fallen. He thought up the Emergency Plan, which handed out millions to these unfortunate souls from the national funds.

He promised that there should be elections. He was dead straight, and he prepared them very fairly; but although the Admiral got in at Caracas, it was Bétancourt who won the election. Bétancourt had to face up to a tricky situation—not a

240

single day without some plot being hatched, not a single day without having to win a battle against the forces of reaction.

I had just bought the biggest café in Caracas, the Grand Café in the Sabana Grande: over four hundred seats. This was the café where Julot Huignard, the hammer-man of Lévy's jewellery shop, had said we should meet when we were in the corridor of the Santé way back in 1931. 'Keep your spirits up, Papi! We'll meet at the Grand Café in Caracas.' Here was I at the rendezvous. Twenty-eight years later, to be sure, but still here—and I owned it. But Huignard had not kept the appointment.

The political state of the country did not make Bétancourt's job an easy one. A vile, cowardly attempt on his life suddenly upset the still youthful democracy. Under the remote control of Trujillo, the dictator of San Domingo, a car stuffed with explosives went off right by the president as he was driving to an official ceremony. The head of the military household was killed, the chauffeur very badly wounded, General Lopez Henriquez and his wife horribly burnt, and the president himself had his forearms dreadfully injured by the flames. Twenty-four hours later, with his hands bandaged, he addressed the Venezuelan nation. It seemed so unbelievable that some people claimed that the man who spoke was his double.

In such an atmosphere Venezuela too, though blessed by the gods, began to be attacked by the virus of political passion. There were cops everywhere, and among the officials, there were some who made evil use of their political connections.

Officials belonging to different ministries came and badgered me many times. Inspectors of every kind appeared: inspectors of drinks, of municipal taxes, of this and of that. Most of them had received no training and they only had the job because they belonged to some political party or other.

What's more, since the government knew about my past, and since I was inevitably in contact with various bent types who passed through even though I lived honestly and had nothing to do with them in the way of business, and since on top of that I had been granted asylum here, while proceedings against me were still in force in France, the pigs took advantage of my position to carry out a kind of blackmail, playing on my past. For example, they dug up the murder of a Frenchman two years back, in which the killer had never been found. Did I know anything about it? I knew nothing? Wasn't it in my interest, considering my position, to know a little?

Oh, this was beginning to be a splendid party, this was. I had had about enough of these bastards. It might not be very serious for the moment, but if it went on and I blew up, God knows what would happen. No, no blowing up here, not in this country that had given me my chance of being a free man once more and of making a home for myself.

There was no point in going round and round the mulberry bush: I sold the Grand Café and the other joints, and Rita and I went off to Spain. Maybe I'd be able to start some kind of business there.

But I could not manage to get going. The European countries are too well organized. In Madrid, when I had obtained the first thirteen permits to open a business, they kindly told me I needed a fourteenth. It seemed to me that was just one too many. And Rita, seeing that I was literally incapable of living far from Venezuela and that I missed even the sods who badgered me, agreed that although we had sold everything, we should go back there.

15: *Camarones*

CARACAS once more. This was 1961, and sixteen years had passed since El Dorado. Night-life had changed a great deal in Caracas, and buying a joint as healthy, good-looking and important as the one I'd sold, the Grand Café, was impossible to find and even more impossible to build up. And then again there was a ridiculous law that the people who had bars and sold alcoholic drinks corrupted public morals: this meant all kinds of abuses and exploitation on the part of certain officials, and I didn't want to get back into that racket at all.

Something else was needed. I discovered not a mine of diamonds but a mine of very big prawns, the kind called *camarones*, and of even bigger ones called *langostinos*. And all this was back at Maracaibo once again.

We settled down in an elegant flat: I bought a stretch of shore and founded a company called the Capitan Chico, after the district that included my beach. Sole share-holder, Henri Charrière; managing director, Henri Charrière, director of operations, Henri Charrière; chief assistant, Rita.

And here we were, launched into an extraordinary adventure. I bought eighteen fishing-boats. They were big craft, each with a fifty-horsepower outboard and a net five hundred yards long. A crew of five to each boat. As one fully-equipped boat cost twelve thousand five hundred bolivars, eighteen of them meant a lot of money.

We transformed the little villages round the lake, doing away with poverty and the dislike for work (since the work I gave was well paid), and bringing a new life in place of the old listlessness.

These poor people owned nothing, so without any guarantee from them we gave one full set of fishing gear for each crew of five. They fished as they chose and the only undertaking they had to give was to sell me the *langostinos* and *camarones* at the market price less half a bolivar a kilo, because all the equipment and its upkeep was paid for by me.

The business ran at a tremendous pace, and it fascinated me. We had three refrigerated trucks that never stopped hurrying about the beaches to pick up my boats' catch.

I built a pier on the lake about a hundred feet long, and a big covered platform. Here Rita managed a team of between a hundred and twenty and a hundred and forty women who took off the heads of the *camarones* and *langostinos*. Then, washed and washed again in ice-cold water, they were sorted for size, according to how many would go to one American pound. There might be ten to fifteen, or twenty to twenty-five, or twenty-five to thirty. The bigger they were, the more they fetched. Every week the Americans sent me a green sheet which gave the market price for *camarones* each Tuesday. Every day at least one DC-8 took off for Miami, carrying 24,000 lb of *camarones*.

I should have made a lot of money, if I had not been such a fool as to take a Yankee partner one day. He had a moon face, and looked worthy, stupid and straight. He spoke neither Spanish nor French, and as I spoke no English, we could not quarrel.

This Yankee brought in no capital, but he had rented the freezers of a well-known brand of ice that was sold all over Maracaibo and in the neighbourhood. This meant that the *camarone*s and the *langostinos* were perfectly frozen.

I had to look after the fishing, the supervision of my boats, the loading of each day's catch into my three refrigerated trucks and the payment of the fishermen: and I had to provide these considerable sums out of my own pocket. Some days I would go down to the beach with thirty thousand bolivars and come home without a cent.

All this was well organized; but nothing runs itself without a hitch, and I had a continual war with pirate buyers. As I've said, it had been agreed with the fishermen who used my equipment that I should buy their catch at the market price less half a bolivar a kilo, which was fair. But the pirate buyers risked nothing. They had no boats: they just had a refrigerated truck and that was all. They turned up on the beaches and bought *camarones* from no matter who. When a boat brought in eight hundred kilos of *camarones*, half a bolivar a kilo more made a difference of four hundred bolivars for my fishermen between what I gave them and what the pirate offered. You would have to be a saint to resist a temptation like that. So whenever they could, my fishermen took the pirate's money. That meant I had to protect my interests almost day and night; but I liked the battle—it gave me intense satisfaction.

When we sent our *camarones* and *langostinos* to the States, the payment was made in the form of a letter of credit, once the bank had seen the shipping papers and a certificate that the quality of the goods and their perfect deep-freezing had been checked. The bank paid eighty-five per cent of the total and the remaining fifteen per cent was received when Miami told Maracaibo that the consignment had arrived and had been found satisfactory.

It often happened that on Saturdays, when there were two plane-loads of *camarones*, my partner would go in one to accompany the consignment. On those days the freight cost five hundred dollars more and the Miami cargo-handlers did not work on Saturdays. So someone had to be on the spot to get the consignment out, loaded on to a refrigerated trailer and taken to the buyer's works, either in Miami itself or at Tampa or Jacksonville. And as the banks were closed on Saturdays there was no way of working the letters of credit: there was no way of insuring, either. But on Monday morning, in the States, the shipment sold for ten or fifteen per cent more. It was a sound venture.

Things were running smoothly, and I was delighted with my partner's elegant strokes of business when he flew off at the week-end. Until the day he did not come back.

By stinking bad luck, this happened at the season when there were few *camarones* in the lake: I had hired a big boat at the sea-port of Punto-Fijo to fetch a whole cargo of splendid crayfish from Los Roques. I'd come back loaded to the gunwales with extra-prime-quality goods; and I'd had their heads taken off right there. So I had a very valuable shipment, made up entirely of best crayfish tails, weighing from a pound and a half to a pound and three-quarters each.

And that Saturday two DC-8s loaded with crayfish tails paid for by me, the freight and all the rest paid for by me too, took off with this choir-boy and vanished into the clouds.

Monday, no news: none on Tuesday, either. I went to the bank: nothing from Miami. I didn't want to believe it, but I knew already: I had been done. As it was my partner who dealt with the letters of credit and as there was no insurance on Saturday, he had sold the whole consignment the moment he got there, and walked quietly away with the dough.

I flew into a terrible rage and went off to look for Moonface in America, with a souvenir for him in my pocket. There was no difficulty in picking up his trail, but at each address I found a woman who said he was her lawful wedded husband but she didn't know where he was. And this three times, in three different towns! I never did find my worthy partner.

There I was, flat broke. We had lost a hundred and fifty thousand dollars. We still had the boats, of course; but they were in poor condition: so were the outboards. And as this was a business in which you had to have a lot of ready cash to carry on day by day, we could not stand the loss, nor get on our feet again. We were pretty well ruined, and we sold everything. Rita never complained nor blamed me for having been so trusting. Our capital, the savings of fourteen years of hard work, more than two years of useless sacrifice and continual effort—everything was lost; or very nearly everything.

With our eyes filled with tears, we left the great family of fishermen and workers we had brought into being. They were appalled too; they told us how it grieved them to see us go and how grateful they were to us for having brought them a prosperity they had never known before these two years.

16: The Gorilla

THERE was a knock at the door (the bell was not working) and I went to open it. It was my buddy, Colonel Bolagno. He and his family had always called me Papillon: they were the only people in Venezuela to do so. All the others called me Enrique or Don Enrique, according to how I was doing at the moment. The Venezuelans have a feeling for that; they know straight away if you are prosperous or on the rocks.

'Hi there, Papillon. It's three years since we've met.'

'True enough, Francisco: three years.'

'Why haven't you been to see me in my new house?'

'You never asked me.'

'You don't ask a friend. He comes when he feels like it, because if his friend has a house it's his house too. To invite him would be an insult.'

I made no answer; I knew he was in the right.

Bolagno embraced Rita. He sat there with his elbows on the table, looking disturbed and uneasy: he had taken off his colonel's cap. Rita gave him a cup of coffee, and I asked, 'How did you find my address?'

'That's my business. Why didn't you send it to me?'

'A great deal of work and a great deal of worry.'

'You have worries?'

'All I want.'

'Then I've come at the wrong moment.'

'Why?'

'I came to ask you to lend me five thousand bolivars. I'm in a jam.'

'Impossible, Francisco.'

'We are ruined,' said Rita.

'Ah, so you're ruined? You're ruined, Papillon? It's true you're ruined? Is that why you did not come to see me, so as not to let me know about your worries?'

'Yes.'

'Well, just you let me tell you you're a sod. Because when you have a friend, he's there so you *can* tell him your worries and so you can rely on him to do something to get you out of a

247

hole. You're a sod not to have thought of me, your friend, to back you up and give you a hand. I heard about your difficulties from other people, and that's why I'm here to help you.'

Rita and I were so moved we scarcely knew where we were: we could not say a word, we were so touched. We had never asked anyone for anything and that was a fact; but there were a good many people I had helped a lot and who even owed me their jobs, and although they knew we were ruined not one had come to give us a hand in any way at all. Most were French; some straight, others bent.

'What do you want me to do for you, Papillon?'

'Setting up a business we could live off would cost too much. Even if you have the money, you couldn't spare it.'

'Go and get dressed, Rita. We'll all three of us go and eat at the best French restaurant in town.'

By the end of the meal, it was agreed that I should look for a business and tell him how much it would cost to buy. And Bolagno said, 'If I have the money, there's no problem; and if I haven't enough, then I'll borrow from my brothers and my brother-in-law. But I give you my word I'll get hold of what you need.'

All the rest of that day, Rita and I talked about his wonderful tact. 'When he was just a corporal at El Dorado,' I said, 'he gave me his only civilian suit, so that I could leave decently dressed; and now today here he is giving us a hand to make a fresh start.'

We paid our overdue rent and moved to a pleasant, well-situated café-restaurant in the top avenue of Las Delicias, still in the Sabana Grande district. It was called the Bar-Restaurant Gab, and that was where we were at the time of Long Charlie's arrival.

Charles de Gaulle, then president of the republic, came on an official visit, invited by Raul Leoni, the president of Venezuela.

Caracas and the whole of Venezuela celebrated the occasion. The people, the real people, the ones with horny hands, straw hats and rope-soled shoes, all these open-hearted people without exception were waiting, filled with emotion, to cheer

Charles de Gaulle.

The Gab had a charming covered terrace, and I was sitting there quietly drinking pastis with a Frenchman. He explained the mysteries of the processing of fish-meal; and in a low voice he also told me about an invention he was just perfecting—one that would bring him in millions, once it was accepted. The discovery was cinema in relief; he whispered and looked sideways to seem more confidential and also to tell me how much money I could invest in his researches.

It is always amusing to listen to the line of a guy that wants to do you, and his patter was so smooth and it so charmed me that I did not notice a neighbour pricking up his ears and leaning over to listen to us. Not until I unfolded a little note from Rita, who was at the cash-desk and who had sent it discreetly by one of the waiters: 'I don't know what you are talking about, but there's no doubt your neighbour is very interested in catching what you say. Looks like a foreign pig.'

To get rid of the inventor, I strongly advised him to carry on with his researches, and I told him I was so sure he would succeed that I should certainly have come in with him if only I had any savings, which was unfortunately not the case. He went away: I got up, turned round and faced the table behind me.

Sitting there I saw a well-built guy, too well-built and too well-dressed, with a tie and all, and a steel-blue suit; and there on the table in front of him, a pastis and a packet of Gauloises. No need to ask his trade; nor his nationality either.

'Excuse me, are those French cigarettes you are smoking?' I asked in Spanish.

'Yes: I'm a Frenchman.'

'Really? I don't know you. Tell me, you wouldn't be one of Long Charlie's gorillas, by any chance?'

The well-built guy stood up and introduced himself. 'I'm Commissaire Belion, in charge of the General's security.'

'Pleased to meet you.'

'And what about you? Are you French?'

'Come off it, Commissaire. You know very well who I am; it's not just by chance you're here on my café terrace.'

'But . . .'

'Don't go on. You put the Gauloises right out on your table

so that I should talk to you. Right or wrong?'

'Right.'

'Another pastis?'

'OK. I came to see you because since I'm responsible for the President's security, I'm getting the embassy to draw up a list of people who might have to leave Caracas before the General arrives. The list will be shown to the minister of the interior and he'll take the necessary steps.'

'I'm on the list?'

'Not yet.'

'What do you know about me?'

'That you have a family and that you are going straight.'

'What else?'

'That your sister is Madame X and she lives at such and such an address in Paris and that the other one is Madame Y, who lives in Grenoble.'

'After that?'

'That proceedings against you lapse next year, in June 1966.'

'Who told you?'

'I knew it before I left Paris, but it's been notified to the consulate here.'

'Why didn't the consul let me know?'

'Officially he doesn't know your address.'

'Well, thanks for the good news. Can I go to the consulate and be told officially?'

'Whenever you like.'

'But tell me, Commissaire, how come you're sitting on the terrace of my restaurant this morning? It's not just to give me the news about proceedings having lapsed, nor to let me know my sisters haven't changed their address, eh?'

'Correct. It was to see you. To see Papillon.'

'You only know one Papillon, the guy in the Paris police file, a heap of lies, exaggerations and twisted reports. A file that never even described the man I was before, still less the man I have become.'

'Quite sincerely I believe you: and I congratulate you.'

'So now you've seen me, are you putting me on the list of people to be expelled during de Gaulle's stay?'

'No.'

'Well now, do you want me to tell you why you're here, Commissaire?'

'That would be interesting.'

'It's because you said to yourself, a guy on the loose is always a guy on the lookout for dough: now although Papillon may have become a good citizen, he's still on the loose, he's still an adventurer. He might refuse a considerable sum for doing something against de Gaulle himself; but as for picking up a fat packet for just helping to prepare an attack—why, that's something else again, and very possible.'

'Go on.'

'Well, you've got it dead wrong, dear Commissaire. In the first place because I wouldn't get mixed up with any political crime, not even for a fortune; still less one against de Gaulle. Secondly, who could possibly gain by such a thing in Venezuela?'

'The OAS.'

'Right. That's not only very possible but even very probable. They've pulled things off so many times in France that in a country like Venezuela, it's a piece of cake.'

'A piece of cake? Why?'

'The way they're organized, the OAS men don't have to get into Venezuela by the ordinary ways, the ports or airfields. The land frontiers are enormous—Brazil, Colombia, British Guiana—not to mention a coastline of over a thousand miles. They can come in just when they want, on the day and at the time that suits them, without anyone being able to do anything about it. That's your first mistake, Commissaire. But there's another, too.'

'What's that?' asked Belion, smiling.

'If these OAS guys are as sharp as people say, they've taken great care not to contact the French living here. Because since they know the cops are going straight to the Frenchmen, their very first precaution must be to go nowhere near any single one of them. And don't forget, no evil-intentioned guy is ever going to stay in a hotel. There are hundreds of people here who'll let a room to no matter who without declaring him. So you see there's no point in looking for people who might make an attempt on de Gaulle's life among the Frenchmen here, crooks or not.'

When Belion left he told me to come and see him when I returned to Paris; and he behaved straight with me. Unlike some other Frenchmen I was not expelled from Caracas during de Gaulle's stay—a stay that passed off with no trouble at all.

And like a fool I went along and cheered de Gaulle.

And like a fool the mere presence of this great leader who had saved my country's honour made me forget it was that same country which had sent me to penal for life.

And like a fool I would have given one of my fingers to shake his hand or be there at the embassy's reception in his honour: a reception to which I was not invited, of course. But the underworld was able to take an indirect revenge, because some old retired French whores slipped in: they had turned over a new leaf, as you might say, by making a good marriage, and there they were with their arms full of flowers for de Gaulle's delighted wife.

I went to see the French consul, and he read me out the notification that proceedings against me lapsed next year. One year more and I'd go to France.

Our situation improved rapidly, and I went back into all-night bars, buying the Scotch Club in Chacaito, in the very middle of Caracas. This was an odd business because I went into it in the first place to come to the rescue of a poor French hairdresser who some ugly bastards were trying to strip. Later this Robin Hood caper paid off very well.

So for several years there I was living by night again. The Caracas night-life was growing more and more vulgar, losing that touch of bohemianism that was its charm. The men who lived it up were no longer the same, and these new customers lacked culture and good manners.

I stayed in the bar as little as possible and I lived in the street almost all the time, wandering about the neighbouring districts. I came to know the kids of Caracas, the urchins who drifted about all night looking for a few cents, and the wonderful inventiveness of these children whose parents lived in rabbit-hutches. Not always model parents, either; for there were a good many who, in their poverty, had no hesitation in exploiting their children.

And these kids bravely launched themselves into the night to bring home the amount required of them. They were any age between five and twelve; some were shoe-shine boys, others waited at the door of all-night joints, offering to guard the customer's car as he went in, and others rushed to open the car door ahead of the doorman. A thousand dodges, a thousand clever gimmicks to add bolivar to bolivar until they had ten or thereabouts so that at five or six in the morning they could go home.

Often, when a customer I knew was just going to get into his big car, I would urge him to be generous, using this formula, 'Be handsome, now! Think of the money you've spent in this joint—a hundredth part of what you've splashed about would be a godsend to this poor kid.' Nine times out of ten it worked, and the playboy would give the kid a ten- or twenty-bolivar note.

My best friend was called Pablito. He was rather small and thin, but he was tough and he fought older, bigger boys like a lion. For there were conflicting interests in this struggle for life, and if a customer had not specially pointed out one boy to guard his car, then when the man came out again, the quickest off the mark got the coin. That meant a pitched battle.

My little friend was bright, and he had learned to read from the papers he sold from time to time. There was none like him at outstripping all competition when a car drew up; and he was the quickest at running little errands—fetching things the bar was short of, like sandwiches or cigarettes.

Every night my little Pablito carried on the struggle so that he could help his grandmother: she was a very, very old grandmother, it seemed, with white hair, faded blue eyes and rheumatism—rheumatism so bad she could not work at all. His mother was in gaol for having crowned a neighbour with a bottle when he tried to steal her radio. And he, at nine, was the one and only breadwinner in the family. He would not let his grandmother, his little brother or his little sister come out into the streets of Caracas, either by day or by night. He was the man of the house, and he had to look after all his people and protect them.

So I helped Pablito when he had had a bad night or in cases of emergency, money for his grandmother's medicines, or for a taxi to take her to see a doctor at the free hospital.

'And she has these bouts of asthma too, my grandmother. So you realize what that costs, Enrique?'

And every night Pablito gave me a report on his grandmother's health. One day there was an important request: he needed forty bolivars to buy a secondhand mattress. His grandmother could not lie in a hammock any more, because of her asthma: the doctor said it compressed her chest.

He often used to sit in my car, and one day the policeman on guard was talking to him, leaning on the door and playing with his revolver: without the least bad intention he put a bullet into Pablito's shoulder. They rushed him to hospital and operated. I went to see him the next day. I asked where his hut was and how to get to it; he said it was impossible to find it without a guide, and the doctor would not let him get up in that condition.

That night I looked for Pablito's friends, hoping one of them would take me to his grandmother. The terrific solidarity of street-arabs: they all said they did not know where he lived. I didn't believe a word of it, because every day a whole gang of them waited for one another to go home together.

I was interested and puzzled, and I asked the nurse to call me when Pablito had a visitor she knew was one of the family or a neighbour. Two days later she phoned me and I went to the hospital.

'Well, Pablito, and how are you coming along? You look worried.'

'No, Enrique; it's only that my back hurts.'

'Yet he was laughing only a few minutes ago,' said his visitor.

'Are you one of his family, Madame?'

'No. I'm a neighbour.'

'How are his grandmother and the little ones?'

'What grandmother?'

'Why, Pablito's grandmother.'

'But Pablito hasn't got a grandmother.'

'Well, well, well.'

I took the woman aside. Yes, he had a little sister; and yes, he had a little brother: but no grandmother. His mother was not in prison: she was a wreck of a woman, very dim-witted.

That wonderful Caracas street-kid did not want his friend Enrique to know his mother was half-crazy, and he had invented this splendid asthmatic grandmother so that his buddy the Frenchman, giving because of her, might relieve his poor mother's unhappiness and distress.

I went back to my little friend's bed: he was ashamed to look me in the face. Gently I pulled his chin up: his eyes were closed, but when at last he opened them I said, '*Pablito, eres un tronco de hombre.*' (You're a real man.)

I slipped him a hundred-bolivar note for his family and walked out, thoroughly proud and pleased with myself for having such a friend.

17: Montmartre—My Trial

1967: proceedings against me had lapsed. I left for France by myself; to keep the business running properly you had to have authority and courage and the power of making yourself respected: and only Rita could do that. She said to me, 'Go and embrace your people in their own homes; go and pray at your father's grave.'

I went back to France by way of Nice. Why Nice? Together with my visa, the French consulate in Caracas had given me a document notifying the lapse of proceedings; but as he handed them to me, the consul said, 'Wait until I have instructions from France about the conditions under which you can return.' They did not have to spell it out. If I went back to the consul and he had received the reply from Paris, he would tell me I was *forbidden the department of the Seine for life*. But I had the firm intention of taking a trip to Paris.

This way I avoided getting the notification; and seeing I had neither received it nor signed it, I would be committing no offence, unless the consul learned that I was off and told the police at the Paris airport to hand me the notification. Hence my two stops—I should arrive at Nice as though I were coming from Spain.

1930–1967: thirty-seven years had gone by.

Thirteen years of the 'road down the drain'; twenty-four years of freedom, twenty-two of them with a home, which meant that I could go straight, reintegrated into society.

In 1956, a month with my people in Spain, then a gap of eleven years, though during these eleven years our many letters had kept me in living contact with my family.

1967. I saw them all. I went into their homes, I sat at their table, I had their children on my knee and even their grandchildren. Grenoble, Lyons, Cannes, Saint-Priest and then Saint-Peray, where I found Tante Ju in my father's house, still faithful at her post.

I listened to Tante Ju as she told me why Papa had died before his time. He watered his garden himself and he carried the cans for hours and hours over a distance of more than two hundred yards. 'Just imagine that, my dear, at his age! He could have bought a rubber hose, but Lord above, he was as stubborn as a mule. And one day, as he was carrying these watering-cans, his heart failed.'

I could just see my father lugging those heavy cans all the way to his beds of lettuces, tomatoes and haricot beans. And I could see him obstinately persisting in not getting the hose his wife, Tante Ju, kept begging him to buy. And I could see him, that country schoolmaster, stopping to draw breath and to mop his forehead, advise a neighbour or give a botany lesson to one of his grandsons.

Before going to see his grave in the cemetery, I asked Tante Ju to go with me on his favourite walks. And we went at the same pace he used to go, following the same stony paths lined with rushes, poppies and daisies until a milestone, or some bees, or the flight of a bird would remind Tante Ju of some little happening long ago that had touched them. Then, quite delighted, she would tell me how my father had told her about his grandson Michel being stung by a wasp. 'There, Henri, do you see? He was standing just there.'

I listened, with my throat constricted, thirsty for more, still more of the smallest details about my father's life. 'You know, Ju,' my father had said to her, 'when my boy was very small, five or six at the most, he was stung by a wasp when we were out for a walk: not once, like Michel, but twice. Well, he never cried at all; and on top of that, we had the greatest difficulty stopping him going off to look for the wasps' nest to destroy it. Oh, Riri was so brave!'

I did not travel on into the Ardèche: I went no farther than Saint-Peray. For my return to my village I wanted Rita to be with me.

I got out of the train at the Gare de Lyon; and put my bags in the left-luggage office so as not to have to fill in a registration form at the hotel. And then once more there was the asphalt of Paris under my feet, after thirty-seven years.

But this asphalt was not *my* asphalt until I was in my own district, Montmartre. I went there by night, of course. The only sun the Papillon of the thirties knew was that of the electric lights.

And here it was, Montmartre: the Place Pigalle and the Pierrot café and the moonlight and the Passage Elysée des Beaux-Arts and the types whooping it up and the laughter and the tarts and the ponces that anyone in the know could tell straight off just by the way they walked, and the joints crammed tight with people at the bar. But all this was just my first impression.

Thirty-seven years had gone by: nobody took any notice of me. Who was going to look at an old man of sixty? The tarts might even ask me upstairs and the young men might be so disrespectful as to elbow me out of my place at the bar.

Just one more stranger, a possible client, a provincial manu-facturer—that's what this well-dressed, tie-wearing gent must be; a middle-class guy, another who had lost his way at this late hour and in this dubious bar. You could see right away he wasn't used to being in these parts; you could feel he was uneasy.

Sure I was uneasy, and that was understandable. These were not the same people nor the same mugs; at the first whiff you could tell that everything was mixed up now, everything confused. Pigs, lesbians, phony ponces, pouffes, wide-boys, squares, blacks and Arabs; there were only a few types from Marseilles or Corsica, speaking with a southern accent, to re-mind me of the old times. It was a completely different world from the one I had known.

There wasn't even what there had always been in my time—tables with groups of poets, painters or actors, with their long hair that reeked of Bohemia, and an avant-garde intelligence. Now every silly little jerk had long hair.

And I wandered from bar to bar like a sleepwalker, and I climbed stairs to see if there were still the billiard-tables of my youth on the first floor, and I civilly refused a guide's offer to show me Montparnasse. But I did ask him, 'Do you think that since 1930 Montmartre has lost the soul it had in those days?'

I felt like slapping him down for an answer that insulted my own personal Montmartre: 'Oh, but, Monsieur, Montmartre is immortal. I've lived here forty years, seeing I came when I was ten, and believe me, Place Pigalle, Place Blanche, Place Clichy and all the streets running off them are just the same and always will be the same for ever.'

I fled from the dreary little sod and walked along under the trees on the raised part in the middle of the avenue. From here, yes—so long as you didn't see the people clearly, so long as you only saw their shapes—from here, yes, Montmartre was still the same. I went slowly on towards the very spot where I was alleged to have shot Roland Legrand on the night of 25–26 March 1930.

The bench, probably the same bench repainted every year (a public bench might perfectly well last thirty-seven years with its wood that thick), the bench was there, and the lamp-post was there, and the bar over the way was there, and the half-closed shutters on the house opposite, they were still there. But say something, won't you, wood and stone and tree and glass! You saw, you must have been there then, seeing you're here now; you were the first, the only, the true witnesses of the tragedy; you know very well the man who fired that night was not me. Why didn't you say so?

People went by, unconcerned; people went by, never noticing this sixty-year-old man leaning against a tree, the same tree that had been there when the shot was fired.

Twenty-four I was in 1930, when I used to run down the Ruc Lepic, that street which I can still walk up pretty briskly. The ghost has come back in spite of you all; he's pushed back the gravestone under which you buried him alive. Stop, stop, you half-blind creatures passing by! Stop and have a look at an innocent man who was condemned for a murder in this very place, on this very ground, before these same trees and these same stones—stop and ask these dumb witnesses, ask them to speak out today. And if you lean close, if you beg them, implore them to speak, you will hear them just as I hear them, whispering faintly, 'No, this man was not here at half past three on the night of 25 to 26 March thirty-seven years ago.'

'Where was he, then?' the doubters will say. Simple: I was in the Iris-Bar, maybe a hundred yards from here. In the Iris-Bar, when an honest taxi-driver burst in, crying, 'There was a shot outside just now.'

'It wasn't true,' said the pigs. 'It wasn't true,' said the boss and the waiter of the Iris, prompted by the pigs.

Once again I see the inquiry; once again I see the trial: I could not avoid being brought face to face with the past. You want to live through it again, man? You really want to? Nearly forty years since and you still want to go through that nightmare again? You're not afraid this going back will make you long for a revenge you gave up long ago? Are you sure of your strength, sure that dipping yourself in this filth won't mean you cannot wait for dawn and the shops to open to buy a cabin-trunk and stuff it with explosives for you know where? No: I'm perfectly certain of it: not one of them has anything to fear from me—let them perish, if the worms haven't eaten them already.

Well, my old Papi, there's no difficulty about going through the Grand Guignol piece you were the hero of, and the victim. Sit down there, on this same green bench, the one that saw the killing just opposite the Rue Germain-Pilon, right here on the Boulevard de Clichy, by the Clichy Bar-Tabac, where the tragedy began after the inquiry.

It's the night of 25–26 March: half past three in the morning. A man comes into the Clichy and asks for Madame Nini.

'That's me,' says a tart.

'Your man's just been shot in the guts. Come on; he's in a taxi.'

Nini runs after the unknown guy, together with a girlfriend. They get into the taxi, where Roland Legrand is sitting on the back seat. Nina asks the unknown guy who told her to come too. He says, 'I can't,' and disappears.

'Quick, the Lariboisière hospital!'

It was only during the drive that the taxi-man, a Russian, learned that his passenger was wounded: he had not noticed anything before. The moment his fare was unloaded at the hospital he hurried off to tell the police what he knew: he had been hailed by two men arm-in-arm outside 17, boulevard de Clichy: *only one of them got in*—Roland Legrand. The other told him to drive to the Clichy Bar and followed on foot. This man went into the bar and came out with two women; then he vanished. The two women told him to drive to the Lariboisière hospital: 'It was during the trip that I learned the man was wounded.'

The police carefully wrote all this down; they also wrote down Nini's declaration that her boy-friend had played cards all that night in that same bar where she plied her trade, had

260

played cards with an *unknown man*; he'd played dice and had a drink at the bar with some men, still *all of them unknown*; and that Roland had left after the others, *alone*. Nothing in Nini's statement to show that anyone had come to fetch him. He went out by himself, after the others, the unknowns, had left.

A commissaire and a cop, Commissaire Gérardin and Inspecteur Grimaldi, questioned the dying Roland Legrand in the presence of his mother. The nurses had told them his condition was hopeless. I quote their report, it's been published in a book written to pull me to pieces, with a preface and therefore a guarantee by a *Commissaire divisionnaire*, Paul Romain. Here it is. The two pigs are questioning Legrand:

' "Here beside you you have the police commissaire and your mother, the holiest relationship in the world. Tell the truth. Who shot you?"

'He replied, "It was Papillon Roger."

'We asked him to swear that he had really told the truth. "Yes, Monsieur, I have told you the truth."

'We withdrew, leaving the mother beside her son.'

So what happened on the night of 25 March 1930 was clear and straightforward: the man who fired was Papillon *Roger*.

This Roland Legrand was a pork-butcher and a ponce who put his girl-friend Nini out to work for him: he lived with her at 4, rue Elysée des Beaux-Arts. He was not really a member of the underworld, but like all those who hung around Montmartre and all the genuine crooks he knew several Papillons. And because he was afraid they might arrest another Papillon instead of the one who had killed him, he was exact about the Christian name. For although he was fond of living as a ponce, like all squares he also wanted the police to punish his enemy. A Papillon, sure: but Papillon *Roger*.

Everything came flooding back to me in this accursed place. I must have run through this file in my head a thousand times and more; I'd learned it by heart in my cell, like a Bible, because my lawyers had given it to me and I'd had time to engrave it on my mind before the trial.

So there was Legrand's statement before he died; and the declaration of Nini, his girl. Neither of them named me as the killer.

Now four men come upon the stage. On the night of this job they went to the Lariboisière hospital to ask:

(1) if the wounded man was in fact Roland Legrand
(2) what condition he was in

The pigs were told at once and they began a search. Since these men did not belong to the underworld and were not concealing themselves, they had come on foot and they left on foot. They were picked up as they were walking down the Avenue Rochechouart and kept in custody at the station in the XVIII arrondissement.

Their names were:

Georges Goldstein, 24; Roger Dorin, 24; Roger Jourmar, 21; Emile Cape, 18.

All the statements they made to the commissaire of the XVIII arrondissement station on the very day of the killing were fresh from the oven. Goldstein stated that in a gathering of people he had been told that a man called Legrand had been wounded—shot *three times* with a revolver. Thinking it might be his friend Roland Legrand, who was often in that district, he walked to the hospital to find out. On the way he met Dorin and then the two others and asked them to go with him. The others knew nothing about the business and they did not know the victim.

The commissaire asked Goldstein, 'Do you know Papillon?'

'Yes, a little. I've met him now and then. He knew Legrand; *that's all I can tell you.*'

So what of it? What does this Papillon mean? There were five or six of them in Montmartre! Don't get worked up, Papi. As I go through all this again, I'm still twenty-four and I'm re-reading my file in my cell at the Conciergerie.

Dorin's statement: Goldstein asked him to go with him to the Lariboisière to inquire after a friend *whose name he did not mention.* Dorin went into the hospital with him and Goldstein asked if the Legrand who had been brought in was seriously wounded.

'Do you know Legrand? Do you remember Papillon Roger?' asked the commissaire.

'I don't know Legrand, either by name or by sight. I do know a man called Papillon, having seen him in the street. He is very well known and they say he is a terror. I know nothing more.'

The third man to be questioned, Jourmar, said that when Goldstein came out of the hospital, having gone in alone with Dorin, he said, 'It's certainly my mate.'

So before he went in, he was not sure about it, right?

The commissaire: 'Do you know Papillon Roger and a man called Legrand?'

'I know a man called Papillon who hangs around Pigalle. The last time I saw him was about three months ago.'

The same with the fourth thief. He didn't know Legrand. A Papillon, yes, but only by sight.

In her first statement the mother also confirmed that her son had said Papillon *Roger*.

It was only after these first statements that the really dirty business began. Up until then everything had been plain, clear-cut and exact. All the chief witnesses gave their evidence in complete freedom before a local commissaire without being prompted, threatened or guided.

In short, Roland was in the Clichy bar before the tragedy; and all the people present were unknown. They may have been playing cards or dice, which meant they were acquaintances of Roland's, but still they were unknown. What was odd and indeed disturbing, was that they remained unknown until the very end.

Second point: Roland Legrand was *the last to leave the bar, and he left it by himself*: his own girl said so. Nobody came to fetch him. A very little while after he went out he was wounded by an unknown man whom he positively identified on his deathbed as Papillon *Roger*. The man who came to tell Nini was also an unknown; and he too was to remain unknown. Yet he was the one who helped Legrand into the taxi immediately after the shooting—an unknown man who did not get in but who walked along with the cab as far as the bar where he was going to warn Nini. And this essential witness was to remain unknown for good, although everything he had just done proved that he belonged to the underworld, to Montmartre, and that he was therefore known to the pigs. Strange.

Third point: Goldstein, who was to be the prosecution's chief witness, *did not know* who had been wounded and went to the Lariboisière hospital to find out whether it was his friend Legrand.

The only clues as to this Papillon were that he was called Roger and that he was said to be a terror.

Were you a terror at twenty-three, Papillon? Were you dangerous? No, not yet; but maybe you were on the way to becoming both. And it's certain too that I was a tough guy, an 'undesirable' then; but it's also certain that at only twenty-three, I could not have become set for ever as one particular type of man. It's also certain that at that age, having been only two years in Montmartre, I could not have been either the head of a gang or the terror of Pigalle. Certainly I disturbed public order; and certainly I was suspected of having taken part in big jobs, but nothing had ever been proved against me. Sure they had pulled me in several times and grilled me pretty hard at 36, quai des Orfèvres, but without ever having been able to get anything out of me, neither a confession nor a name. Sure, after the tragedy of my childhood and after my time in the navy and after the government had refused me a steady career, I had made up my mind to live outside that society of clowns and to let them know it. Sure, every time I was picked up and grilled at the quai des Orfèvres for an important job they thought I was mixed up in, I insulted my torturers and humiliated them in every possible way, even telling them that one day I should be in their place, the shits, and that they would be in my power. So of course the pigs, humiliated through and through, might have said to themselves, 'This Papillon, we'll have to clip his wings the first chance we have.'

But still, I was only twenty-three! My life was not only mere resentment and rancour against society and the squares who obeyed its damn-fool rules: it was also *life itself*, continually on the move, sending off showers of sparks. It's true there was some serious nonsense; yes, but it was not wicked nonsense. Besides, when I was pulled in there was only one condemnation on my file: four months' suspended sentence for receiving stolen goods. Did I deserve to be wiped off the face of the earth just for having humiliated the pigs and just because I might turn dangerous one day?

And it all began at the point when the criminal police took

the business over. The word went round Montmartre that they were looking for all the Papillons—Little Papillon, Pussini Papillon, Papillon Trompe-la-Mort, Papillon Roger, etc.

As for me, I was just plain Papillon; or sometimes to avoid confusion, Charrière Papillon. But it was no part of my way of life to hobnob with the pigs, and I moved off fast: yes, that was true, I went on the run.

And why did you do that, Papi, since it wasn't you?

You ask that now? Have you forgotten that by the time you were twenty-three you had already been tortured several times at the quai des Orfèvres? You were never really fond of being knocked about, nor of all those exquisite tortures invented by the head pig of those days, the trough where they shove your head under the water until you are perishing for want of air and you don't know whether you're dead or alive, the pigs who give your balls five or six twists and leave them so swollen you walk like an Argentine gaucho for weeks on end, the paper-press in which they crush your nails till the blood spurts and they come off, the beating-up with a rubber truncheon that wounds your lungs so blood pours out of your mouth, and the twelve- or fifteen-stone porkers who jump up and down on your belly as if it was a spring-board. Is it your age, Papi, or have you lost your memory? There was not just one reason for going on the run right away, but a hundred. It was a break that didn't carry me too far, since I wasn't guilty. There was no need to go off abroad; just a little hide-out near Paris would be enough. Soon they'd pick up the Papillon Roger in question, or if not pick him up then at least identify him; and then fine, you jump into a taxi and you're back in Paris. No more danger for your balls or your nails or all the rest.

Only this Papillon Roger never was identified. There was no culprit.

Then all at once a wanted man was produced like magic. This Papillon Roger? Simple: you just wipe out the Roger and you pick up plain Papillon, the nickname of Henri Charrière. The trick's done: all that's left is to pile up the evidence. It's no longer a matter of an honest, impartial inquiry into the truth, but of the total fabrication of *a culprit*.

Policemen, don't you see, need *to bring off the solution of a murder-case* so as to deserve promotion in their very noble, very honest career. Now this Papillon has everything going for him as a culprit. He's young, and there is something of the ponce about him ... We'll say his girl's a whore. He's a thief, and he's been in trouble with the police several times; but he's either got off on a dismissed charge or he's been acquitted.

And then into the bargain the guy is an awkward sod; he's awkward when we arrest him, he sneers at us, humiliates us, calls his little dog Chiappe [chief of the Paris police in those days] and sometimes he says to our colleagues, 'You'd be well advised to grill a little more gently, if you want to reach retirement age.' These threats of punishing us one day for our 'modern' and 'thoroughgoing' methods of interrogation worry us. So go right in, man. We're covered on all sides.

So that was the sinister beginning of it all, Papi. Twenty-three you were, when these two lousy pigs flushed you out at Saint-Cloud on 10 April, while you were eating snails.

Oh, they went right in, all right! What drive, what zeal, what steadiness, what passion, what diabolical cunning to succeed in getting you into the dock one day, for the court to fetch you that blow—a blow that knocked you out for thirteen years!

It wasn't so easy to turn you into the guilty man, Papi. But the inspector in charge of the job, Mayzaud, a Montmartre specialist, was so eager to send me down that it was open war between him and my lawyers even in the court, as you can see in the papers of that time, with insults, complaints and foul blows; and ready to hand this accursed Mayzaud had the draper's son, the plump little Goldstein, one of those phony little bastards who lick the underworld's feet in the hope of being accepted. Very amenable, this Goldstein! Mayzaud (he said so himself at the trial) met him maybe a hundred times *by chance* during the inquiry. This precious witness *on the very day of the killing* stated that in a crowd of people he had heard that someone called Roland had got three bullets in the guts; he had then gone to the hospital to ask about the exact identity of the victim and the danger of his wound—a statement cross-checked by three friends who had nothing whatsoever to do with it; more than three weeks later, on 18 April, after many contacts with Mayzaud, this same Goldstein made the following declaration: 'That on the night of 25–26 March, before the killing, he had met Papillon [me] together with two unknown men' [still more?]. Papillon had asked him where Legrand was. Goldstein: 'At the Clichy.' Papillon left him and straight away he went to warn Legrand. While he was talking to Legrand one of Papillon's two companions came in and asked Legrand to come outside. Goldstein himself went out a little later and saw Papillon and Legrand talking quietly; but he did not linger. Later, coming back to the place Pigalle, he *once more* met Papillon who told him he had just shot Legrand and asked him to go to the Lariboisière and see what state he was in, and if he was still alive, to advise him to keep his mouth shut.

For of course, Papi, you who were described to the court as a terror, a member of the underworld all the more dangerous because of your intelligence and cunning; so would you in fact be such an idiot that having shot a guy right there on the boulevard, you would hang around the place Pigalle, right on the spot, until Goldstein comes that way again? Do you stand there like a milestone on some little Ardèche lane, so that the pigs only have to come trotting along to ask you how you are doing?

But this Goldstein was not such a fool as all that: the day after his statement he buggered off to England.

Meanwhile I stood up for myself stoutly. 'Goldstein? Don't know him. I may have seen him; may even have exchanged a few words with him like you do with people always around the same district, without knowing who you're talking to.' I really could not manage to fit a snout to that name; so much so that it was only when we were brought face to face that I succeeded in identifying him. And I was so taken aback that a little square I didn't know should make such a detailed charge against me, that I wondered what crime he could have committed—nothing much for sure, he being such a dreary little sod—for the pigs to have such a hold on him. I am still wondering; sexual offences? Cocaine?

Without him, without his successive statements that *every time* brought new material to the case the pigs were building up, without him nothing held together. Nothing.

And now there appeared something that at first sight looked miraculous but later turned out to be exceedingly dangerous—

indeed fatal. A diabolical police plot, a horrible trap that I and my lawyers fell into head first. I thought it meant safety, but it was disaster. Because there was nothing solid in the file: Goldstein's successive bits of evidence were all very improbable. The file had so little body to it that my alleged killing lacked even a motive. Since I had no cause to dislike the victim and since I was not raving mad, I was as out of place in this job as a hair in the soup; and any jury at all, even one made up of the dullest idiots on earth, could hardly fail to realize it.

So the police invented a motive: and the one who provided it was a pig who had been working Montmartre for the last ten years, Inspector Mazillier.

One of my lawyers, Maître Beffey, liked wandering about Montmartre in his off time; and he met this pig, who told him he knew what had really happened on the night of 25–26 March and that he was prepared to tell—and this implied that what he had to say would be in my favour. Beffey and I said, either he's motivated by professional honesty or else—which is more likely—there's some rivalry between Mayzaud and him.

And *we* called him as a witness. *We* did.

But what Mazillier had to say was not at all what we had expected. He stated that he knew me well, that I had done him many favours, and he added, 'Thanks to the information provided by Charrière I have been able to carry out several arrests. As for the circumstances in connection with the murder, *I know nothing about them.* Yet I have heard it said [Lord, how many 'I have heard it said's' we had during my trial!] that Charrière was the object of ill-will on the part of persons unknown to me who disapproved of his relations with the police.'

And there we were with the cause of the murder! I'd killed Roland Legrand during a quarrel because he was spreading it around Montmartre that I grassed, that I was an informer.

And when was this statement of Inspector Mazillier's made? 14 April. And when did Goldstein make his, the one that went back on his statement on the day of the killing? 18 April, *four days after Mazillier's.*

But the other judges—apart from the investigating magistrate Robbé, who was in the pigs' pocket from the start—the other judges were not ready to swallow the ugly brew prepared by these bastards. When the court of first instance was presented with this padded, elastic evidence, this mass of rumours, lies and prompted statements, they sensed there was something fishy about the whole thing. Because although you often put them all into the same bag, Papi, as if judges, pigs, jurymen, the law and the prison administration were all part of the same conspiracy you must admit that there have been some exceedingly honest judges.

As a result, the court *refused* to send me before the assizes with that phony file and sent all the evidence back to the investigating magistrate, insisting upon *further inquiry*.

The pigs were utterly infuriated; they found witnesses everywhere—in prison, just about to be let out or just having been let out. But the further inquiry produced nothing, absolutely nothing, not the slightest clue nor the least beginning of new and serious evidence.

In the end, without anything fresh—still a badly-made bouillabaisse with no rascasse—the file was at last allowed to be sent up to the assizes.

And now came the clap of thunder. Something happened that is almost never seen in the legal world: the public prosecutor, the man whose job it is to protect society and to get promotion by putting as many defendants as possible behind bars—the public prosecutor who had been given the brief to act against me, took it with the tips of his fingers, as though he were holding it with tongs, and put it back on the desk, saying, 'I shan't act in this case. It smells fishy and prefabricated: give it to someone else.'

How splendid he looked, Maître Raymond Hubert, when he came to tell me this extraordinary news at the Conciergerie! 'Can you imagine it, Charrière! Your file is so unconvincing, a prosecutor has refused to have anything to do with it and has asked for the brief to be given to someone else!'

... It was cool that night on the bench in the boulevard de Clichy. I walked up and down under the shadow of the trees; I did not want to walk into the light for fear of interrupting the magic lantern as it poured out these pictures from thirty-seven years ago. I turned up the collar of my overcoat. I pushed back my hat a little to air my head—the intensity of all this total recollection had made it hot and sweaty. I sat down again, pulled my coat over my legs, and then, with my back to the avenue I slid my legs over the bench and sat the other way round, my arms leaning on the back as they had leant on the rail of the dock during my first trial in July 1931.

Because there was not just one trial at the assizes for me. *There were two*. The first in July, the other in October.

It all went too well, Papi! The court was not blood-red, like a slaughterhouse; it was more like an enormous boudoir. In the flooding light of that marvellous July day, the hangings, the carpets and the judges' robes were almost pale pink. And in this court, a smiling, kindly, rather sceptical presiding judge, so little convinced by what he had read in the file that he opened proceedings like this: 'Charrière, Henri, as the indictment does not entirely correspond with what we should have liked to see in it, will you explain your case to the court and the jury yourself?'

The president of an assize court asking the defendant to lay open his case! You remember that sun-filled July assize and those wonderful judges? It was too good to last, Papi. Those judges conducted the proceedings with such impartiality, the president calmly and honestly looking for the truth, asking the pigs embarrassing questions, worrying Goldstein, pointing out his contradictions and allowing my lawyers and me to ask him awkward questions—it was too splendid; I tell you again, Papi, it was sunlit justice, a holiday-sitting with the judges in your favour.

There you could fight and stand up for yourself, Papi. Fight against whom? Oh, there was no lack of enemies—they were there in droves.

The first important witness, already primed by the pigs: the mother. I don't think it was out of bad faith that she had adopted the pigs' insinuations. She really did so unconsciously.

Now the mother no longer said that she and the commissaire had heard 'Papillon Roger', or that Legrand had added (when?) that a friend of his called Goldstein knew Papillon well. Now she stated that what she had heard was, 'It's Papillon: Goldstein knows him.' She had forgotten the *Roger* and she had added the 'Goldstein knows him', words that Commissaire Gérardin and Inspecteur Grimaldi did not hear. Odd that a commissaire should not write down something as important as that, don't you think?

Maître Gautrat, the lawyer appearing for the family, wanted me to ask the victim's mother to forgive me. I said to her, 'Madame, I do not have to ask your forgiveness because I did not kill your son. I express my sorrow for your grief; that is all I can do.'

But Commissaire Gérardin and Inspecteur Grimaldi changed nothing of their first statement: Legrand had said 'It was Papillon Roger', that's all.

And now the key witness came forward: Goldstein. This witness, a recording machine prepared at 36, quai des Orfèvres, had made five or six statements: three of them were used. Each one accused me; it did not matter if they were contradictory—each time they brought a fresh piece of wood to the framework the police were building up. Sitting there on the bench, I could see him as if he were just in front of me. He spoke in a low voice: he scarcely raised his hand when he said 'I swear it'. When he had finished his statement, Maître Beffey went for him. 'Goldstein, how many times have you met Inspector Mayzaud "by chance"? He himself states that he has met you and talked to you about this case "by chance" several times. It's curious, Goldstein. In your first statement you said you knew nothing about the affair; then you knew Papillon; after that you said you had met him on the night of the crime, before it was committed; then he tells you to go to Lariboisière and see how Legrand is getting on. How do you explain these differing statements?'

Goldstein's only reply was to repeat, 'I was afraid, because in Montmartre Papillon is terribly dangerous.'

I made a gesture of protest and the president said to me, 'Defendant, have you any questions to ask the witness?'

'Yes, Monsieur le Président.' I looked straight at Goldstein. 'Goldstein, turn this way and look me in the face. What is it that makes you lie and accuse me falsely? What crime of yours does Mayzaud know about? What crime are you paying for with these lying statements?'

The shit trembled as he looked me in the face, but he did manage to bring out the words 'I'm telling the truth' quite distinctly.

I could have killed the swine! I turned towards the court. 'Gentlemen of the court, gentlemen of the jury, the public prosecutor says I am an intelligent, sharp-witted, knowing character; but the witness's evidence shows me to be a perfect idiot and I'll prove it to you. Confiding something as important as this, telling a man you've just killed his friend means, if you are intelligent, that you must know him very well; whereas admitting such a thing to a man you don't know at all is the act of a total imbecile. Yet I don't know Goldstein.' And turning towards Goldstein I went on, 'Goldstein, please name one single person in Paris or in the whole of France who can say he has seen us talking together even once.'

'I don't know anyone who could testify to that.'

'Right. Please name a bar, restaurant or eating-place in Montmartre, Paris, or anywhere in France where we have eaten or drunk together even once.'

'I've never eaten or drunk with you.'

'Very well. You say the first time you met me that extraordinary night I had two men with me. Who were they?'

'I don't know them.'

'Nor do I, either. Now say quickly, without hesitating, where I told you to meet me to give me the answer—the answer you were to bring back from the hospital—and say whether you mentioned that place to the men who went with you. And if you did not mention it to them, why not?'

No answer.

'Reply, Goldstein. Why don't you reply?'

'I didn't know where to find you.'

Maître Raymond Hubert: 'So my client sends you on an errand as important as this—he sends you to find out Roland Legrand's condition, and you did not know where to give him the answer? It is as absurd as it is unbelievable!'

Yes, Papi, it was unbelievable all right; but it was even more unbelievable that the whole indictment had been allowed to be built up on the successive accusations of this dreary straight who, although carefully prepared by the pigs, did not even have wits enough to give a quick answer.

The president: 'Charrière, the police claim that you killed Legrand because he called you an informer. What have you to

272

say to that?'

'I've had dealings with the police six times and each time I came away with the charge dismissed or an acquittal, except for my four months' suspended sentence. I've never been arrested with another man; I've never had another man arrested. It is impossible to accept that when I am in the hands of the police I don't talk, and that when I'm at liberty I inform on my friends.'

'An inspector says you are an informer. Call Inspector Mazillier.'

'I state that Charrière was an informer, one who enabled me to arrest several dangerous individuals; and that this was known in Montmartre. As to the Legrand affair, I know nothing about it.'

'What have you to say to that, Charrière?'

'It was on Maître Beffey's advice that I asked for this inspector to be called at the inquiry: Maître Beffey had told me Mazillier knew the truth about the murder of Legrand. And now I see that both my counsel and I fell into a horrible trap. Inspector Mazillier, when he advised Maître Beffey to call him, said he knew all about the killing; my counsel believed him, and so did I. We imagined he was either an honest cop or that there was some rivalry between him and Mayzaud that led him to give evidence about this crime. But now, as you see yourself, he says he knows nothing about it.

'On the other hand, it's clear that the inspector's statements at last provided the missing motive for my alleged crime. This statement, coming from a policeman, was a godsend: it preserved the framework of the accusation and gave some body to an indictment that just didn't hold together. Because there's no doubt that without the help given by Mazillier, the indictment would have fallen to pieces, in spite of all Inspector Mayzaud's efforts. The dodge is so obvious that it's astonishing the prosecution should ever have used it.'

I fought on and I said, 'Gentlemen of the court, gentlemen of the jury, if I'd been a police informer, one of two things would have happened: either I should not have killed Raymond Legrand for calling me a grass—because a type as low as that takes such an insult without batting an eyelid—either I should not have killed him at all, or, if I had shot him, being

273

furious, you can be dead certain the police would have played the game: they would never have gone out for my blood with all this zeal and all this clumsiness, because I was so useful to them. More than that, they would have closed their eyes or have fixed some gimmick that would have made it look as though I was acting in legitimate self-defence. Plenty of precedents of that kind could be quoted; but fortunately for me they don't apply. Monsieur le Président, may I ask the witness a question?'

'Yes.'

Knowing what I was up to, Maître Raymond Hubert asked the court to free Inspector Mazillier from his professional secrecy, otherwise he would not be able to reply.

The president: 'By its discretionary powers, the court releases Inspector Mazillier from his professional secrecy, and requires him, in the interests of truth and justice, to answer the question the defendant is about to put to him.'

'Mazillier, name one single man in France, the colonies or abroad you have arrested because of my information.'

'I cannot reply.'

'You're a liar, Inspector! You can't reply because there's never been one!'

'Charrière, moderate your language,' said the president.

'Monsieur le Président, I'm defending two things here, my life and my honour.'

But the incident went no farther. Mazillier withdrew.

And the other witnesses, how they came rolling up! All dressed in the same cloth, cut and sewn in the same fashion, all the handiwork of the pigs at 36, quai des Orfèvres, Paris.

And your last explanation, Papi, don't you remember that? The last and the most logical of them all. I can still hear it. 'Gentlemen, be straight with me and listen to what I have to say: Legrand got only one bullet; he was shot once only; he remained on his feet, he walked off alive, he was allowed to quietly take a taxi. That means the man who shot him did not want to kill him; otherwise he'd have fired four, five, six shots the way we do in the underworld. Anyone who knows Montmartre knows that. Right or wrong? So suppose it was me, and suppose I confess and say "Gentlemen, this man, for such-and-such a reason, right or wrong, had a row with me or accused me of something; he put his hand in his pocket, and as he was an underworld type like me I was afraid so I fired just one shot to defend myself." If I said that, at the same time I'd be giving you the proof I didn't mean to kill him because he went off on his own feet and alive. Then I would end up by saying to you, "Since an inspector says I'm very useful to the police, I ask you to accept my confession and that what I have told you is true, and to treat the business as unintentional homicide." '

The court listened in silence: thoughtful, it seemed to me. I went on, 'Ten times, a hundred times, both Maître Raymond Hubert and Maître Beffey have asked me the question, "Was it you who fired? If it was you, say so. You'll get five years at the outside, maybe even less: you can't be sent down for more. When they arrested you you were twenty-three, so you'll still be very young when you come out." But, gentlemen of the court and gentlemen of the jury, I can't take that path, not even to save myself from the guillotine or penal servitude, *because I'm innocent and I've been framed by the police.*'

All this in that sunny courtroom where they let me explain things properly. No, Papi, it was too good; it was going too well; you felt that the court was worried and that victory was possible. Poor pretentious kid, couldn't you see it was too good to last?

For this was the point where Mayzaud quickly thought up a gimmick: one that beyond doubt showed his diabolical nature. Feeling he had lost the game and that his fifteen months of effort might be reduced to nothing, he did what was forbidden. During a pause in the hearing he came to see me in the room where I was alone among the *Gardes républicains* and which he had no right to enter. And he came up to me and he had the nerve to say, 'Why don't you say it was Corsican Roger?'

Completely taken aback, I said, 'But I don't know any Corsican Roger.'

He talked for a moment, walked quickly out, went to the prosecuting counsel and said to him, 'Papillon's just confessed to me that it was Corsican Roger.'

And now what this accursed Mayzaud wanted to happen did happen. The trial was stopped, in spite of my protests. Yet I still fought on and I said, 'For the last eighteen months Inspector Mayzaud has been saying there's only one Papillon in this case and that it's me; Inspector Mayzaud says there's no doubt that I am Legrand's killer; Inspector Mayzaud says he not only asserts it but that he's brought honest, unanswerable witnesses who prove my guilt without the shadow of a doubt. Since the police have found all the necessary witnesses and proofs against me, why is their whole framework collapsing? So isn't this whole mass of evidence a pack of lies? And is just one new name tossed into the arena enough for it to seem uncertain any more that Papillon is guilty? Since you say you've got all the proofs of my guilt, is it merely on the existence of some imaginary Corsican Roger that the trial is to be stopped and started all over again? Just because of some imaginary Corsican Roger, thought up by Mayzaud if you believe me, or thought up by me, if you trust him once again? It's impossible: I demand that the proceedings should go on: I demand to be judged. I beg it of you, gentlemen of the jury and Monsieur le Président!'

You'd won, Papi, you'd very nearly won; and it was the honesty of the prosecuting counsel that made you lose. Because this man, Cassagnau, stood up and said, 'Gentlemen of the jury, gentlemen of the court, I cannot proceed ... I no longer know ... The incident must be expunged ... I ask the court to put the trial back and order a further inquiry.'

Just that, Papi, just those three phrases of Maître Cassagnau condemned you on a phony indictment. Because if this upright lawyer had had something clear, straight and unanswerable in his hands, he would not have said 'Stop the trial, I can no longer proceed.'

He would have said, 'Just one more of Charrière's inventions: the defendant wants to lead us astray with his Corsican Roger. We do not believe a word of it, gentlemen; here I have everything that is required to prove Charrière guilty, and I shall not fail to do so.'

But he did not say that: and why not? Because in his conscience he did not fully believe in his brief, and because he must have begun asking himself questions about the honesty of the pigs who had put it together.

You were a kid of twenty-three: and that was how, at the very moment they were shamefully losing, the pigs pipped you at the post, knowing very well their Corsican Roger was pure boloney. They hoped that before the next assizes they could think up some other ploy. Their twisted minds reckoned that another court, another president, another prosecuting counsel and the atmosphere of the next assizes would not be so favourable to me, and that the boudoir would turn into a slaughterhouse.

The trial was stopped and they ordered a supplementary inquiry, *the second in this case.*

One of the newspapers said, 'Such a lack of conviction is most unusual.'

Of course the supplementary inquiry provided *no new facts whatsoever*. Corsican Roger? Of course he was never found. During this further inquiry the *Gardes républicains* were straight: when they were asked about the incident in July they gave evidence against Mayzaud. In any case, how could a man who proclaimed his innocence and who proved it logically and who felt the court favourably inclined towards him, how could this man throw the whole thing up and suddenly say 'I was there but I wasn't the one who fired: it was Corsican Roger'?

And what about the other trial, Papi? The next assizes, the last, the decisive hearing: there where the dry guillotine began to work, there where at twenty-four your youth and your faith in life received the great hammer-blow of a life-sentence; there where Mayzaud, sure of himself once more, apologized to the prosecuting counsel and admitted having made a mistake in July; there where you shouted at him 'I'll rip off your mask, Mayzaud!' ... do you really want to live through all that again?

Do you really want to see that courtroom again, and that grey, unhappy day? How many times do I have to tell you that thirty-seven years have gone by since then? Do you want to feel that savage blow on the jaw again, that swipe which forced you to struggle for thirty-seven years to be able to sit on this bench in the Boulevard de Clichy, in your Montmartre? Yes, indeed; I want to go down those first steps of the ladder that took me to the very bottom of the pit of human baseness, I want to go down them one by one again, so as to have a better notion of the road I have travelled.

You remember? You remember how different it was when

you came into the second courtroom, a good-looking boy in a perfectly cut double-breasted suit? Yet it was the same court.

In the first place the sky was so low and rainy they had to light the chandeliers. This time everything was draped in red, blood-red. Carpets, hangings, judges' robes—as if they had all been dipped in the basket that holds the heads of guillotined men. This time the judges were not about to go off for their holidays; they had just returned from them: it was not the same as July.

The old stagers of the law courts, the barristers and so on, know better than anyone how the weather, the time of the year, the character of the presiding judge, his mood that day, the mood of the prosecuting counsel and the jury, the defendant's and his lawyers' fitness—their form—can sometimes influence the scales of justice.

This time the president did not pay me the compliment of asking me to explain my case myself; he was quite satisfied with the monotonous voice of the clerk of the court reading out the indictment.

The twelve bastards who made up the jury had brains as damp and dreary as the weather; you could see that in their moist, dull, half-witted eyes. They eagerly supped up the boloney of the indictment.

There was absolutely nothing human about the prosecuting counsel, the purveyor-in-chief for the guillotine.

I felt all this the moment I came in and glanced quickly round the court. 'Look out, Papillon, it's not in a court like this that you're going to be able to stand up for yourself properly.' And I had sized it up exactly; during the two days the trial lasted they hardly let me speak at all.

And now came the same statements, the same evidence, as in July. No point in going over it in detail; it was the same party beginning all over again with the one difference that if I felt outraged and if I sometimes burst out, they shut me up at once.

Only one really new fact, the appearance of the taxi-driver Lellu Fernand, the witness for my alibi, who had not had time to give his evidence before the postponement in July—the only witness the pigs had never been able to find: a myth, according to them.

Yet he was an essential witness for me, because he had stated that when he went into the Iris Bar saying 'there's just been a shot', *I was there*.

Lellu confirmed his statement: they accused him of being a put-up witness.

Here on this green bench, fury seized hold of me again; I felt neither the cold nor the drizzle that had begun to fall.

Once again I saw the boss of the Iris Bar come into the witness-box and state I could not have been in his place when Lellu came in to say there had been a shot outside, because he had forbidden me to enter his bar a fortnight earlier. That meant I was such a bloody fool that in a job as serious as this, with my freedom and perhaps my life at stake, the alibi I gave was just the very place where I was not allowed to go! And his waiter confirmed his evidence. Naturally they forgot to add that permission to stay open until five in the morning was a favour granted by the police and that if they told the truth they would be going directly against the pigs, which would mean their closing-time would be brought back to two o'clock. The boss was defending his till and the waiter his tips.

Maître Raymond Hubert did all he could and so did Maître Beffey—a Maître Beffey so disgusted that he reached the point of open war with Mayzaud, who, in confidential police reports, tried to damage his standing as a barrister by giving details of sexual matters that had nothing to do with the case.

Now it was the end. I was the last to speak. What could I say? 'I'm innocent. I've been framed by the police. That's all.'

The jury and the court withdrew. An hour later they returned and I stood up while they went back to their places. Then in his turn the president rose: he was about to read the sentence. 'Prisoner at the bar, stand up.'

And so firmly did I believe I was in the court, here under these trees in the Boulevard de Clichy, that I jumped to my feet, forgetting that my legs were pinned against the back of the bench, which made me fall back on my arse.

So it was sitting, not standing as I ought to have been, that there under the boulevard trees in 1967, I heard the toneless voice of the president who, in October 1931, pronounced this sentence. 'You are condemned to penal servitude for life.

Guards, take the prisoner away.'

I was just about to hold out my hands; but there was no one to put on the handcuffs; there were no *Gardes républicains* beside me. There was no one except a poor old woman lying curled up at the far end of the bench, with newspapers on her head to protect her from the cold and the rain.

I untwisted my legs. Standing at last, I let them get over their stiffness and then, lifting the papers, I put a hundred-franc note into the hands of this old woman, sentenced to extreme poverty for life. For me, 'life' had only lasted thirteen years.

And still keeping under the trees in the middle of the Boulevard de Clichy I walked along to Place Blanche, pursued by the last image of that trial—myself standing to receive the unbelievable blow that wiped me out of Montmartre, my Montmartre, for nearly forty years.

I had scarcely reached that wonderful square before the magic-lantern went out, and all I saw were a few bums sitting there at the exit from the métro, squatting with their heads on their knees, asleep.

Quickly I looked round for a cab. There was nothing here to attract me, neither the shadow of the trees that hid the glare of artificial light nor the brilliance of the square, with its Moulin Rouge blazing away at full blast. The one reminded me too much of my past and the other shouted 'You don't belong here any more.' Everything, yes, everything had changed: get out quick if you don't want to see that the memories of your twenties are dead and buried.

'Hey! Taxi! Gare de Lyon, please.'

And in the suburban train that took me back to my nephew's, I went over all the newspaper articles that Maître Raymond Hubert gave me to read after my conviction. Not one of them could avoid speaking of the doubt that had hung over the whole case; *Le Journal* gave it the headline 'A Dubious Case'.

I looked up these papers when I came back to France. Here are a few samples. *Le Matin* of 27.10.31: 'Thirty witnesses were called. Perhaps one would have been enough—the unknown who put the wounded man into the taxi, told his "wife" and then vanished; but this unknown remains the unknown whom thirty successive testimonies will probably not succeed in identifying.'

La France of 28.10.31: 'The defendant replied calmly and firmly ... The defendant: "It grieves me to hear that," he said. "This Goldstein has not the least reason to wish me ill, but he is in the hands of Inspector Mayzaud, like so many others of his kind who have uneasy consciences, and that's the truth of it."'

L'Humanité of 28 October. This article deserves to be quoted at length.

Charrière-Papillon condemned to penal servitude for life

In spite of the persisting doubt as to the identity of the real Papillon, of the Papillon who is said to have killed Roland Legrand on the Butte one night in March, the jury of the Seine convicted Charrière.

At the beginning of yesterday's hearing, the witness Goldstein, upon whose statements the whole charge rests, gave evidence. This witness, who remained in continual contact with the police and whom Inspector Mayzaud said he had seen more than a hundred times since the tragedy, made his statements on three separate occasions, each deposition being more serious than the last. It is clear that this witness is a loyal helper of the criminal police.

While he was uttering his accusations, Charrière listened closely. When Goldstein had finished, Charrière cried, 'I don't understand, I don't understand this Goldstein: I have never done him any harm and yet he comes here and pours out lies whose only aim is to get me sent to penal servitude.'

Inspector Mayzaud was recalled. This time he claimed that Goldstein's evidence was spontaneous. But sceptical smiles were seen in court.

For the prosecution Siramy made a rambling closing speech in which he observed that there were several Papillons in Montmartre and even elsewhere. Nevertheless he asked for a conviction, though without being exact as to the sentence, which he left to the jury.

Maître Gautrat, representing the family, comically held up penal servitude as a school of 'moral betterment' and then asked that Charrière should be sent there for his own good, so as to be made an 'honest man'.

The counsel for the defence, Maîtres Beffey and Raymond Hubert, pleaded innocence. It did not follow that since Corsican Roger, otherwise Papillon, could not be found, Charrière, otherwise Papillon, was therefore guilty.

But after a long retirement the jury came back, bringing in the verdict of guilty, and the court sentenced Henri Charrière to penal servitude for life, awarding the family one franc damages.

For years and years I have asked myself this question: why did the police go all out for a little crook of twenty-three who they *themselves* said was one of their best helpers? I have only found a single answer, the only logical one: they were covering up for someone else; and this someone else was a *genuine informer*.

The next day, in the sun, I went back to Montmartre. I found my old haunts again, the Rue Tholozé and the Rue Durantin; and the market in the Rue Lepic; but the faces, the faces, where were they?

I went into 26, rue Tholozé to see the concierge, pretending to be looking for someone. My concierge had been a big fat woman with a hairy wart on her cheek. She had vanished, and a woman from Brittany had taken her place.

The Montmartre of my youth had not been stolen; no, everything was there, absolutely everything; but it had all changed. The dairy had turned into a laundromat, the local bar into a chemist's and the fruit shop into a self-service store.

The Bandevez bar, at the corner of the Rue Tholozé and the Rue Durantin, used to be the meeting-place for women from the post office in the Place des Abbesses; they came and drank their little glass of *blanc-cassis*, and to make them fly off the handle we solemnly reproved them for getting blind drunk while their poor husbands were working. Well, the joint was still there; but the bar had been moved to the other side and the two tables were no longer in their right place. What's more, the owner of the bar was a *pied-noir* from Algeria and the customers were Arabs or Spaniards or Portuguese. Where can the old boss have vanished to—the type from the Auvergne?

I went up the steps that lead from the Rue Tholozé to the Moulin de la Galette. At least the handrail had not changed: it still ended as dangerously as ever. It was here that I had picked up a poor little old man who had fallen on his nose, not seeing well enough to make out that the rail stopped so soon. I stroked the rail: I saw the scene again and I heard the old man thank me: 'Young man, you are truly kind and very well brought-up. I congratulate you upon it, and I thank you.' These simple words so disturbed me that I did not know how to set about picking up the gun I had dropped as I leaned over him; I did not want him to see that the good young man was maybe not as kind as all that.

Yes, my Montmartre was still there all right. It had not been stolen from me—they had just stolen the people, the pleasant smiling faces that used to say, 'Hi, Papillon, how are you doing?' Those, yes, those had been stolen from me, and I felt a terrible pang in my heart.

That evening I went into a rough bar. I chose the oldest of all the old guys there and I said to him, 'Excuse me, but do you know So-and-so?'

'Yes.'

'Where is he?'

'Inside.'

'And So-and-so?'

'Dead.'

'And So-and-so?'

'Don't know him. But you ask a lot of questions. Who are you?'

He raised his voice a little on purpose, to attract the others' attention. It never misses. An unknown type who just walks into a man's bar like that without introducing himself or having a friend—you have to find out what he's after.

'My name's Henri. I'm from Avignon and I've been in Colombia. That's why you don't know me. Be seeing you.'

I did not linger but hurried off to catch my train so as to sleep outside the *département* of the Seine. I took these precautions because at no price did I want them to notify me that

I was forbidden to be there.

But I was in Paris, I was there. You're there, man! I went and danced at the little places round the Bastille. At Boucastel's and at the Bal-à-Jo I shoved my hat back and took off my tie. I even had the nerve to ask a skirt to dance just as I used to do when I was twenty, and in the same way. And as we waltzed to the sound of an accordion almost as good as Mimile Vacher's when I was young, the chick asked me what I did for a living and I told her I kept a house in the provinces: so I was looked upon with great respect.

I went and had lunch at La Coupole, and as if I had returned from another world I was simple-minded enough to ask a waiter whether they still played bowls on the flat roof. He had been there twenty-five years but my question absolutely stunned him.

And at La Rotonde I looked for the painter Foujita's corner, but in vain: my eyes gazed hopelessly at the furniture, the lay-out of the tables and the bar, looking for something that belonged to the past: disgusted at seeing that everything had been turned upside-down and that they had destroyed everything I had known and loved, I walked straight out, forgetting to pay. The waiter grabbed my arm at the entrance to the Vavin métro just by, and as manners have been forgotten in France he bawled the amount of the bill into my face and told me to pay up quick if I didn't want him to call a cop. Of course I paid, but I gave him such a paltry tip that as he left he threw it at me. 'You can keep that for your mother-in-law. She must need it more than me!'

But Paris is Paris. As brisk as a young man I walked right up the Champs-Elysées and then right down again, the Champs-Elysées lit with thousands of lights, with that light of Paris that warms you through and through and casts its wonderful spell, giving you a song in your heart. Ah, life is sweet in Paris!

There was not the least over-excitement in me, not the least longing for violence as I stood there at the Porte Saint-Denis or in front of the old *L'Auto* office in the Faubourg Montmartre, where Rigoulot, then champion of the world, used to lift a huge roll of newsprint. My heart was quiet as I passed in front of the club where I used to play baccarat with Stavisky;

and I went to watch the Lido show alone and perfectly calm. And quietly I mixed in the turmoil of the Halles for a few hours—they, at least, were more or less the same as before. It was only when I was in Montmartre that bitter words rose in my heart.

I stayed eight days in Paris. Eight times I went back to the scene of that famous murder.

Eight times I stroked the tree and then sat on the bench.

Eight times, with closed eyes, I put together all I knew of the inquiry and my two trials.

Eight times I saw the ugly faces of all those swine who manufactured my conviction.

Eight times I whispered, 'This is where it all began, the theft of those thirteen years of your youth.'

Eight times I repeated, 'You have given up your revenge; that's fine; but never will you be able to forgive.'

Eight times I asked God that as a reward for giving up my revenge the same kind of thing should never happen to anyone else.

Eight times I asked the bench whether the false witness and the shifty pig had cooked up their next statement in this very place.

Eight times I went away, less and less bowed down, so that the last time I walked off as straight and supple as a young man, whispering to myself, 'You won after all, man, since you're here, free, fit, beloved and master of your future. Don't you go trying to find out what has happened to those other types—they belong to your past. You're here, and that's close on a miracle. God doesn't work them every day. You can be dead sure that of all the people concerned in this business, you're the happiest.'